Faulkner's *Light in August*

A Description and Interpretation of the Revisions

Frontispiece: Page 59 of the Virginia manuscript of William Faulkner's *Light in August*. (Courtesy Mrs. Paul D. Summers, Jr., and the William Faulkner Collections, the University of Virginia Library)

Faulkner's *Light in August*

A Description and Interpretation of the Revisions

Regina K. Fadiman

Published for the Bibliographical Society
of the University of Virginia

by the University Press of Virginia
Charlottesville

THE UNIVERSITY PRESS OF VIRGINIA
Copyright © 1975 by the Rector and Visitors
of the University of Virginia

First published 1975

Library of Congress Cataloging in Publication Data

Fadiman, Regina K.
Faulkner's Light in August

1. Faulkner, William, 1897-1962. Light in August
I. Title. PS3511.A86L5717 813'.5'2 74-8242 ISBN 0-8139-0584-2

Printed in the United States of America

To my husband

who shares with William Faulkner

his first name and at least one rare virtue—

infinite patience

Preface

THIS STUDY IS devoted to the manuscript of a novel that, although acknowledged to be one of Faulkner's major works, has provoked considerable critical controversy. The disagreement focuses on almost every aspect of the novel, technical and thematic. Some claim that it lacks plot unity; others deplore its ambiguity and contend that the characters are insufficiently motivated. Those who defend it rely on interpretations that are often poles apart and can never be reconciled. Many critics, however, fail to examine the total work, selecting only those aspects of the novel that suit their predilections. Thus, *Light in August* has been diversely classified as the particular novel of Faulkner's most firmly rooted in society, as his strongest indictment of our Calvinistic heritage, and as a Christian allegory. Faulkner has been both highly praised and severely attacked for his treatment of the Negro theme in the novel. Of late, the anthropological critics have been speculating about the mythic archetypes on which the characters and plots are presumably based. Often these widely disparate interpretations and evaluations reveal more about critical methods and preconceptions than about the book.

The lack of agreement on so many aspects of the novel strongly suggests that the parts are being confused with the whole and that there is a need for a thorough examination of the whole before a valid interpretation can be made. A close examination of the manuscripts can, therefore, be useful in establishing certain facts and in offering speculations based on an empirical investigation of the documents. Because such a study entails a close reading of the manuscripts and the published text, it can clarify some of the confusion still prevalent about the narrative facts and also point out the particular ambiguities and inconsistencies that, for one reason or another, cannot be resolved. In light of the disputes over the novel, a thorough analysis of the revisions is greatly needed. In the pages to follow I have attempted to fulfill some part of this need.

My methods, however, are somewhat unorthodox, for this study neither provides a genetic text nor limits itself to a strict bibliographical description. Instead, it employs process criticism, which I define as an interpretation of a completed work derived from an examination of the methods and stages of its revision. Because of the peculiar nature of the manuscript and because I am primarily concerned with structural alterations, my procedure necessarily entails lengthy descriptions of the revisions, accompanied at each stage by explanations of their significance to the work as a whole. I have attempted, therefore, to select from the massive numbers and types of changes those revisions that seem to be the most fundamental in their effect on the novel. I have also tried whenever possible to find consistent patterns of change, which help to provide multiple evidence for the theories I have derived.

My conclusions about the stages of revision have been drawn from the external evidence found in the canceled single numbers and the canceled number-sets that appear in the manuscript, the varying inks and papers, and the numerous passages affixed to the base pages. The typescript provides further evidence for certain of these conclusions. Changes of diction and punctuation, as well as printing conventions, have been employed to identify shifts of time, of scene, and of narrative point of view.

Internal evidence has also been helpful in forming conjectures about the stages of the narrative's composition. There are numerous inconsistencies and contradictions in both the manuscript and the published text which indicate that Faulkner added many episodes and passages after he had written a nearly complete version of the novel. In compressing and rearranging the previous draft, he neglected to resolve these inconsistencies and contradictions. Chapter 5 of this study is devoted to a detailed discussion of such anachronisms.

My first chapter provides a detailed description of the extant manuscripts relevant to *Light in August*; it also compares Faulkner's methods of revision with those apparent in other manuscripts written during the same period. Studies dealing with the revisions of Faulkner's other works are cited to corroborate my generalizations concerning the documents related to *Light in August*. In addition, the first chapter lists the assumptions for which the following three chapters provide evidence.

The manuscript provides a clear record of the techniques Faulkner employed to revise his novel. His alterations during the process of composition resulted in a significant shift in the ultimate meaning of the work, for its new form shaped its new content. In a larger sense the manuscript contains a record of the work habits and methods of revision of the artist who is considered by many to be the major American novelist of the twentieth century; it offers, therefore, valuable insights into Faulkner's imaginative genius and into the creative process itself.

Because of the heuristic nature of this project, many of my conclusions must remain purely speculative. Little is yet known about the inception of *Light in August*. But I hope that my findings will be useful to future students of Faulkner manuscripts and that when more information is available, whatever misconceptions I may have held will be corrected. It is comforting to remember the axiom of one of my professors, who facetiously reminds his students that every researcher has a "scholarly obligation to error." In fulfilling that trust, he leaves a heritage to future scholars, who can be kept busily occupied in correcting the errors of those who preceded them.

Among the many people who have assisted me in various ways, I would particularly like to express my gratitude to the following:

Mrs. Paul D. Summers, Jr., for granting me permission to quote from the unpublished manuscripts of her father, William Faulkner; Random House, Inc., for permission to quote from the published text of *Light in August*, copyright 1932 and renewed 1960 by William Faulkner; The Humanities Research Center, the University of Texas at Austin, for permission to quote from the four-page manuscript of *Light in August* at the University of Texas; Mr. Floyd Stovall for permitting me to use the Faulkner papers at the University of Virginia; Mr. Linton R. Massey, whose Faulkner collection has been made accessible to scholars and students; Mr. Edmund Berkeley, Jr., Curator of Manuscripts; Mr. William Ray, Senior Assistant in Manuscripts, and Mr. Rowe E. Portis—all of whom gave unstintingly of their time to help me when I worked in the University of Virginia Library and who patiently replied to the many written queries that followed my departure; Professor Warren Roberts and Mrs. Mary M. Hirth, Librarian of the Academic Center Library, who so kindly and frequently supplied information concerning the Faulkner manuscripts at the University of Texas; Professors Joseph Blotner, Carvel Collins, James B. Meriwether, and Stephen Dennis for their gracious replies to my requests for information about additional manuscripts; and Professor Blake Nevius, who started me on the path of one of the most exciting adventures that scholarship can provide, who helped me to travel that path, and who was at the end of it with sage counsel and advice.

Contents

Tables

Faulkner's *Light in August*

A Description and Interpretation of the Revisions

I

The Background and the Documents

WILLIAM FAULKNER'S seventh novel (and his eleventh book) was published by the now defunct firm of Harrison Smith and Robert Haas on October 6, 1932, when its author was thirty-five years old. In addition, four short stories were published in 1930, sixteen in 1931, and eight more by December 1932.[1] With the exception of reviews of two of his works, the complete issue of *Contempo* magazine, February 1, 1932, was also written by Faulkner.[2]

The catalog above has a particular bearing on Faulkner's activities during the year he was writing the only extant complete manuscript of *Light in August*, now in the William Faulkner Foundation Collection at the University of Virginia Library. According to its title page, Faulkner began the manuscript in Oxford, Mississippi, on August 17, 1931. On the final page he wrote the place and date of completion: "Oxford, Miss./19 Feb. 1932."

---

[1]There are no facts available at this time about the publishing contract or other conditions concerning the publication of this novel. Bennett Cerf, former editor of Random House, which now owns the copyrights to the novel, replied to my request for information concerning the first edition that there is nothing in the files of Random House pertaining to the arrangements with the first publishers. Carvel Collins answered my request for information about the publishing terms of *Light in August* as follows: "*As a rule* he [Faulkner] did not contract for a book at a time; by the period in which he wrote *Light in August I believe* he was merely 'with' a publishing house, which expected to bring out each work as Faulkner finished writing it" (Collins to Fadiman, May 25, 1970). The title of the novel will be abbreviated to *LIA* in future note references.

These figures include only material published for the first time and exclude *Salmagundi* (Milwaukee: Casanova Press), published April 30, 1932, which contains three essays and five poems reprinted without revisions.

[2]Vol. 1, no. 17.

The Background

The year 1931 was a turning point in Faulkner's literary career, at least with respect to wider public recognition and financial rewards. The first book to be published in that year was *Sanctuary*, on February 9. It was followed, on September 21, by *These 13*, a collection of short stories, five of which had been previously published, either in 1930 or early in 1931, but were revised for this collection. A limited edition of the short story *Idyll in the Desert* was published in book form by Random House on December 10, and on June 27, 1932, *Miss Zilphia Gant*, another short story, appeared in book form, also in a limited edition. In other words, although only six books and five short stories by Faulkner were published from December 15, 1924, to February 9, 1931, after the latter date three books (two of them consisting of only a single short story), *Contempo*, and twenty-eight stories had been published by October 6, 1932, the date on which *Light in August* appeared.[3]

The explanation for the sudden increase in interest in William Faulkner was, of course, the notorious *Sanctuary*. Michael Millgate describes the reception of the book: "Despite the general incomprehension displayed by the reviewers, or perhaps because of the rather lurid reputation they had given the book, *Sanctuary* was a modest commercial success, and Faulkner himself became a minor celebrity."[4] As a result of this popular success Faulkner received an offer to write screenplays in Hollywood and reported for work at Metro-Goldwyn-Mayer on May 16, 1932. Such recognition brought about a considerable change in the position of the man who had said in 1931: "I never sold a short story until about a year ago. For about six years I didn't average more than $100 a year from my writing. I finished one novel and pretty near finished another one before I sold the first."[5]

---

[3]These figures do not include the short sketches published in New Orleans in 1925-26 in the *Times-Picayune* and the *Double Dealer* or poems published before *The Marble Faun* (Boston: Four Seas Co., 1924). See James B. Meriwether, "The Short Fiction of William Faulkner: A Bibliography," *Proof*, 1 (1971), 293-329, and Harry Runyon, *A Faulkner Glossary* (New York: Citadel Press, 1964), pp. 228-37.

[4]*The Achievement of William Faulkner* (London: Constable, 1966), p. 29.

[5]Unsigned interview in the New York *Herald Tribune*, Nov. 14, 1931, rpt. in

The increase in the number of interviews granted (and probably also requested) demonstrates Faulkner's sudden popularity. Although he always tried to maintain a strict separation between his personal and professional lives and kept his private life as private as possible, these interviews provide some information about his activities and peregrinations during the eighteen months preceding the publication of *Light in August*.

In July of 1931 Faulkner, at home in Oxford, was interviewed by Marshall J. Smith, who reported that the author was working on a book of "13 Short Stories." Smith ends his account: "Today Faulkner is loafing. He says the luxury and calm, the quiet and solitude of his home so apart from the rest of the world is 'conducive to doing nothing.' "[6] But from what follows, it seems most unlikely that Faulkner was loafing.

After the July interview with Smith, Faulkner began the Virginia manuscript of *Light in August* on Monday, August 19. In October he attended a Southern Writers' Conference in Charlottesville, traveled to the University of North Carolina, where the Faulkner issue of *Contempo* was being prepared, and then returned to the University of Virginia in Charlottesville. He granted an interview that was printed in the University of Virginia undergraduate weekly, *College Topics*, on November 2. This interview is virtually the first in which Faulkner talked seriously about his literary opinions, although he had made several provocative statements to Marshall J. Smith during the earlier meeting. Moreover, in the student interview, his willingness and even desire to communicate with youth are evident for the first time, foreshadowing the interest in students that was characteristic of him throughout his life. In the interview he explained that he had "never yet started to write a novel," that he usually began with a character and just started writing. He predicted that the novel form as we know it would "break down completely," adding, "there are too many written these days. But there will always be a market for stories."[7]

Lion in the Garden: Interview with William Faulkner 1926-1962, ed. James B. Meriwether and Michael Millgate (New York: Random House, 1968), p. 20.

[6]*Memphis Press-Scimitar*, July 10, 1931, rpt. in *Lion in the Garden*, p. 8.

[7]*Lion in the Garden*, p. 17.

I have quoted these comments because they express Faulkner's ideas about the form of the novel at the time he started the Virginia manuscript that later became *Light in August*.

By November 14, 1931, Faulkner was in New York. The *Herald Tribune* printed an interview that was originally carried under the heading "Slavery Better for the Negro, Says Faulkner."[8] The interviewer asked Faulkner about racial problems and politics and also asked several questions about his reading tastes and his attitude toward book reviews. The article concluded that he hated to be interviewed or questioned; it also announced that he was a "Southern Sage who scarcely read at all." The *Herald Tribune* presented the most unflattering portrait of Faulkner to date and may have done more than its part in establishing the misunderstanding about the man and his ideas that persisted in the minds of so many for so long. But Faulkner seems to have disliked big cities, in particular those with literary colonies that attracted parasites; he apparently took delight in putting his worst foot forward when he was interviewed. Millgate has described the reminiscences of some of the people who met Faulkner in New York that same autumn and concluded that Faulkner disliked most of the aspects of the New York social and literary world.[9] This antipathy might in part explain the hostile tone of the *Herald Tribune* article.

Mrs. Faulkner confirmed the fact that her husband found New York inimical to his creative temperament. Marshall J. Smith, in an interview published in the *Memphis Press-Scimitar*, November 30, 1931, reports her as saying that the noise and confusion of a city did not go well with her husband's writings. She added, " 'The reason I'm going to New York is to keep people away from him. He has an apartment on the 28th floor of a building and his last letter said that he liked it better, for he could forget the noise and see the sun and the sky.' " She also mentioned that her husband was working on a manuscript for a movie that Tallulah Bankhead was to "use," thereby adding still

---

[8]Ibid., p. 19.

[9]*Achievement of William Faulkner*, pp. 31-33.

another project to what must have been Faulkner's literary juggling act that autumn.[10]

On November 28, 1931, the *New Yorker* published a thumbnail sketch of Faulkner in the "Talk of the Town," reporting that "he spends most of his days alone, working on his next novel, which is to be called *Light in August*. It's about a quarter done."[11] This interview is the first to mention the title of the book Faulkner was then writing.[12]

Five days before the manuscript was completed, one final interview appeared, written by Henry Nash Smith, who saw Faulkner in Oxford shortly before writing the article published in the *Dallas Morning News*, 14 Feb. 1932. During his talk with Smith, Faulkner said: " 'I usually get to work pretty early in the morning, and by 10:30 or 11 I'm through. But I can sit down and write almost any time. The stories seem to shape themselves as they go along. I'm working on two novels now, and it may take me two years to finish one of them.' "[13]

Several additional items pertain to the period immediately preceding the completion of the Virginia manuscript. Anthony Buttitta reported some years after Faulkner's Chapel Hill visit in 1931 that Faulkner had the manuscript of *Light in August* with him during the visit. Later, in January 1932, Buttitta visited Faulkner and wrote, "The long proof sheets of *Light in August* were on his writing table."[14] This information seems odd in view of the fact that the manuscript was not completed until February 19, 1932. Furthermore, *William Faulkner, "Man Working,"*

---

[10]*Lion in the Garden*, pp. 25-26. There is no record of this manuscript for a movie in any of the bibliographies or listings of manuscript collections that I have seen. But it may be mentioned, if it survived, in a Ph.D. dissertation dealing with Faulkner's career in Hollywood that I have not seen: George R. Sidney, *Faulkner in Hollywood: A Study of His Career as Scenarist* (Ann Arbor, Mich.: University Microfilms, 1959).

[11]*Lion in the Garden*, p. 23.

[12]Anthony Buttitta said that Faulkner's purpose in coming to New York was to autograph the limited editions of *Idyll in the Desert* ("William Faulkner, That Writin' Man of Oxford," *Sat. R.*, May 21, 1938, p. 7).

[13]*Lion in the Garden*, p. 32.

[14]"William Faulkner, That Writin' Man of Oxford," p. 7.

1919-1962, A Catalogue of the William Faulkner Collection at the University of Virginia, lists a holograph letter from Faulkner to his literary agent, Ben Wasson, received on January 26, 1932, in which the author said that *Light in August* was not yet typed.[15] And when he invited Buttitta to Oxford, Faulkner wrote that he was trying to finish the novel. It seems unlikely, therefore, that he was correcting proof sheets of a novel that he was still writing by hand and had not yet typed.[16]

Once *Light in August* was published, Faulkner claimed, in a recently published four-page typescript containing rare autobiographical material, that he was really finished with it and had lost all interest in it. In this brief autobiography Faulkner wrote that he waited two years after *As I Lay Dying* before he began writing *Light in August.* "The written pages grew in number. The story was going pretty well. I would sit down to it each morning without reluctance yet still without that anticipation and that joy which alone ever made writing pleasure to me. The book was almost finished before I acquiesced to the fact that it would not recur. . . . I received a copy of the printed book and found that I didn't even want to see what kind of jacket Smith had put on it." He explained his disenchantment on the grounds that he "was now aware before each word was written down just what the people would do." He was deliberately "choosing among possibilities and weighing and measuring each choice by the scale of the Jameses and Conrads and Balzacs." He knew that he had read too much and had reached a stage that every young writer must go through "in which he believes he has learned too much about his trade."[17]

---

[15]Comp. Linton R. Massey (Charlottesville: Univ. Press of Virginia, 1968), item 954, p. 105.

[16]Perhaps Buttitta mistook the proof sheets of *Miss Zilphia Gant* (June 27, 1932) for those of *LIA.*

[17]James B. Meriwether, ed., "An Introduction for *The Sound and the Fury,* William Faulkner," *SoR,* 8 (1972), 709-10. *The Sound and the Fury* will be cited hereafter as *TSATF.*

Actually, Faulkner did not wait two years before beginning *LIA.* He completed the manuscript of *As I Lay Dying* on Dec. 11, 1929, and began the semifinal draft of *LIA* on Aug. 17, 1931. Because many of the passages in this draft have been retrieved from previous drafts, there is reason to believe that he started *LIA* even sooner.

Between the appearance of *Sanctuary* on February 9, 1931, and *Light in August* on October 6, 1932, Faulkner was a very busy literary man, although he disliked being designated as such. The list of his works published between those dates is a long one. Moreover, he expended a great deal of energy merely in mailing the stories he had written previously to various magazines and to his agent, Ben Wasson. The schedule he kept of the circulation of these stories has been reproduced.[18] At least twenty were mailed from one magazine to another in the years 1931 and 1932. John Faulkner says, perhaps more loosely than the facts indicate, that "after *Sanctuary* came out the *Post* wrote Bill and said they wanted to apologize for having turned his stories down and if he would send them back they would put him in a preferred bracket and buy them at a thousand dollars apiece. Bill sent them sixty!"[19]

It was against this background that *Light in August* was composed. What effect the suddenly charged atmosphere had on the manuscript and on the book it is impossible to say. But it seems obvious that although Faulkner thought his loss of "ecstasy" in writing *Light in August* came from having read and learned too much, it can be equally well explained by his having worked too hard for too long in order to get his novels and stories before the public. Ironically, when recognition finally came, it was accorded to the wrong book. Faulkner himself was always proudest of *The Sound and the Fury* and once remarked that in order not to shame it and *As I Lay Dying* he rewrote *Sanctuary*. Although he did not object to earning "eating" money in any way he could and although he apparently ignored both critical and public approval or disapproval, he must have been deeply disappointed at the reception of the two books he wished so much not to shame. His brother insists that his "skin was too tender to withstand the barbs fired at him."[20]

[18]James B. Meriwether, *The Literary Career of William Faulkner, A Bibliographical Study* (Princeton, N.J.: Princeton Univ. Library, 1961), pp. 169-80.

[19]*My Brother Bill: An Affectionate Reminiscence* (New York: Trident Press, 1963), p. 156.

[20]Ibid., p. 172.

The Documents

Faulkner once said, "I know what that 'flash' of inspiration is, but I also try to put some discipline into my work."[21] There are few signs of the initial flashes of inspiration in the extant manuscripts of *Light in August*. James B. Meriwether has noted that Faulkner "apparently took pains to save only the finished work," and Carvel Collins has said that he "destroyed the early stages of most of his manuscripts."[22] The remaining drafts, however, provide ample evidence of the discipline Faulkner put into his work.

The Texas Manuscript

Several pages of what may have been the beginning of *Light in August* have survived Faulkner's destructive urge and are now preserved at the Academic Center Library of the University of Texas. Meriwether has described three of these four pages as a "discarded beginning to the novel, with the Reverend Hightower in his study."[23] The manuscript is written by hand in blue ink, with the title *Light in August* at the top of the first page. Although the pages are unnumbered they are consecutive; no paste-on slips are affixed to any of them.[24]

There is also a hand-written fragment at the Academic Center Library in Texas heretofore unrecorded. The writing appears far to the right of the page and the passage clearly pertains to Joe Christmas.[25] These four leaves will be discussed subsequently in

[21]*Lion in the Garden*, p. 72.

[22]Meriwether, *Literary Career*, p. 60. The quotation from Collins is taken from a letter (May 27, 1970) responding to my request for information about the starting date of *LIA*. He said that he did not know just when the first words were put on paper because Faulkner did not save the early stages of his work.

[23]*William Faulkner: An Exhibition of Manuscripts*, comp. James B. Merewether (Austin: Univ. of Texas Research Center, 1959), p. 15. Mr. Meriwether wrote me (June 22, 1970) that he saw at a dealer's another rejected opening of *LIA* but does not know its present whereabouts.

[24]The first page has been reproduced in *William Faulkner: An Exhibition of Manuscripts* and appears on two unnumbered pages preceding page 10 of the pamphlet. The third page of the Texas manuscript is not inscribed fully to the bottom.

[25]Mary Hirth, Librarian of the Academic Center Library at the University of

detail in relationship to their bearing on the revisions of *Light in August.*

The Virginia Manuscript

A complete, 188-page, hand-written manuscript can be found in the University of Virginia Library. If the pages in Texas can be said to represent an early stage of the novel, the Virginia manuscript can be described as a composite version that includes many stages of composition and revision. It is the last hand-written version of *Light in August* and directly precedes the typescript prepared for the publisher. (The first 170 pages of the publisher's typescript are also at the University of Virginia.) Meriwether has described the Virginia manuscript as follows: "The text is continous and complete, despite a duplication in the numbering. There is an unnumbered title page, with the title Dark House crossed out and Light in August written above it; below it is written Oxford, Mississippi/17 August, 1931. The pages of the text are numbered as follows: 2, 3, 3 through 187. At the bottom of the final page is Oxford, Miss./19 Feb. 1932."[26]

A more complete description of this document is in order because it is by far the most useful, as well as the most baffling, of the extant manuscripts of the novel. But unfortunately the description will demonstrate that the Virginia manuscript presents a literary riddle wrapped in a mathematical mystery inside a cryptographer's enigma.

Most of the narrative is inscribed on heavy, parchmentlike sheets of paper showing no watermarks and measuring about 8 9/16 inches wide and 11 1/6 inches long. The title page is exactly eight by eleven inches. Nothing is written on the versos of any of the leaves. Of the 188 leaves of the manuscript, 159 measure 0.004 millimeters in thickness and have carefully ruled margins

---

Texas, has described the four manuscript pages to me by letter, January 21, 1970, as follows: "The manuscript is written in blue ink and no sections have been glued on to the base page. So far as I can determine, the fourth page did come at the time of the other three. It is so much like the others, the paper seems to be the same and also the shade of ink. The original is . . . far to the right of the page with a blank space on the left of almost two-thirds of the width of the page. The first three pages are bound together. The fourth page is separate."

[26]Meriwether, *Literary Career*, pp. 66-67.

in black ink at the top and on the left side of the page. The left vertical margins are 2¾ inches wide and have been used frequently for insertions and additions to the text. The top horizontal margins vary between 2¼ to 2½ inches and have been hand-bisected to the line of the left margin at the beginning of each chapter.

The remaining twenty-nine pages also show no watermarks; they measure 0.003 millimeters in thickness and have margins drawn rather carelessly by hand in dark blue-black ink.[27] The variance in paper and in the demarcations of the margins leads immediately to speculation as to when and why the thinner sheets were added to the manuscript. It is quickly apparent that although these pages were probably among the last added, they contain, by and large, material from previous drafts of the novel. But what is puzzling about these "new" pages is that none of them occur in chapters 5 through 12, those particular chapters that deal with Joe Christmas directly rather than indirectly, as seen or discussed by the other characters in the novel.

There are, moreover, 157 inscribed slips, varying in length from a few lines to an entire page, meticulously pasted to seventy-nine of the manuscript's 188 pages. In most instances these slips were cut from previous drafts, although a particular few appear to have been written expressly for this version of the novel.[28] A listing of the distribution of the paste-on slips can be found in the Appendix, table 5. The highest concentration occurs in chapters 5 and 14 of the manuscript, both of which concern Joe Christmas. These two chapters consist almost entirely of sections affixed to the base pages of the manuscript. I shall discuss the significance of this phenomenon and also cite the passages that look as if they were written after the basic narrative structure of the novel had been devised when I put forward

---

[27]I shall frequently refer to the paper measuring 0.003 mm. as tissue paper and the paper measuring 0.004 mm. as parchment. Although these terms are inaccurate, they are more descriptive of the visual distinction between the two papers and far less cumbersome to use than the decimals.

[28]Russell Roth notes that Faulkner rewrites whole passages rather than correct word for word "as though he does not want to straighten or deaden the original impulse behind the words" ("The Brennan Papers: Faulkner in Manuscript," *Perspective*, 2 [1949], 223-24).

my theory on the stages of the novel's development. Meanwhile, it is well to keep in mind that most of the new material, or the material that was added for this version of the narrative, can be found on the base pages of the manuscript.

These pages, including the paste-on slips, are relatively clean. In fact, there are so few actual changes of diction on the manuscript leaves that one must assume that most of these leaves represent a copying-out of one or more previous drafts.[29] However, because the order of certain episodes has been altered, new transitional material between paste-on slips can be found on the base page and also, as stated previously, certain entirely new passages, probably not carried over from the earlier drafts.

That the manuscript includes among its leaves passages written at different times and originally in a different order can be inferred not only from the numerous sections affixed to its base pages but also from the many varied colors and shades of ink on its sheets. The title page reveals two titles, each inscribed in a different ink. The first, *Dark House*, inscribed slightly to the right of center of the recto, has been written and underlined three times in brown ink. The date and place have also been inscribed in brown in the lower left. Black ink is used to delete *Dark House;* the final title, *Light in August*, also written in black ink, has been placed above the discarded title, in the direct center of the same page. Several headnotes, also written in black ink, can be found above the opening pages of certain chapters. One and one-half base pages are written in purple ink, as are seven paste-on slips in chapters 2 and 3. In addition, there are four pages inscribed in an extremely bright blue ink. With the exception of manuscript pages 70-75, these bright blue ink pages are probably the only first-draft material of any significance in the manuscript.[30]

---

[29]Occasionally a line is duplicated or appears out of context and is scratched out; these also indicate that Faulkner was copying out a previous version. There are sometimes extension lines that fill in space to prepare for the insertion of a paste-on slip. Occasionally a paste-on slip displays an arrow and line from the margin, but nothing has been written in the margin, thus indicating that the section was taken from an earlier draft. The extension lines also sometimes serve as indicators for paragraphing.

[30]The precise leaves bearing these various inks will be cited as evidence in the chapters to follow.

Despite this colorful ink spectrum, it is obvious that the matrix, or bulk, of the manuscript was written in a dark blue-black that became lighter as the author arduously copied out his work. The flow of the dark lines, however, is frequently interrupted by a paste-on slip of a much paler shade of blue. Occasionally this process is reversed. Finally, certain base pages and certain sections pasted to the dark blue or light blue ink pages appear to have been written in a different shade, more closely resembling royal blue.

Thus it becomes apparent that this manuscript represents a composite of several previous drafts or subdrafts of parts of the novel.[31] Two additional features of the manuscript bear out this conclusion and provide valuable evidence for reconstructing some of the stages of the novel's development.

First, excluding the final pages of chapters, nearly all the leaves of the manuscript are fully inscribed to the bottom of the sheet. However, the first manuscript page 3 and pages 35, 64, 69, 73, 74, 75, 85, 115, and 146 are "short" pages, either written and added to the manuscript after the pages that follow them or formerly used to conclude chapters in a previous ordering of the novel's episodes. Two of these short pages, however, may have been truncated to indicate a printing space, sometimes used for the passage of time or a shift in subject matter (MS 64, 73).

Second, the foliation of the manuscript provides important clues to its revisions. The network of canceled numbers is extremely complicated, so that I strongly urge any reader attempting to follow my argument to consult frequently the tables of canceled numbers in the Appendix. In the manuscript, where there are no canceled numbers, the single, final number is placed in the extreme upper left corner, about $1/6$ inch (2 to 3 millimeters) from the left and top edges of the sheet.

---

[31] Stephen Dennis lists several kinds of evidence toward the conclusion that the Virginia typescript of *Sartoris* is a composite typescript. Among these are overlappings of the text between consecutive pages. The overlappings vary in length from a phrase or two to an entire paragraph ("The Making of *Sartoris:* A Description and Discussion of the Manuscript and Composite Typescript of William Faulkner's Third Novel," Diss. Cornell 1969, p. 72). I shall refer to similar overlappings that may be evidence of rearrangement of material or help to identify earlier and later periods of composition.

Several sheets display single canceled arabic numbers; others have pairs and triads on consecutive textually linked pages. Chapters 7 through 12 are distinguished by five sets of canceled numbers in the upper left corner of each of their fifty-one pages. They form five perfectly ordered sets, with the exception of manuscript pages 70-75, which lack canceled numbers in the same sets. If, however, hypothetical numbers are assigned to these pages, the five sets continue in perfect progression.[32] In addition, certain sheets of chapter 13 display four canceled pairs of arabic numbers on the same sheets, as well as five canceled triads on other sheets, and single canceled numbers on still others. One final set of canceled arabic numbers appears in chapter 15. From one to seven canceled roman numerals, obviously indicating previous chapter divisions and arrangements, appear on the opening pages of chapters 7 through 19 (excepting chapters 14, 17, and 18).

It is obvious from the appearance of the manuscript that Faulkner's earlier aspirations to be a graphic artist were not entirely in vain. One hesitates to describe Faulkner's penmanship as mere handwriting. In fact, he has developed a unique shorthand, or symbol system, reminiscent of the hieroglyphics carved into stone monuments, mysterious runic figures, or even the patterned abstractions of medieval illuminated manuscripts. Faulkner's letters are so minuscule that they are smaller than their printed counterparts in the published version of the novel.

---

[32]The following critics have commented on Faulkner's use of canceled numbers: Meriwether says of *LIA* "that Faulkner's revisions of the manuscript involved rearrangements of this episode [MS 110] is indicated by the different page and chapter numbers which are cancelled" (*Literary Career*, p. 23). Emily K. Izsak notes that "several series of pages in the first and second sections [of *TSATF*] were renumbered so as to indicate both relocations of certain passages and a general expansion of the material" ("The Manuscript of *The Sound and the Fury:* The Revisions in the First Section," 20 [1967], 197). Also see Gerald Langford, *Faulkner's Revisions of* "Absalom, Absalom!": *A Collation of the Manuscript and the Published Book* (Austin: Univ. of Texas Press, 1971), p. 5. Stephen Dennis makes substantial use of changed pagination in reconstructing the stages of *Sartoris*'s development. He states that "the existence of such multiple page numbers suggests that Faulkner shifted pages and sections around within his typescript. This is the evidence which suggested to me that a close study of the *Sartoris* typescript might be fruitful" ("The Making of *Sartoris*," p. 72).

He writes with a fine-point pen that seems a tool more appropriate for an etcher than an author. From an aesthetic point of view the pages of the manuscript have a nice delicacy and regularity in the preponderance of vertical lines and sinuous curves, representing the suffix *-ing*. He apparently objects to horizontal lines, for the letters *t* and *f* are never crossed. Vowels are either entirely eliminated or abstracted to a linear pattern. Actually, Faulkner has invented his own embryonic shorthand, which is often more difficult to decipher than the most complex and obscure code.[33]

[33]Faulkner stated that he himself was unable to read his own writing on occasion and attributed his pinched hand to the days when he had to economize on paper (*Lion in the Garden*, p. 36, which quotes an unsigned interview with Faulkner, printed in 1939 in the *New Orleans Item*). Anthony Buttitta reports that Louise Bonino, employed first by Hal Smith and then by Random House, was the only one besides Faulkner who could read his writing ("William Faulkner, That Writin' Man of Oxford," p. 7). Faulkner explained the illegibility of his handwriting as follows: "I can't write as fast as I need to, and I begin to make symbols because at the time it's plain to me, and I say, 'Oh, I'll remember what that is,'—but then tomorrow of course I don't" (*Lion in the Garden*, pp. 157-58). I might add here that the manuscript of *TSATF* and *As I Lay Dying* are far easier to read, because Faulkner used a more conventional method of printing his letters. But *The Hamlet* presents new problems in translating Faulkner's hand because, by 1940, he had shown a preference for diagonal slashes that give the manuscript the quality of a series of baroque miniatures. For additional descriptions of the physical appearance of Faulkner's manuscripts, handwriting, and typescripts, see Faulkner's interview with Henry Nash Smith, *Lion in the Garden,* pp. 28-32, first published in the *Dallas Morning News*, Feb. 14, 1932; Norman Holmes Pearson, "Faulkner's Three 'Evening Suns,'" *YULG*, 29 (1954), 64; Robert Hilton Knox III, "William Faulkner's *Absalom, Absalom!*" Diss. Harvard 1955, pp. 44-48; James B. Meriwether, "Notes on the Textual History of *The Sound and the Fury*," *PBSA*, 56 (1962), 290; Langford, *Faulkner's Revision of* "Absalom, Absalom!" p. 4. Reproductions of Faulkner's handwriting are available in Meriwether's *Literary Career; William Faulkner: Early Prose and Poetry*, ed. Carvel Collins (Boston: Little, Brown, 1962); *William Faulkner, An Exhibition of Manuscripts*; and *William Faulkner, "Man Working."* There are reproductions of manuscript pages elsewhere too, such as in Joseph Blotner, *William Faulkner's Library—A Catalogue* (Charlottesville: Univ. Press of Virginia, 1964) and Langford, *Faulkner's Revision of* "Absalom, Absalom!" Meriwether and Dennis also have listed many texts in which these reproductions can be found (*Literary Career*, p. 59, and "The Making of *Sartoris*," p. 46). Dennis has provided a full description of the idiosyncrasies of Faulkner's penmanship, spelling, and punctuation. He has also identified changes in Faulkner's handwriting from the earliest stages of his career to the period of writing *LIA*, thus disputing some of the published descriptions that do not take these changes into account. Dennis concludes that the handwriting of the three pages in Texas entitled *LIA* "is still that of the *Sartoris* manuscript, and apparently the change in Faulkner's handwriting from the

The content of the Virginia manuscript reveals that in what is probably the narrative's final holograph form, Faulkner was primarily concerned with structural elements. The narrative chronology, the chapter divisions, the encounters between the characters, the episodes, and the flashbacks have been rearranged and placed in their final positions. Moreover, there is little evidence in its leaves of the struggle for *le mot juste*. Although many changes of diction occur from the Virginia manuscript to the typescript described below, no intervening drafts are known to exist. It is likely that there was only one complete typescript, for Faulkner often said that he habitually wrote his first drafts in longhand and revised and rewrote when he typed the manuscript for the publisher.[34]

The Typescript

Part of the typescript that Faulkner typed himself is also at the University of Virginia. Meriwether has described it as follows:

Typescript setting copy, 466 pp. Some manuscript corrections. The text is incomplete, the last page (p. 470) ending with the words "so humorless that" which appear in the first paragraph of p. 428 of the published book, and p. 469 being missing. The text is preceded by a title page bearing the pencilled number 1, apparently not in Faulkner's hand; the text is numbered as follows: 2 through 121, 122, and 123 [one page, marked with

---

handwriting in *Sartoris* to the hand of the later novels occurred during the writing of *Light in August*" ("The Making of *Sartoris*," p. 46). Dennis's full description of Faulkner's handwriting can be found on pp. 44-47.

[34]*Lion in the Garden*, pp. 34, 72. Faulkner made numerous references to the fact that he wrote "entirely by hand." He is quoted as saying that he did his rewriting on the typewriter, but that first he had to "feel the pencil and see the words at the end of the pencil...." He added that because he wrote so fast his handwriting was nearly illegible, making it necessary for him to type it almost immediately: "If I leave it until tomorrow I can't read it myself..." (William Faulkner, *Faulkner in the University: Class Conferences at the University of Virginia 1957-1958*, ed. Frederick L. Gwynn and Joseph L. Blotner [1957; rpt. New York: Vintage-Random House, 1965], p. 194). These remarks were made some twenty-five years after the composition of *LIA*. Statements closer to the date of its composition quoted earlier in the chapter indicate that Faulkner did not begin his final and only extant typescript of that novel until he had nearly completed the holograph version.

both numbers], 124 through 468, 470 [a page missing between 468 and 470].

He has also noted that the manuscript precedes the typescript and that there are many differences between the texts of the two versions.[35]

The remaining fifty-six pages of the same typescript, numbered 471 through 527, can be found at the Academic Center Library at the University of Texas. Page 471 begins with the phrase "the legion commander withheld" and completes the sentence left dangling on page 470 of the typescript in Virginia. Page 527 ends: " 'My, my. A body does get around. Here we aint been coming from Alabama but two months, and now it's already Tennessee.' " At the bottom of the page in blue pencil enclosed in a circle of the same is written "The End!?" These words are not in Faulkner's hand and were no doubt added by a disgruntled reader.

The typescript, which can be considered fair copy, includes two title pages. Chapter 1 begins on the verso of the second title page. The first title page is numbered 2. There are changes of pagination from chapters 2 through 7 which indicate that Faulkner was already typing the first section of the novel while he was still revising the manuscript. Although Faulkner wrote his literary agent in late January that none of the manuscript was typed and that it was going too well for the author to stop to type any of it, the canceled numbers on the typescript show that Faulkner did in fact begin typing before he had made the final revisions in the manuscript.[36] A list of these numbers has been included in the Appendix, table 4, because the change of pagination in this document provides additional evidence for the reconstruction of the revisions of the manuscript.

In addition to accommodating the typescript to later additions to the manuscript, as well as one sizable deletion, Faulkner corrected with his fine-point pen and dark blue ink certain errors of grammar and facts of chronology. He adjusted the tenses of

[35]Meriwether, *Literary Career*, p. 67.

[36]Joseph Blotner to Fadiman, May 30, 1970. The letter Faulkner wrote to Wasson is listed as item 954 in *William Faulkner, "Man Working"* and was received by Ben Wasson on January 26, 1932.

several verbs, altered an occasional word, and clarified certain narrative facts.[37] The tense and grammar corrections, even as late as the typescript, seem to indicate that Faulkner composed as if he were telling a story orally. In the manuscript he frequently slipped into the present tense and into colloquial rather than standard diction; some of the slippage persisted through the typing stage.[38]

Many passages have been greatly expanded from the manuscript to the typescript, and certain paragraphs appear in a different order. The punctuation, italicized sections, and fused words that now appear in the text have, in many cases, been supplied for the typescript where they were completely lacking or in a different form in the manuscript.

Nevertheless, the major structural revisions are still evident in the manuscript, and these make it the more valuable document for this study of the revisions. The typescript can, however, corroborate some of the assumptions to follow about the purposes of the revisions and stages of growth of the manuscript.

The Corrected Galleys

The only remaining document to be discussed relating to *Light in August* is a complete set of corrected galleys, also at the University of Texas. The corrections "are very minor, mostly typographical errors, nothing to do with text corrections."[39] The galleys, therefore, play no part in this study of the revisions.

Pertinent Manuscripts of Other Novels

That Faulkner in the process of writing *Light in August* made extensive revisions is evident from a casual survey of the Virginia manuscript. Its complex system of canceled numbers most clearly resembles that of the manuscript of the first version of

---

[37]The adjustments of tense, chronology, and narrative fact are not always consistent, as a close reading of the novel reveals.

[38]Russell Roth points out that "one of Faulkner's favorite working devices is to begin his more 'folksy' stories in a completely colloquial, loose, free-wheeling manner, gradually tightening his form and language in successive drafts" ("The Brennan Papers," p. 221).

[39]Mary Hirth to Fadiman, January 21, 1970.

Sanctuary, which Faulkner finished in May of 1929. It differs considerably from the final version, although, according to Millgate, not in the ways Faulkner claimed in his introduction to the Modern Library edition of the novel.[40] Like *Light in August*, the *Sanctuary* manuscript has many paste-on slips, and parts of it are written in the same bright blue and purple inks. In addition, the base pages at the beginnings of some of the chapters provide transitions that prepare for these paste-on slips—a practice that will be noted in the discussion of the *Light in August* revisions. *Sanctuary* also displays many canceled chapter numerals, indicating a rearrangement in the order of episodes and in the introduction of characters. Strangely enough, chapter 2 of *Sanctuary* once began with Horace Benbow in his study, described in words that recall the introduction of Gail Hightower at the beginning of chapter 3 of *Light in August*. Benbow is introduced as follows: "At home, from his study window, he could see the grape arbor. Each spring he watched the reaffirmation of the old ferment, the green-snared promise of unease."

The similarities in the physical appearance of the two manuscripts confirm the fact that Faulkner made extensive revisions in both and used the same methods to effect these revisions. Comparing the Virginia manuscript of *Light in August* to the manuscripts of *The Sound and the Fury* and *As I Lay Dying* (also at Virginia) reveals similar work habits but fewer paste-on slips, salvaged from previous drafts, and fewer canceled numbers documenting changes in the order of the episodes.

The Sound and the Fury manuscript displays bright blue, black, and royal blue inks. Most of the manuscript is written on tissue-type paper with no paste-on slips. Seven pages of thicker paper are inserted into it, indicating that a new episode has been introduced. New pages are added to the beginning, but only three sets of canceled numbers have been employed, visible on seven of the pages. A cursory glance indicates that there is more first-draft material here than in *Light in August*.

Most of the *As I Lay Dying* manuscript is inscribed in bright blue ink, but the "Vernon Tull" section is written in purple ink

---

[40] *Achievement of William Faulkner*, pp. 113-18. These pages compare revisions of all extant documents related to *Sanctuary*.

and the "Darl" section in royal blue. Some of the versos have been used, but the passages written on them have been copied out again and placed elsewhere in the manuscript. The paper is similar to the thinner kind used for the manuscript of *The Sound and the Fury* and the new pages of *Light in August*. Only two leaves show canceled numbers, and there are only three or four paste-on slips in all. Two of these, written in bright blue, are pasted to the purple ink base page of the first "Anse" section.

Thus it would appear that the same kinds of massive structural alterations apparent on the manuscript leaves of *Light in August* were not carried out directly in the extant manuscripts of the other two works. My brief description of these two manuscripts suggests one further point relevant to *Light in August*. The purple ink used on the sheets of *As I Lay Dying* raises the possibility that the few instances of that ink in the *Light in August* manuscript may mean that those passages of the latter were written close to the period of the former. (The manuscript of *As I Lay Dying* is dated October 25, 1929–December 11, 1929.) Evidence will be provided in the next chapter for the supposition that these "purple" passages are the earliest in the manuscript of *Light in August*, though the actual date of their writing must, for the present, remain purely conjectural.

Studies of Faulkner's Work Habits

Faulkner's work habits have been recorded in Meriwether's *The Literary Career of William Faulkner*, Stephen Dennis's "The Making of *Sartoris*," the interviews collected in *Lion in the Garden*, and in the seminars recorded in *Faulkner in the University*. It is particularly relevant to this study to observe, among the manuscripts at the University of Virginia Library, the three different versions of a single episode in the unpublished short story entitled "Love." Two are in holograph form and one is typed. There are also three, possibly four, holograph versions of a single episode (never carried forward to the typescript) among the leaves of a manuscript entitled "Growing Pains" (included among the *Elmer* documents). These fragments illustrate Faulkner's method of rewriting entire episodes, as well as single paragraphs, many times before he considered them worthy of being added to the manuscript.

As yet there have been comparatively few studies of Faulkner's manuscripts. Meriwether noted this circumstance in 1961,[41] and Stephen Dennis, eight years later, said that "Faulkner's manuscripts have not received the amount of attention one would expect."[42] Dennis's dissertation on *Sartoris* is the first full-scale study of revisions that attempts to reconstruct previous drafts of an entire novel. It is an impressive study and should inspire more such investigations of those Faulkner manuscripts that offer the possibility.

Of the studies of revisions listed by Meriwether,[43] only Linton Massey's article on *Sanctuary* deals in detail with the earlier arran   nent of the episodes and discusses the revisions from the point of view of the structural implications of the changed positions of individual episodes.[44] Millgate, in *The Achievement of William Faulkner*, has made preliminary investigations when possible of the manuscripts as they relate to his interpretations of the published texts. Leon Howard's unpublished lecture, "The Creation of a Novel: William Faulkner's *The Sound and the Fury*" (1969), traces Faulkner's experiments in limiting point of view and shows that the final version of the "Benjy" section was an "artful intermingling of fragments composed at different and indeterminable times." Howard also points out that in the "Quentin" section Faulkner wrote an original core story that was woven into the frame story. The major episodes were composed independently and then woven into the two. Separately written fragments were also inserted into the frame story. This technique can also be observed in *Light in August* and will be fully illustrated in the chapters to follow.

Emily K. Izsak's study of the revisions of the first section of *The Sound and the Fury* shows that after completing the manuscript of the first section, Faulkner added certain links in order

---

[41]Meriwether, *Literary Career*, p. 59n.

[42]"The Making of *Sartoris*," p. 8.

[43]Meriwether, *Literary Career*, p. 59.

[44]"Notes on the Unrevised Galleys of Faulkner's *Sanctuary*," *SB*, 8 (1956), 195-208.

to establish connections between it and the third and fourth sections. Izsak provides a thorough analysis of syntactical revisions, also noting shifts of dialogue to different characters, and phrases to different positions. She cites many of the same phenomena that can be observed in the changes from the manuscript to the typescript of *Light in August*, such as the increase in the number of paragraphs and the radical difference in the use of italics.[45]

The introduction of Gerald Langford's recently published collation of the manuscript and published text of *Absalom, Absalom!* points out the importance of manuscript studies in forming critical interpretations. The author notes that tracing the process of revision demonstrates "how the meaning of a fictional work can shape its structure and thus stand revealed by what has become the outward and visible sign, or form, of that meaning."[46] Langford discusses the structural aspects of Faulkner's revisions and notes that certain of the errors of time and chronology are "the unintentional result of Faulkner's reworking of his original chronology."[47]

Langford assumes that the date at the beginning of the manuscript of *Absalom, Absalom!* refers to the actual inception of the composition of the novel. He states: "Like most 'first drafts,' the present manuscript is a composite of reworked passages and other passages written probably only once: this fact is revealed, first, by Faulkner's preservation in the manuscript of various cancelled passages followed by reworked versions, and, second, by his economical practice of simply pasting in, instead of copying over, passages clipped from pages written earlier or later than the pages on which they appear."[48]

Unfortunately, Langford ignores such matters as the types of paper and the shades of ink in the manuscript, which has been described by Millgate as a composite "made up of material written at different times over what may have been a fairly long period." There are many sections affixed to the base sheets, and

[45]"The Manuscript of *The Sound and the Fury*," p. 190, et passim.

[46]*Faulkner's Revisions of* "Absalom, Absalom!" p. 3.

[47]Ibid., p. 4.

[48]Ibid., p. 5.

"these sections, like the base sheets themselves, are in a variety of different inks and even show minor differences of handwriting." The manuscript is dated "March 30, 1935" on the first page and "31 January 1936" on the last.[49] It appears, therefore, that these dates do not refer to the very earliest drafts of the novel but to the beginning of the particular manuscript now in Texas. Moreover, Faulkner himself said on several occasions that he worked on it for a year and then put it away. When he returned to it, he found that "there was a lot of rewriting in that."[50]

In fact, Faulkner said explicitly that he wrote *Pylon* because he got into trouble with *Absalom, Absalom!* and had to get away from it for a while.[51] Since *Pylon* was published in 1935, it seems highly probable that some of the paste-on slips now found in the Texas *Absalom* manuscript were retrieved from drafts written before the date (March 30, 1935) found on its opening leaf. *Absalom* may even be one of the two novels that Faulkner referred to in 1932 when he told Henry Nash Smith that he was working on two novels and that one of them might take him two years to finish.[52] Because *Light in August* was so nearly completed by the date of Smith's visit (February 1932), Faulkner may have been working also on both *Pylon* and *Absalom*, or he may have been referring to only the latter and to *Light in August*. The evidence, however, indicates that Faulkner started *Absalom* several years before he prepared the Texas manuscript and that he took longer than the ten-month span between its dates to compose the novel.[53]

Inasmuch as the manuscript of *Light in August* is similar in appearance to that of *Absalom, Absalom!* it is safe to assume

---

[49] *Achievement of William Faulkner*, p. 150. For a more complete bibliographical description, see *William Faulkner: An Exhibition of Manuscripts*, p. 13.

[50] *Faulkner in the University*, p. 281.

[51] Ibid., p. 36.

[52] *Lion in the Garden*, p. 32.

[53] Noel Polk in a well-documented attack on *Faulkner's Revisions of* "Absalom, Absalom!" also takes exception to Langford's facile assumption of the dating of the novel. See "Review Essay of the Manuscript of *Absalom, Absalom!*" *MissQ*, 25(1972), 358-67.

that the dates on neither manuscript pertain to the earliest stages of composition. Stephen Dennis has commented that the sections pasted to the new manuscript pages of *Sanctuary, Light in August, Absalom, Absalom!* and *The Hamlet* have been taken from early manuscript drafts and that later insertions have been written on the base page between these pastings.[54] This observation is of interest not only to critics concerned with Faulkner's work habits but also to those attempting to trace the stages of growth of the various novels.

Other studies of Faulkner's revisions, which will be cited presently for more specific purposes, also corroborate the suppositions on which my hypothesis is based. In short, most of the critics who have looked closely at Faulkner's manuscripts add evidence in one form or another to substantiate Meriwether's statement that "the writing of nearly every work . . . was characterized by the most rigid discipline, a discipline made equally evident at every stage in the writing, from revisions involving the rearrangements of whole chapters in a novel to the almost endless process of minor stylistic polishing."[55]

Assumptions

Every study of manuscript revisions is unique because every manuscript is unique. But the student of revisions is frequently frustrated when flights of speculation are grounded for lack of sufficient evidence. In following Faulkner's path as he composed *Light in August*, one finds few difficulties in observing the changes between the corrected typescript in Virginia and the published text of the novel, for, with the exception of printing errors, the two are nearly synonymous. But the holograph manuscript contains various draft levels deeply buried and ultimately fused to form a new version of the novel. As Dennis has noted, "*Sanctuary* is the first novel for which Faulkner destroyed one

[54]"The Making of *Sartoris*," p. 4.

[55]Meriwether, *Literary Career*, p. 60. See also James A. Winn, "Faulkner's Revisions: A Stylist at Work," *AL*, 41 (1969), 231-50.

manuscript in order to create another."[56] It is impossible, therefore, to reconstruct a complete previous version of the novel.

Still, although Faulkner "apparently took pains to save only
the finished work," he left many clues in the leaves of the manuscript of *Light in August* to the stages through which it passed
before it was finally completed.[57] Earlier and later sections of
the work can be identified, and new material and the rearrangement of narrative episodes can be observed, as well as changes
of setting and narrative point of view. By using external evidence
in the form of the physical appearance of the manuscript and
internal evidence based on revisions of narrative fact and the
narrative inconsistencies that remain in both the manuscript and
the published text, one can make certain assumptions as to the
direction and purposes of the revisions.[58]

But before I proceed to offer my theories of how the
documents described above came to appear as they do, certain
questions should be posed about documents that apparently no
longer exist. Since only the three final stages preceding the novel
are available in complete form, it is hard to resist speculation on
what may have preceded them.

Certain physical characteristics of the manuscript suggest that
Faulkner may have written an early version of the story in which
Joe Christmas was merely a name or was seen only externally
through the eyes of the other characters. If such a version
existed, the Christmas section would have been written and
added later and the Lena-Bunch-Hightower story altered to
accommodate it.[59] Such a version could explain why there are
no 0.003 millimeter sheets or paste-on slips in the entire Christmas section of the Virginia manuscript, beginning in chapter 5

---

[56]"The Making of *Sartoris*," p. 4. Dennis suggests that a previous version of
Sanctuary can be reconstructed because there are cut down and reused versos in the
manuscript. *The Hamlet* also provides some opportunity for reconstruction because
pages remain from which fragments have been cut.

[57]Meriwether, *Literary Career*, p. 60.

[58]Many critics have observed inconsistencies in the novel. The most complete
listing I have seen is Richard L. Canary's "Caveat Lector: The State of Packaged
Learning," *CE*, 32 (1970), 370-79.

[59]In future references, in the interest of saving space, the Lena-Bunch-Hightower
story will be called the LBH story.

with Joe Christmas the night before the murder and ending with the murder in chapter 12. At this hypothetical stage the novel would have depicted the effect of the murder on three characters accidentally caught up in the catastrophe and on the townspeople of Jefferson and Mottstown, who in one way or another became involved in the sensational event. This possibility is also suggested by the fact that no familiar character from any of the Yoknapatawpha stories appears in the Christmas flashback, although the Armstids, Buck Connor, Buford, Maxey, Verner, and Gavin Stevens all figure briefly in the events of the narrative present.

Contrariwise, it is possible that the novel was written in two separate sections, with the events of the narrative present in one section and the Christmas flashback in the other. The author may have intended from the start to introduce Joe Christmas, not only as the catalyst whose act of murder set off the action of the LBH story, but also as an actor in the drama of the events of the narrative present. The Virginia manuscript reveals some evidence for this theory and even more for the assumption that the story of the present was revised separately from that of Christmas's past.

It also provides evidence for the assumption that there was a shorter version of *Light in August*, lacking the seven chapters of the Christmas flashback. Precisely how much of this version was completed before the flashback was added is hard to judge. But parts of chapters 5 and 12 in which Christmas figures conspicuously were probably present, as well as the Hines story that reveals the facts about his birth. It is the evidence for this version that is apparent in the manuscript and on which I shall base many of my arguments in the following pages.

Although the precise time order of the revisions cannot be reconstructed nor their various stages delineated accurately, the physical characteristics of the Virginia manuscript provide evidence for certain assumptions:

1. It represents Faulkner's semifinal draft of *Light in August*, in which he was primarily concerned with integrating the episodes of the narrative present with those of the Christmas flashback.

2. The dates on the first and last pages refer only to the

beginning and completion of the Virginia manuscript; the retrieved passages written earlier cannot be dated.

3. The canceled numerals indicate that an earlier organization of some episodes has been rearranged and that certain leaves were carried forward intact. These leaves were formerly identified by numbers that varied for the same leaf in successive stages of revision. The previous order cannot be reclaimed because the textual links are gone or have been recopied in the manuscript.[60]

4. Most of the passages inscribed on the paste-on slips have been taken from earlier drafts and subdrafts. In addition, many episodes or portions of episodes have been copied out from previous drafts onto the base pages of the manuscript.

5. Some few paste-on slips were added expressly to the Virginia manuscript and were not retrieved from previous drafts. New material also appears on the base page of the manuscript, often between paste-on slips, although many such slips are contiguous.

6. The novel originally began with the character of Gail Hightower; the earliest leaves to have been written that are still included in the Virginia manuscript are those inscribed in purple ink, describing Hightower. At the same time, Faulkner wrote the other purple ink passages still remaining in the manuscript, describing the first meeting between Lena Grove and Byron Bunch and their discussion about Joe Christmas and Joe Brown. Therefore, all five characters were present at least in name in an earlier draft of the novel.

7. The LBH story was nearly completed when Faulkner added the Christmas flashback (chapters 6 through 12). The former was compressed at the time of copying-out and compiling the Virginia manuscript. This compression was partly effected by means of cutting up an earlier draft written on thicker paper

---

[60]"Faulkner seemed to have trouble with the novel, dragging the manuscript about with him to many places and once—or, possibly, even twice—losing a small part of it. (Maybe that's why the book doesn't seem to 'work' as smoothly as some of his others—though that is just a wild surmise and an unpopular critical opinion.)" (Carvel Collins to Fadiman, May 25, 1970). Joseph Blotner says that two letters listed in *William Faulkner, "Man Working"* reveal the following: "Item 955 says that WF hopes for serial publication of the novel first, that he likes it and hopes Ben [Wasson] will too. Item 956 says that Sam Marx of MGM asked WF about the book but that WF didn't think he could use it" (Blotner to Fadiman, May 30, 1970).

and pasting certain of its passages to the thinner sheets now forming part of the manuscript. In addition, the narrative point of view and the setting of some episodes were altered.

8. After the Christmas flashback was introduced, it was considerably expanded, necessitating additional revisions of chapter 5, which is set in the narrative present, and to chapter 6, which begins the flashback. The expansion was effected in two major stages; this method accounts for many of the inconsistencies of fact found in both the manuscript and the printed text of the novel.

9. Chapters 5 through 12, which present the Christmas story directly, were first revised as an independent unit, treated separately from the remaining chapters. They show, therefore, no leaves or paste-on slips measuring 0.003 millimeters. After the revisions were carried out in the chapters that now precede and follow chapters 5 through 12, chapters 5 and 6 were revised a final time; this explains why chapter 6 is the only chapter of the Christmas flashback lacking the five canceled number-sets. Additional canceled numbers within the flashback apply only to the revisions of the flashback. Manuscript pages 70-75, which lack canceled numbers, replace previous leaves and were among the last added to the manuscript.

Procedures

For the purposes of discussion, I have divided the novel into two parts: the narrative present and the Christmas flashback. The following two chapters deal with the revisions of these two sections. Chapter 4 takes up the particular revisions that appear to have been engineered when the two large sections were joined into a single novel and also revisions within individual chapters that illustrate how the combination was achieved. Chapter 5 turns to the published text to provide additional evidence for the assumptions of the previous chapters, and the final chapter summarizes the hypotheses of the preceding chapters and the significant points about the novel that have been revealed by the study of the manuscript.

To indicate that certain quotations have been scratched out in the manuscript, I have used brackets (⟨ ⟩) around the particular word, phrase, or entire passage that has been voided, except when my text states that I am quoting a deleted passage. When I am in doubt as to the reading of a particular word, I have so indicated by a question mark in brackets following the word. Finally, when I have no clue whatever as to the word or even how many letters it contains, I have marked it "unreadable."

In the interest of consistency and reader accommodation, I have changed Faulkner's shorthand symbols and spelling to standard usage. Where he used such abbreviations as "thru," "thot," "bot," "tho," "lg" (long), "lst" (last), and "yg" (young), I have written out the words in full. I have crossed his *t*'s and supplied *q*'s and *y*'s, for the marks on the manuscript that have no counterpart on the typewriter.

As for punctuation, anticipating that readers might be as troubled as was the professional reader who normalized Faulkner's punctuation on the publisher's typescript, I have occasionally but not always supplied a final period. Faulkner, of course, withstood the pressure to supply the commas and periods the reader suggested, but since I am trying to describe complicated material as coherently as possible, I have taken the liberty of adding a period at the end of quotations which are incorporated into my sentences and which terminate the sentence in which I have used them.

Faulkner's unorthodox use of quotation marks has generally been maintained. It was his habit to employ either single quotation marks or italics to set off the mental processes of his characters. Perhaps by employing both devices, Faulkner intended to distinguish between two levels of consciousness or two degrees of intensity. For dialogue within dialogue, Faulkner followed the conventional practice of employing single quotation marks within double ones, and in quoting him I have done the same. I must point out, however, that the manuscript is not consistent in the use of any of these devices; the text in this respect is generally more consistent.

The emphasis in this study will be on the structural revisions that Faulkner made during the process of composing the Virginia manuscript. Diction changes will be noted only when they are pertinent to structural revisions or to the changed intention of the work. For the reader's convenience, I have, when quoting from the manuscript, given page references to both the manuscript and the published text, although there are many differences between the two in diction and paragraph length. Conversely, when referring specifically to the text, I have also provided the number of the manuscript page on which a different version of the quotation from the text can be found. Because my investigation is principally concerned with the reorganization of episodes and memories of episodes, the diction changes in most instances are not significant.

In the chapters to follow I shall try to present evidence for the general statements above about the growth and development of *Light in August* and attempt to illustrate how Faulkner's revisions shaped the novel. As I proceed it will become evident that Faulkner had a persistent compulsion to revise and rework his material. He was a meticulous and canny craftsman, thoroughly professional in the exploitation of all his resources and the thrifty salvaging of prior work.

In sum, since the manuscript primarily demonstrates the author's alterations in narrative structure, it illustrates the skill of his craftsmanship more readily than his "flashes of inspiration." It reveals that much more than the mere writing or telling of a story goes into the finished work and aptly bears out the percentages of inspiration and perspiration that, taken together, comprise genius. Although I must cite inconsistencies in narrative detail to give evidence for my conjectures, it is not my purpose to quibble over trivialities or to magnify insignificant aspects of a powerful and vital work of art. Instead, a study such as this one should communicate admiration for the painstaking and seemingly limitless efforts Faulkner invested in its composition.

II

The Narrative Present

IT IS STILL possible to discern in the Virginia manuscript of *Light in August* the shape of an earlier version of the novel that included most of the episodes in which Lena Grove, Byron Bunch, and Gail Hightower figure but in which Joe Christmas was far less conspicuous. Although he was frequently discussed, he was seldom seen. In fact, Faulkner had so nearly completed this earlier version that the fates of the major characters were already resolved before he filled out the story of Joe Christmas. Leaves on which the earlier version was copied out still remain in the manuscript, as well as passages inscribed on paste-on slips, salvaged when Faulkner cut up his prior draft and used large sections of it intact in the semifinal draft. Since most of these passages are comparatively clean, Faulkner must have copied out at least one previous draft, the original of which he subsequently destroyed.

It is my firm conclusion, after adding up the evidence in the manuscript, that Faulkner had written most of the story of the narrative present before he composed the long Christmas flashback. Many of the manuscript's inconsistencies of detail (some of which have been carried over to the published text) are a result of the later insertion of the Christmas story into the nearly completed LBH story.

I shall attempt in this chapter to isolate the episodes still remaining in the novel that were part of this earlier version. The evidence for my assumptions will be drawn from the physical appearance of the manuscript and from changes of diction, tone, and narrative fact. But before attempting to trace the stages in the growth of the semifinal draft in Virginia, I shall describe and discuss three of the four work sheets that preceded it.

The Texas Manuscript

As far as extant records show, the story of the novel begins with the three holograph pages, now at the University of Texas, about Gail Hightower. Many words and phrases have been crossed out, interlined, and added from the margins, indicating that these sheets may actually be the first draft of the Hightower story. In less than two and one-half pages and in a completely straight-forward manner, an omniscient narrator describes Hightower in his study, the painted sign outside his window, and the Negro nurse and children who peer at the sign. Hightower is at the window, writing, with the open Bible beneath his other hand. His recurrent vision of the shots, shouts, galloping horses, and the rush of invisible horsemen is described in detail. His back-ground is filled in briefly: "His father began to tell him about that night when he first began to hear, and when he began to remember he could not remember when he had not known the story." The omniscient narrator explains that Hightower was a late and only child, born when his father had long since "gotten out of life." His mother was a woman "whom everyone believed to have passed her climacteric." To the child it had seemed "that it was that black rush in the darkness and not a man who had gotten him . . . that he also had been attenuated out of all time by the stubborn thunder of an accomplished event."[1]

All the facts familiar from the novel about Hightower's childhood, his house, sign, and garden are reported on the first page of this early version.[2] On the second page the narrator describes Hightower with his wife en route by train to assume his clerical duties in Jefferson. He tells her excitedly about the raid on the henhouse in Jefferson in which his grandfather had participated during the Civil War; she tries in vain to silence him. The wife in this draft is an actual character, not merely, as in

---

[1]The quotations in this section are from the Texas manuscript; its pages are not numbered. The first page of the manuscript is reproduced in *William Faulkner: An Exhibition of Manuscripts.* In quotations from the manuscript I have eliminated Faulkner's deletions and have regularized his spelling.

[2]Michael Millgate discusses this early version of *LIA* and also quotes from the Texas manuscript. He points out that all the images associated with Hightower in the novel are already present in the early draft (*Achievement of William Faulkner,* p. 131).

the completed novel, Hightower's most agonizing memory. On the train to Jefferson Hightower "sat, slender and young, twisted on the green plush of the seat, facing her, his face a little wild with the recapitulation of that incident which had fathered two men, while 3 or 4 passengers watched him curiously." Mrs. Hightower, referred to only as "she," warns her husband that some member of his future congregation might also be aboard the train, and her warning forces Hightower to remember that they must both behave with perfect probity to "compensate for their youth in the eyes of the prospective flock." " 'A little child shall lead them,' he had said to comfort her, who would need so much reassuring, with her weak health to begin with, but to himself, 'I hope I can do as well there as he did. I must,' he said hearing again the dark thunder rushing into the night, 'I must do it.' "

The third page is less than half-filled. The narrator describes Hightower's arrival in Jefferson and reports that a member of his new flock had indeed been on the train, that the "ordeal of his first Sunday in the pulpit had not arrived before the story had got around that his dignity was a pose, that beneath it he was a little unbalanced." The page ends with a dialogue between Hightower and his wife in which she states that she does not understand why he keeps talking about the Civil War; she reminds her husband that people think it is very curious of him, particularly since he is a minister. Later that night he is awakened by her crying in the darkness and her bemoaning the fact that she is an orphan with nowhere to go. After he lights the lamp, they kneel on the floor to pray.

As summarized, many elements of the Hightower story, or at least those that constitute the exposition, already exist in this brief sketch. But they are not filtered through Hightower's mind and memory nor related to Byron Bunch as sympathizer and ultimately judge.

The Earliest Sections of the Virginia Manuscript: Chapters 2-4

A second extant version of many of the same passages may be found in chapter 3 (MS 24-30) of the semifinal draft, here referred to as the Virginia manuscript. Even without a carbon-14 test, one can identify the earliest material in the manuscript. The "purple" passages of the ink spectrum described previously (chap. 1) clearly demonstrate that a second version of *Light in August* also once began with "Gail Hightower in his study, alone." The present manuscript page 24 (T 52),[3] written completely in purple ink, shows that it was once page 2, for the number 2 is also written in purple ink, but the number 4 has been added in dark blue-black. Moreover, the headnote quoted just above, but not used in the text, has been added later, in the same ink as the number 4.

Manuscript page 24 now begins chapter 3 by describing Hightower, in slightly different language from the text, and continues through the short description of his wife's death (T 54). The purple ink continues on the next sheet to the space indicating the shift to Byron Bunch, who is introduced on the base page in light blue-black ink (MS 25; T 55). For additional proof that both manuscript pages 24 and 25 were once used to begin the novel, a purple 3, canceled in blue-black ink, and the number 25, written in the same blue-black, can be found on manuscript page 25. Two more passages of chapter 3 are inscribed in purple ink, one each pasted to manuscript pages 26 and 27.[4] Chapter 3 will be discussed in more detail presently, but in order to demonstrate that Lena Grove and Byron Bunch were also a part of the purple ink draft, it is necessary to turn back to the second chapter of the manuscript.

The first part of chapter 2 (MS 13-23; T 27-51) is devoted to a flashback describing Joe Christmas and Joe Brown as seen through the eyes of Byron Bunch when all three worked together at the planing mill in Jefferson. It is enlivened by the colloquial dialogue of the other men at the mill who comment on this strange pair. After the episode in which both men quit their

---

[3]All pages cited from the published text refer to the first printing of *Light in August* (New York: Harrison Smith and Robert Haas, 1932). The Modern Library College Edition (New York: Random House, 1968) has been reproduced photographically from the first printing, October 6, 1932. References to the manuscript will be abbreviated as MS and to the published book as T.

[4]All pages and paste-on slips inscribed in purple ink consist of paper measuring 0.004 mm.

jobs, there is a space to indicate a shift in narrative time, followed by the omniscient narrator's brief summary of Byron Bunch's life in Jefferson. This passage brings the reader to the Saturday of the immediate present and prepares for the introduction of Lena Grove.

The action of the narrative present begins: "Then Byron fell in love. . . . It happens on a Saturday afternoon while he is alone at the mill. Two miles away the house is still burning" (MS 19; T 44). Beginning with manuscript page 20 and continuing through page 22, five passages written in purple ink on the thicker paper are affixed to thinner base pages; these paste-on slips are corrected in the dark blue ink of the base page.

It is in these sections affixed to the base page that Byron Bunch talks to Lena Grove and tells her about Joe Christmas, Joe Brown, and the fire at Miss Burden's. Consequently, it can comfortably be assumed that these passages were taken from the same draft that provides the purple ink descriptions of Hightower in chapter 3 and also that in that draft Lena, Bunch, and Hightower were in some way concerned with Joe Brown and the man with the funny name of Joe Christmas (T 48).

From the evidence above, one can identify those fragments of the first-draft level of the LBH story that now form part of the semifinal draft. Although Faulkner said that the idea of *Light in August* came from seeing a "young girl with nothing, pregnant, determined to find her sweetheart," the first chapter of that draft began with Gail Hightower and somewhere within it occurred Byron's and Lena's first meeting.[5]

It is doubtful that the present chapter 1 formed a part of the earliest draft, for a significant change of diction from the manuscript to the book can be seen in the second paste-on slip of manuscript page 21. Lena is talking to Byron, while quietly he watches her. In the manuscript she is "telling him more than she knows that she is telling, or that she even knows about the man who has betrayed and deserted her and she's not even aware that she has been deserted and like everyone else to whom she has told her story, he knows almost at once that her name is not Mrs. Bunch." (The last word was intended by the author to be

---

[5]*Faulkner in the University*, p. 74.

Burch.) The novel now reads, "As she has been doing now to the strange faces among whom she has travelled for four weeks with the untroubled unhaste of a change of season" (T 47).

This revision seems significant because the manuscript version of this scene summarizes briefly the necessary information about Lena provided in chapter 1, but the diction does not in any way convey the tone of the first chapter. Since the Hightower chapter once began an earlier draft, it is quite possible that the present chapter 1, describing Lena on the dusty road, having come "all the way from Alabama a-walking," (T 1) did not exist at the time the purple ink leaves were inscribed.

Originally Byron Bunch may have been the narrator instead of the auditor of most of the Hightower story in chapter 3 (MS 24-30). Byron does not appear by name in any of the passages written in purple ink in that chapter, but his presence is indicated by an insertion from the margin, written in blue ink. For example, one paste-on slip in purple ink begins, " '⟨And so⟩ after about almost a year in Jefferson. . . .'" From the margin Faulkner had added "and they told Byron how after about a year in Jefferson . . ." (MS 26; T 57). In fact, from manuscript pages 26 to 29 Byron Bunch appears by name only on the base page of the manuscript and never in any of the paste-on slips. All these slips are written in either purple or royal blue ink on the parchmentlike paper used for the earlier draft (MS 26, 27, 28).

On these pastings, retrieved from an earlier draft and placed in chapter 3 of the manuscript, the speaker who relates the episodes of Hightower's life in Jefferson uses colloquial and sub-standard diction. This narrator can be found not only in the purple ink pastings but in those written in royal blue as well; his diction has been corrected in the printed text. The quotation marks indicating that the passages were originally in the form of direct dialogue in the manuscript have been removed for the indirect dialogue of the text. But the manuscript still reveals the presence of the former narrator, who uses such phrases as "wouldn't no longer" and "him preaching" and "she had done crawled across the floor." He says of the K.K.K. episode: " 'But he wouldn't tell who done it. And a lot of the folks knowed that was wrong.' " These linguistic characteristics have been modified by Faulkner, in the blue-black ink in which the base page is written, to conform to the more standard usage of the published text. The original narrator was fond of "I reckon," whereas the present narrator prefers "very likely."

Thus, sizable revisions are apparent on the manuscript leaves of chapter 3, made for the purpose of engaging Byron Bunch as auditor of the Hightower story. But the story itself was carried over from an earlier draft and the original narrator can still be found on the thicker paste-on slips throughout the chapter. One such slip attached to manuscript page 28 shows an odd variation of a single detail: Hightower, leaving the church after his wife's sensational death, in order to avoid having his picture taken by the photographer waiting outside, covers his face with his hat, instead of his hymnbook. Faulkner has changed "hat" to "hymn-book" where it occurs on manuscript page 28, but he has not made the correction in chapter 20 on manuscript page 182, at which time Hightower himself is remembering the episode. Hence, the earlier draft of the LBH story must have included a version of Hightower's later reflections on his catastrophic failure as a minister in Jefferson.

A jarring mixture of tones, notable in the voice of the omniscient narrator, also helps to distinguish between the earlier and later passages of chapter 3. This narrator is not the one who "reckons" but the narrator who describes Hightower at the beginning of the chapter (in purple ink) and Hightower's obser-vations of Byron at the end (in royal blue ink) in such terms as "the puny, unhorsed figure moving with that precarious and meretricious cleverness of animals balanced on their hinder legs" (T 70). This rather supercilious narrator presents Hightower's thoughts as being sardonic and patronizing, whereas the narrator of the newer passages reports that Hightower says of the people of Jefferson: " 'They are good people. . . . And so it is not for me to outrage their believing nor for Byron Bunch to say that they are wrong' " (T 69). Fortunately, Faulkner adjusted the narrator's more offensive diction in the first page of the chapter from "but now and then a Negro nursemaid in charge of a child or two would pause and spell them out loud [the letters of Hightower's sign] with that dull stupid and vacuous idiocy of her idle and illiterate race," to "with that vacuous idiocy of her idle and illiterate kind" (MS 24; T 53). "Kind," of course, could apply to nursemaids as a group rather than to Negroes as a race. The substitution needs no comment except that it is one small indication of the changed attitude of the narrator (and perhaps the author) and one slight but early clue to the progressive change in the intention of the work itself.

Chapters 2 and 3 dive deep into the well of the past, surfacing at the end of each chapter to return to the world of the present. In chapter 4 (MS 31-40) Faulkner concentrates on the events of Saturday and Sunday of the immediate present. Here, setting and point of view work together to unify the four episodes that comprise the chapter. The manuscript shows that the author has snipped material from disparate parts of at least one previous draft and, on this occasion, used Byron Bunch as narrator to take in the seams of what may have been a more loosely designed garment. By placing the action in Hightower's study, with Hightower now in the role of auditor, and by using Byron as reporter of both the Lena Grove and the Joe Christmas story, Faulkner has managed to relate to each other, if somewhat indirectly, all four characters. Consequently, the episode of Byron's and Hightower's meeting on Sunday night serves as a frame for the more significant plot developments that Byron reports.

Of the four episodes related by Byron to Hightower, two concern Lena and two deal with the murder. Byron first tells the story of Lena's appearance at the mill and then carries the plot forward to describe his own attempt to save her from the knowledge that the man she is seeking, Lucas Burch (referred to as Joe Brown by everyone but Lena from this point on), is involved in the search for a murderer. Byron also tells of his taking her to Mrs. Beard's boarding house to spend the night. In addition, he recounts the discovery of the fire and corpse by a farmer making his usual Saturday visit to town, and repeats in detail Joe Brown's eager testimony, given readily once he is aware that Miss Burden's nephew in New Hampshire has offered a reward of one thousand dollars to the man who captures the murderer. The final leaf of the chapter, a thicker one than the four preceding it, provides the information that "they took some bloodhounds out there today," but that Christmas has not yet been caught. It ends with Byron's description of Lena descending from a wagon on the Jefferson square the preceding day (MS 40; T 93-94).

Two obvious characteristics can be seen in the pages to which paste-on slips have been affixed. First, certain of these passages were originally written as dramatic scenes rather than as action discussed after the fact.[6] This changed point of view is particularly evident in manuscript page 34, which begins, " 'That's what I thought,' Byron said, quickly, eagerly" (T 79) and ends, " 'Would it surprise you to hear that that fellow Christmas hadn't done no worse than that in his life?' " (T 81). Most of this sheet, consisting of a dialogue between Byron and his landlady, Mrs. Beard, was probably written with neither Hightower nor his study in mind, for Hightower appears only on the base page as a reminder to the reader of the immediate present and the location of the scene.

Secondly, there are several other indications that the order of these episodes was readjusted when they were incorporated into the Virginia manuscript. For instance, as Bunch begins to tell Hightower the story of the countryman's discovery of the fire, manuscript page 36 reads, " ⟨Then⟩ it was yesterday morning' " (T 83). "Then," of course, has been deleted because it would be a non sequitur here, and "morning" has been added from the margin. And on the same sheet there is also a margin reminder that the scene between Bunch and Hightower occurs on Sunday night.

The revision reveals that Byron Bunch did, in fact, tell Hightower in the previous draft the story of the murder and of Brown's testimony, for Hightower does appear in the paste-on slip of thicker paper that includes "Byron ceases and looks, glances at the man beyond the desk. Hightower has not moved" (MS 36; T 85). But Hightower never appears in a paste-on slip of the thicker paper during the recital of the Lena episodes. Thus, it can be assumed that the Lena episodes were not originally told to Hightower but reported by the omniscient narrator as they were enacted. This method may have been used before chapter 1 was written in order to provide a more direct view of

---

[6]Norman Holmes Pearson observes that Faulkner's revisions often show that the angle of reference was primarily changed("Faulkner's Three 'Evening Suns,' " p. 62).

Lena, for in chapter 4 she closely resembles her portrait of chapter 1.

From the discussion above, it is apparent that all the episodes from the end of chapters 2 through 4 of the text (T 45-94) involving Lena's meeting with Byron, the scene at the boarding house, the Hightower biography, Byron's report of the fire and the murder, Christmas's and Brown's bootlegging activities, and Brown's testimony were a part of an earlier draft, although the order of these passages has been rearranged. But it is hard to discern whether the first six leaves of chapter 2, describing Christmas and Brown as seen through the eyes of the men at the planing mill, consist of episodes copied out from this same previous draft (MS 13-18; T 27.1-42.11).[7] Some earlier version, however, of Christmas and Brown at the mill must have existed because one short passage, written on parchment and pasted to manuscript page 17, shows signs of having been composed before anything else on those sheets (T 38.3-17).

Again the passage is in the form of a dialogue within a dialogue, recounted by a voice that employs substandard diction, such as "wouldn't have no trouble doing that" (MS 17; T 38). Perhaps it is the voice of the mysterious stranger who originally told part of the Hightower story in chapter 3 of the manuscript or even, since he is not mentioned directly in the passage, the voice of Byron Bunch.

In repeating the mill hands' remarks about Brown and Christmas, the narrator refers to the character Mooney by the name of Ad and also mentions for the first time the new car in which the two mavericks have recently been seen. The new car is later mentioned by Brown when he tells the sheriff that it was given to Joe Christmas by Joanna Burden (MS 38; T 89). This second reference also occurs on a parchment pasting from an earlier draft. But, curiously, throughout the two chapters that describe Joe Christmas's affair with Joanna Burden, no car is ever mentioned in either the manuscript or the text. In fact, Joe Christmas always walks into town.

There are also several allusions to another seemingly vestigial detail, which can be found on two of the parchment paste-on

---

[7]The last four words of T 42.11 are inscribed on MS 19.

slips of chapters 2 and 4, as well as in two recopied passages. These strange references allude to the rumor of a violent incident in which Brown and Christmas were involved on the road to Memphis. A close reader of the novel must wonder what happened, for the exact details are never given and the hints seem only to function for the purpose of illustrating Christmas's proclivity for violence. In the Burden sections of the Christmas flashback, the narrator reports that Joe began to sell liquor (T 247) and that he took frequent business trips to Memphis, where he betrayed Joanna with other women (T 249), but the episode that so absorbs Christmas's acquaintances in the earlier chapters of the novel is never mentioned. It might, therefore, be interpreted as the remains of an incident more fully developed in the earlier draft. Its inclusion in the published text, as well as its fragmentary nature, leads to the assumption that there must have been some previous version of the mill hands' observing and discussing their fellow worker, Joe Christmas.

Chapter 5: Stage 1

Chapter 5 of the Virginia manuscript is extremely different in various ways from chapter 5 of the published text (MS 41-49; T 95-110). I shall be describing the stages and kinds of revisions apparent in this chapter when I ultimately attempt to trace the complicated path by which Faulkner reached his final version of this remarkable tour de force. My present purpose, however, is to try to demonstrate that many of its passages were retrieved from the same draft as those of chapters 2 and 4.

The manuscript version of chapter 5 holds key evidence for the postulation I have offered—namely, that Faulkner had written almost the entire version of the dramatic action of the narrative present before he added the Christmas flashback. From the appearance of this chapter, I have concluded that the major episodes of Joe Christmas's last night as a free man in Jefferson were carried forward from the earlier version to the semifinal draft of the manuscript.

No canceled numbers appear on the manuscript pages of chapter 5, but there are seventeen slips carefully pasted to its nine pages. Although there is not a shred of the tissue-type paper, several shades of blue ink are observable, among them the royal blue that was used for the passages in chapter 3 spoken by the semiliterate narrator. Significantly, in both chapters 3 and 5 this ink is found on the paste-on slips rather than on the base page.

Other clues, however, seem more reliable. Looking at the list of canceled numbers in the Appendix, table 2, one can see two pairs of numbers (35, 36; 43, 44) in chapter 12 on manuscript pages 108 and 109; they are much lower than the final pagination and do not form part of the five canceled number-sets. These numbers overlap two canceled pairs (34, 35; 43, 44) on the first two leaves of chapter 13, and they also form a series with a third pair of numbers there (45, 46). Manuscript page 108, moreover, shows a canceled roman numeral VII. It looks, therefore, as if these leaves were originally paginated when the episodes they contain occurred far earlier in the novel and were carried over intact from a copying-out of a previous draft.

Manuscript pages 108 and 109 are introduced by the headnote "Escape of Christmas into the country, first night." They include passages that supply a major clue in the search for Christmas (T 267.21-270.31). After the murder, Joe jumps into a passing car, terrifying its youthful white occupants because, without realizing it, he is grasping a gun. When he leaps from the car, he flings away the gun, which is later discovered by the eager bloodhounds.

Because of the low numbers found on manuscript pages 108 through 111, one can conclude that these leaves were retrieved from a previous draft in which the gun clue was manifest. In addition, the passage in which the bloodhounds discover the gun appears in a long paste-on slip attached to manuscript page 113, which also includes the description of the country boy's visit to the sheriff (T 281.6-282.11). Consequently, these two episodes as well were probably carried forward from an earlier version.

Since this direct but extremely brief and fragmentary view of Joe Christmas has been traced to a previous draft, it seems likely that more of the matter of Christmas may have been lifted from that draft and pasted to the leaves of the Virginia manuscript. And, in fact, almost all of chapter 5, from manuscript page 44 to the end, is written on clean, textually linked paste-on slips, with pages 47 and 48 showing nothing at all inscribed on the base page.[8] It looks, therefore, as if the paste-on slips of pages 44-49 (beginning "the cool mouth of darkness," T 100-110) once directly preceded the last two leaves of chapter 12, before the earlier sections of chapter 12 were written.

Two additional factors point to the conclusion that before turning from Christmas to his pursuers, Faulkner wrote at least one long, powerfully sustained episode tracing Joe's wandering during the twenty-four hours preceding the murder. Both factors, although of a different order, concern matters of diction.

At the end of chapter 5, moments before the murder, Christmas rises and moves toward the house (MS 49; T 110). Near the end of the new sections of chapter 12 and just before the older leaves (MS 108, 109), Christmas repeats the identical action that terminates chapter 5: "He rose. He moved from the shadow and went around the house" (MS 107; T 266).

Why does Joe rise twice at precisely the same moment? One explanation may be that the first "rising" was part of an earlier manuscript and, conversely, that the second was added so much later that the author forgot, when he composed the long Christmas flashback, that Joe had already risen and was moving toward the house. The repetition adds evidence for the theory that most of chapter 5 was written to form a part of the earlier version and that the flashback was added after that version was nearly complete. In revising, Faulkner probably allowed the repetition to remain because it functioned effectively to guide the reader back to the exact moment of the narrative present in which he had last encountered Joe Christmas.

A second prominent feature of the diction of the manuscript version of chapter 5 dramatically illustrates the changed intention of the total work, for in that earlier version Joe Christmas actually had Negro blood.

One positive statement to that effect on the narrator's part can be found in a paste-on slip on manuscript page 48: "The Negro smell, was behind and below him now; upon his sweaty

[8]There is a long paste-on slip attached to MS page 45 that was not retrieved from the same draft. This slip will be fully discussed in my next chapter.

face blew faintly now the smell, carbolical, asceptical of the hospital. His heart beat and beat, slowly while his ⟨unreadable⟩ cooled black blood talking [?] now only to death."

A previous passage inscribed in a paste-on slip on manuscript page 47, describing Christmas's unwilling visit to Freedman Town, presents Joe as standing there in a "kind of shocked outrage and fury, as though somehow he had betrayed himself unawares [?]." He sees the "dimlighted city, hospital sprawled" and hears "above and about him, the bodiless fecund murmur of the voices of Negro women." For the text Faulkner has explained that to Joe these voices seem to be "murmuring, talking, laughing, in a language not his" (MS 47; T 106-7). Also the sentence found on manuscript page 44 beginning "but the black blood was not talking now" has been deleted from the text (T 101). These revisions, although seemingly slight, illustrate how Faulkner neutralized the color of Joe Christmas's blood.

The remaining revisions of chapter 5 will be discussed in the following chapters of this study to demonstrate how it was subsequently altered after Faulkner wrote the Christmas flashback. But before terminating the present discussion, I shall risk a conjecture about the original shape of chapter 5. Earlier I pointed out that instead of being separated by sixty manuscript sheets as they now are, the paste-on slips at the end of chapter 5 were probably once contiguous to the present manuscript pages 108 and 109. In that order, the parallel must have been more clearly drawn between the two episodes in which Joe, unaware that he is doing so, brandishes two lethal weapons at two sets of innocent victims: Jupe and his company of Negroes (T 109-10) and the white girl and boy in the commandeered car (T 267-70). For just as Joe's wanderings earlier in the chapter symbolically illustrate the color dichotomy that torments him, these later episodes also focus on color, as well as illustrating the extreme dissociation between Joe's thoughts and his actions.

The Composite Pieces of Chapters 13 and 14

My quest for the hidden draft levels buried within the Virginia manuscript next leads to chapter 13. From this point on, the

clues are more scattered and more difficult to identify and inter-
pret. There are several helpful canceled numbers, a generous
supply of paste-on slips, and other clues in the form of inconsistencies of narrative fact—all of which strongly point to a
previous version of the episodes of the week following the
murder, a version that was based on a different calendar of
events. In identifying this previous version, I shall be forced to
dismantle some of the chapters, but I hope that when they are
reassembled the process will serve to illustrate Faulkner's gift
for achieving significant syntheses.

As readers of the novel have surely noticed, there are two
versions of the discovery of the fire and of Miss Burden's corpse,
as well as of Brown's return to give evidence to the sheriff and
claim the reward. The second version occurs in the present
chapter 13 (MS 110-22) and is told by the omniscient narrator
focusing on the sheriff and the reaction of the crowd, excitedly
gathered to observe the scene of carnage. Certain of these episodes now in chapter 13 were, in an earlier draft, placed directly
after those of the present chapter 5, for, as stated above, the
low canceled numbers on the first two leaves of the manuscript
of chapter 13 (MS 110, 111) form two complete number-sets
when added to the two pairs on manuscript pages 108 and 109.
The two canceled roman numerals (VI and VII) found on manuscript page 110, show too that these four pages were once
actually part of a chapter that was placed far earlier in the novel.[9]

The first two parchment leaves of chapter 13 are followed by
textually linked slips pasted to two new tissue-type pages. On
these four pages (MS 110-13) the narrator describes the townspeople's reactions to the murder and the sheriff's activities after
the murder has been discovered. Manuscript pages 110 and 111
include the description of the townspeople and conclude with
the sheriff's frustrated attempt to gain information from the
Negro he has seized (T 271.1-276.12). On the next two leaves
the questioning of the Negro is continued; then the sheriff re-

---

[9]MS page 110 was lent by Faulkner to the exhibition of his manuscripts at
Princeton. Meriwether described it in his catalog of the exhibition as follows: "That
Faulkner's revisions of the manuscript involved rearrangement of this episode is indi-
cated by the different page and chapter numbers which are cancelled" (*Literary
Career*, p. 23).

turns to town to see Miss Burden's will; Brown appears; the dogs are "disgorged" on "the bleak platform, in the sad dawn of that Sunday morning" and are taken to the cabin to pick up Christmas's scent (T 279-80). Finally, the boy and his father report the episode described at the end of chapter 12, in which Christmas, gun in hand, had stopped a passing car and commandeered a ride. The posse goes forth again. The dogs, "with their apparent infallibility for metal in any form," find Joanna's old Civil War cap-and-ball pistol but cannot discover Christmas's trail (T 281). The members of the posse, discouraged, return to Jefferson on Monday morning.

The events listed above, as noted in the preceding discussion of chapter 5, must all have occurred in the previous draft, written and copied out before Faulkner added the Christmas flashback. Not only do two of these sheets still show their previous foliation, but certain revisions of diction demonstrate that the passages were written with a different version in mind. On the base page of manuscript page 112 Faulkner originally placed the dogs' arrival on "Monday AM." "Monday" has been replaced by "Sabbath." Also, the last paste-on slip of manuscript page 113 shows some uncertainty. After the foray of the first posse, Faulkner has crossed out and added again, in black ink, "then it was Monday morning" (T 282). Black ink is generally used in the manuscript for late revisions and for headnotes that do not appear in the text. Furthermore, in a paste-on slip in the manuscript, the country boy "told of having been on the way home in a car later *Saturday* night and of a man who had stopped him with a pistol," whereas the text reads, "The boy told of having been on the way home in a car late *Friday* night, and of a man who stopped him a mile or two beyond the scene of the murder, with a pistol" (MS 113; T 281; my italics).

By applying a magnifying glass to the joints of chapter 13, one can see that the first four pages, describing the beginning of the search for Christmas, were not originally linked to Byron's second meeting with Hightower on Tuesday night. For one thing, the passage of time and the transition from the posse's second foray on Monday to Byron and Hightower on Tuesday occur on the base page of manuscript page 113. The sheet ends, "They sit opposite one another in the study, the desk, the lighted

lamp between, talking of Lena on the emergency cot."[10] On this
Tuesday evening Byron and Hightower debate lengthily the
morality of moving Lena to the cabin formerly occupied by
Christmas and Brown on the Burden plantation. The scene ends
with Byron's remark "Then you won't help me. You won't say
what I ought to do" (MS 117). The text reads "Then what do
you think we—I ought to do? What do you advise?" (T 290).
Hightower insists that Byron leave Jefferson but adds that Byron
no longer needs Hightower's help, since Byron is already being
helped by the devil (T 291). Yet when Byron and Hightower
meet for the third time, an odd anachronism can be found on
both manuscript page 120 and in the text. Byron does not
stumble this time on the bottom step; Hightower, suspecting
that he has successfully engineered Lena's move to the cabin,
says," 'But at least you are going to tell me about it. What you
have already done, even if you didn't see fit to talk about it
beforehand' " (T 295).

By observing that this move was discussed on approximately
four sheets of this same chapter and that only one and one-half
leaves intervene before the argument starts again, one can conclude not only that the preceding discussion was written after
the last three pages of the chapter but also that these last three
pages were composed, revised, and copied out for an earlier
draft.[11] Moreover, a single line on the base page ends manuscript
page 119 with " 'that sounds like it may be either hope or threat,
Byron,' Hightower said" (T 295). Approximately the same line
is deleted at the beginning of manuscript page 120.[12] And at this
meeting the reader recognizes the Hightower of the earlier draft

[10]On page 310 of the typescript Faulkner has also crossed out "talking of Lena
Grove asleep on the emergency cot in Mrs. Beard's bedroom. 'I am going to find
another place for her,' Byron said." Page 311 of the typescript begins, "Byron sits
again on the hard chair . . ." (T 282). The overlapping may indicate that new pages
were added after Faulkner had typed this page.

[11]The last of these three pages, MS 122, once continued on with a line beginning
"the first definite," which was written and crossed out at the bottom of the leaf. A
paste-on slip once covered these words but was ripped off.

[12]The sentence is turned into a question in the novel. That MS 119 is a new page,
added to combine two scenes, is apparent from the fact that the Bunch-Hightower
meeting on the paste-on slip is written in much lighter blue ink than the passages on
the base page.

of chapter 3, with his "faintly overbearing note of levity" (MS 119; T 295). For further evidence that manuscript pages 120-22 formed part of the hidden draft, four triads of low canceled numbers can be observed, all but one of which now overlap the pagination of chapters 5 and 6.

Chapter 14 (MS 123-30) has been combined from at least two drafts and revised numerous times. It has no canceled numbers but shows the highest ratio of paste-on slips to the total number of pages of any chapter in the manuscript—twenty-three in all. The last five of its eight pages measure 0.003 millimeters, whereas the first three measure 0.004.

The opening page comments on the fact that Lena is comfortably settled in the cabin; the rest of the chapter tells the story of the pursuit of Christmas and his week in the woods. There is no way of knowing the precise day on which the sheriff discovers that Lena is now living on Miss Burden's plantation because shortly after his discovery the reader is thrust into the scene in which the Negro arrives in town at three o'clock Wednesday morning to tell the story of Christmas's sudden outburst at the church. The story begins after a space on the base page with the words "At three o'clock" (MS 124; T 304); they directly follow the paste-on slip that terminates the episode of the sheriff's discovery of Lena.[13] Thus, one can assume that the Wednesday episode of the posse in search of Christmas did not originally occur in that position. As it stands, it throws the entire episode of Christmas at the church, as well as the final attempt to capture him, into a flashback, the events of which occurred before the opening of the chapter.

On page 313 of the text, the narrator turns from the disgruntled sheriff to the fleeing Christmas, after the "noise and the alarms, the sound and fury of the hunt dies away." This shift in focus occurs on manuscript page 127; the narrator maintains his close-up view of Christmas to the end of the chapter.

---

[13]Byron took Lena to the Burden plantation on Wednesday evening, before his second meeting with Hightower in chap. 13 (T 296). The second meeting occurs on Wednesday because it directly follows Hightower's marketing excursion, when he learns that Christmas was seen at the Negro church (T 292). In chap. 14 the sheriff conducts the search of the church at eight o'clock Wednesday morning (T 308-9).

For several reasons, it looks as if the last three and one-half manuscript pages were written and revised separately from the earlier part of the chapter and combined with the pages describing the hunt in order to link together in a single chapter the pursuers and the pursued. First, there is the utterly detached tone of the early part of the chapter in which the narrator describes Christmas's arrogant, contemptuous behavior after he has terrorized the Negroes at the church and left behind for the sheriff an unprintable, unsigned note (T 307.20-309.12). The tone here differs considerably from the narrator's sympathetic attitude toward Christmas in the later sections in which, in a series of reflective scenes and lyric descriptions, Joe becomes one "with loneliness and quiet that has never known fury or despair" (T 313).

Next, although Christmas recollects several encounters during his week of flight, there is no reference to any reminiscence of the havoc he had created at the church. A revision, moreover, from manuscript to text of the day of the week confirms the hypothesis that the search-and-escape episodes were written independently at different periods.

One night Christmas lies "all night in a haystack," awakening "in time to watch the farm house wake" (T 314). He thinks about how hungry he is and tries to remember how many days have passed since he has had supper in Jefferson on the Friday evening of the murder. But, approaching the kitchen door, he finds that "the name of the day of the week seemed more important than the food." He hears "his mouth saying quietly: 'Can you tell me what day this is?'" (T 314). "Its Tuesday," replies the frightened woman of the text (T 315). But in the manuscript she has twice remarked, "Its Wednesday" (MS 128).[14]

A direct contradiction, therefore, can be found in the manuscript, for if Christmas had been at the church on Tuesday night and, after his fight, had hidden in the bushes outside, he could not have been lying all the same night in the haystack outside the farmhouse. Nor could he have exchanged his shoes for the brogans at daylight on Wednesday morning (T 312).

[14]The typescript shows the following uncertainty: "⟨Tuesday⟩, ⟨Wednesday⟩, ⟨Thursday⟩, ⟨Tuesday⟩."

There are also confusions of tense in the manuscript on the first of the paste-on slips that focuses directly on Joe Christmas (MS 127; T 313.6). In some cases Faulkner has tried the same verb in both the present and past tenses, then scratched out both. For the remaining verbs he has used the past tense where the text now uses the present, and vice versa. The effect of the tenses in the manuscript is to place the action of the first two paragraphs (after the space) on the Wednesday that Christmas obtained the brogans. But the changes of tense in the text and the new material added on the base pages of the manuscript place the entire period of Christmas's week in the woods into a flashback, the individual episodes of which he remembers on the Thursday night before he decides to go to Mottstown. The arrangement of paste-on slips reveals that these episodes were originally written chronologically and then purposely reshuffled to create the hazy quality of Joe's trancelike state in which each day blurs into another. There has been some attempt, though, to relate Joe's flight to the expeditions of his pursuers, evidenced in the change discussed earlier of the manuscript's "Wednesday" to the "Tuesday" of the text.

A version of Christmas's week in the woods, employing Christmas as center of consciousness, was probably written at the same time as the earliest passages of chapter 5. Faulkner seems to have had the habit of immersing himself in the story, as well as in the psyche, of a single character and following that character's development through most of the episodes that concerned him, irrespective of where those episodes would ultimately appear in the novel. But a second version of the same week was already written—a version in which we have a totally objective narrator, who concentrates on the characters of Brown and the sheriff. That version included the episode at the Negro church to which two discarded lines on the opening leaf of chapter 13 obliquely refer: "He threw the pistol away and walked from the road into the dark woods and vanished from the knowing sight and hearing of man for 4 days. That was Friday night or Saturday A.M. (MS 110).

The reference to four days unquestionably anticipates the Tuesday night catastrophe at the church; it once served to link that episode to the opening sections of chapter 13, both of which are narrated from an objective point of view. It also refers back to the end of chapter 12, in which Joe disposes of the gun. For these reasons, one can identify the search passages of chapter 14 as belonging to the earlier draft that included the present manuscript leaves 108 through 111.

But how much of the flight was actually written for the draft that told only the events of the narrative present before Faulkner added the long flashback? The question is difficult to answer from the scanty evidence of the manuscript. Nevertheless, certain characteristics of the language do indicate that parts of chapters 5 and 14 were written at the same time to echo each other. In both chapters, the author describes in similar terms the peace Christmas found in the woods. In the former, Joe, "hanging motionless and without physical weight . . . seemed to watch the slow flowing of time beneath him, thinking *All I wanted was peace*" (T 104). He also thinks, while watching the people peacefully playing cards on the veranda, " 'That's all I wanted. . . . That don't seem like a whole lot to ask' " (T 108).

On manuscript page 129 of chapter 14 can be found the following passage, not carried forward to the published text: "It is just dawn, daylight. He rises and begins to walk. He is quite weak now, and his mind goes with quiet and neutral clarity, as though it were the mind of neither man nor woman, of nothing living in life. Then with that quiet amaze: 'that was all I wanted. That don't seem a lot to ask in 30 years.' "

In addition to the similarity in diction, there is the question of Christmas's use of "30 years." That figure also appears in chapter 5 in a passage in which the author explains that although Joe had been aware of the stars for thirty years, not one of them had any meaning for him "by shape or brightness or position" (T 98). It is reminiscent of the passage in chapter 14 that describes Joe as "a foreigner to the very immutable laws which earth must obey" (T 320). But even more significant to the matter of identifying the concealed draft is the use of "thirty years" in these passages. As the published text stands, the thirty years quoted above refers only to the years after Christmas had left the orphanage. But the figure may have originally been used to provide the information that Joe Christmas was thirty when he was killed. I shall elaborate on this speculation later in this chapter.

The Texas Fragment and the Age Problem:
Chapters 15 and 16

Chapter 15 (MS 131-38) provides more proof for the assumption that the passages focusing directly on Christmas in chapter 14 were written separately and perhaps later than the chapters following them and also shows certain signs that many passages of the present chapter 15 were carried forward from the previous draft. The chapter has only one 0.003 millimeter leaf, its second (MS 132). This leaf bears three large, contiguous, textually linked paste-on slips of the 0.004 millimeter paper, with only two or three incomplete sentences at the top and bottom of the base page. The following parchment leaf (MS 133) begins with a short, textually linked parchment paste-on slip. All these pastings and all the subsequent sheets of the chapter appear to have been carried forward from an earlier draft. But the first sheet of the chapter must have been added after Faulkner wrote the passages focusing directly on Joe Christmas alone in the woods.

The chapter begins: "On that Friday when ⟨he⟩ Christmas was captured in Mottstown . . ." (MS 131). But when Faulkner rewrote that first page, he neglected to rearrange his previous day-by-day account of the week following the murder, for on manuscript page 134, copied out from the earlier version, appear the words " 'then ⟨this⟩ yesterday morning he come into Mottstown in broad daylight, on a Saturday with the town full of folks.' "[15] "Saturday" still remains in the text (T 331).

Most of the townsman's description of Joe's capture and the eccentric, unfathomable behavior of the Hineses seems, because of the confusion of dates, to have been part of the earlier draft. But there are certain name changes from manuscript to text that

---

[15]Peter Swiggart and Richard L. Canary have observed the novel's inconsistency on this point (Swiggart, *The Art of Faulkner's Novels* [Austin: Univ. of Texas Press, 1962], p. 146, and Canary, "Caveat Lector," p. 372).

might indicate that Mrs. Hines's attempt to see the sheriff originally occurred in Jefferson. The deputy mentioned in chapter 15
was first called Buford, but his name was changed to Russell in
the manuscript (MS 136; T 335). Also, old Doc Hines was once
deposited by his wife in front of Bind's Store, which became
Grimm's Store in the typescript and was changed there and in
the text to Dollar's Store (T 338). Both Buford and the Grimms
live in Jefferson; Grimm is a hardware merchant there.

One fragment of a discarded version of Christmas's capture,
obviously a very early work sheet, still remains. It is the fourth
manuscript sheet, described in my first chapter, now to be found
in Texas. An omniscient narrator relates the episode as follows:

He was captured in broad daylight, single-handed, on the main
street of a town not 20 miles from the scene of his crime and
not a week after it. Captured by a white man who stopped him
and asked his name, and ⟨in the life [?] of he said that his⟩ after
a moment he said that his name was Joe Brown—a name only
half spurious and patently ⟨invented⟩ unpremeditated. ⟨The need,
the necessity; not even apparently not⟩

The place of the capture is not specified, but it is obviously
not Jefferson. The day on which "he" was captured is clearly
not the Friday of the semifinal draft and of the text, for it is
"not a week" after the crime. But there can be no doubt that
the "he" referred to is Joe Christmas, because the pseudonym
he chose was only "half spurious." That he was a Negro can be
inferred from the narrator's specifying that he was captured by
a white man. One wonders, though, why the "he" of the passage
clutched desperately at a false name, choosing one "patently
unpremeditated." It seems inconsistent on the narrator's part to
use such diction when he could so easily have mentioned that
"he" took the name of his accomplice or partner, Joe Brown.

There are several plausible explanations of this four-line
scratching: Faulkner may have planned to describe Christmas's
capture much earlier, before telling of the connection between
Brown and Christmas and of any of the events of Christmas's
life; or, at this writing, the two characters of Brown and Christmas may have been fused into one. Obviously these few lines
provide too flimsy a piece of evidence to support so radical a

proposition as the latter, although in both the copied-out manuscript page and the text a curious line describing Brown appears: "Kind of a murderer trying to catch himself to get his own reward" (MS 40; T 94). The fragment, however, indubitably illustrates a vastly different intention on the part of the character who committed the crime, for he was seeking an alibi in inventing a false identity. As the reader of the novel knows, Joe Christmas made no attempt to protect himself or to avoid discovery when he was apprehended on the street in Mottstown. In fact, he was not captured; he surrendered.

The Texas fragment, consequently, provides important evidence for the theory that the Mottstown episodes were indeed written before the story of the events in Joe's life that led up to them. Even from this brief sketch, one can observe a far different Joe Christmas from the character of the final version. Furthermore, in the later additions Joe not only matures spiritually and intellectually but physically as well. It was a younger man who was captured on the streets in broad daylight, an older one who surrendered.

It is evident, even from the novel, that there is a discrepancy about Joe Christmas's age. At the opening of chapter 15 the narrator says that the Hineses had come to Mottstown thirty years before and that for the five years following their appearance there, Hines had returned home only once a month because he held some position in Memphis (MS 131; T 322). According to this information, Joe Christmas on that Friday when he appeared in Mottstown would have been thirty years old because it was during the first five years of Joe's life that Hines worked in Memphis as janitor of the orphanage in which he had placed his grandson.[16]

In chapter 16 Mrs. Hines tells the story of Joe's birth and says she has not seen him since he was an infant, thirty years ago

[16]William H. F. Lamont states that the confusion concerning various dates in *LIA* results from Faulkner's very casual use of the number *thirty*. He uses *thirty* in much the same way as the writers of the Bible use *forty* ("The Chronology of *Light in August*," *MFS*, 3 [1957], 360-61). Lamont gives no evidence from other Faulkner novels for this casual use of *thirty*. The Virginia manuscript shows far too many revisions effected to achieve precision in matters of elapsed time for me to agree with Lamont's statement.

(MS 142; T 350). But, contradicting the narrator of the previous chapter, she claims that five years after Joe was born she and her husband moved to Mottstown and that her husband never again returned to Memphis (MS 145; T 361). Joe, according to her reckoning, would still be thirty years old in the narrative present. Mrs. Hines adds that she and her husband made one additional move between Arkansas, where Joe was born, and Mottstown. The length of their stay in this unnamed town was probably five years; the town is not named, obviously by intention, since Faulkner substituted for the word "Mottstown" the vague "there" twice in the manuscript and also carried it over to the novel (MS 145; T 359).

The reiteration of "thirty" obviously confuses the reader who knows that Joe was about eighteen when he "entered the street which was to run for fifteen years" (T 210) and that he finally reached Mottstown after living in Jefferson for at least two and one-half years. For according to that set of figures Joe Christmas is not thirty, but thirty-five, or nearly thirty-six, on the Friday before his death when he is apprehended in Mottstown. Moreover, Faulkner carefully adjusted Joe's age from the thirty of the manuscript to the thirty-three of the text, at the point in chapter 10 where the street with imperceptible corners ended on a Mississippi country road (MS 88; T 213).[17]

The question of Joe's age in the narrative present is relevant at this point only because the confusion seems to have crept in when Faulkner turned his attention directly to Joe Christmas and developed his story beyond the short segments of the earlier draft. In chapter 3 of this study, I shall show how, as Faulkner built up, and added to, the Christmas flashback, the contradictions in the matter of age developed. As demonstrated here, the inconsistencies serve to indicate further that most of the action of the narrative present was written before the flashback was added.

It is hard to solve the puzzle of exactly how the story of the Hineses and the story they tell of Joe Christmas's birth and first five years at the orphanage were altered and reordered to appear

---

[17]Langford enumerates similar time changes and inconsistencies in dating in the manuscript of *Absalom* (*Faulkner's Revisions of* "Absalom, Absalom!" p. 12).

in the present chapters 15 and 16. Several stray canceled numbers on their leaves suggest that they may have originally formed a single chapter, before the first leaves of chapter 15 were revised to accommodate the end of chapter 14, describing Christmas's decision to go to Mottstown (see Appendix, table 1). The inconsistency about whether the Hineses had lived in Mottstown for twenty-five or thirty years obviously occurred when the new manuscript page 131 was written. But there is no inconsistency in any of Mrs. Hines's statements that she has not seen her grandson in thirty years. Accordingly, it seems plausible to assume that Mrs. Hines's testimony has been retrieved from an earlier version in which Christmas died at the age of thirty.

Several more inconsistencies still in the text in Doc Hines's story of Joe at the orphanage point to the assumption that chapter 6, the first of the flashback, was written at a different time from the episodes Hines tells to Hightower in his study. Hines says that Joe Christmas was hidden behind the dietitian's bed (T 364), whereas the omniscient narrator of chapter 6 describes Joe's hiding place as a cloth curtain that served as a closet, screening off one corner of the room (T 112).[18] Even more confusing is Hines's statement that after he saw Joe leave the orphanage in a buggy, God said to him, "'You can go now' " (T 365), for in chapter 6 Hines disappeared fully a month before Joe drove off with McEachern (T 131-32). Hines, moreover, does not mention that he kidnapped Joe, nor does the omniscient narrator of chapter 6 tell of two scenes that Hines reports in chapter 15: Joe's pitiful question to Hines—" 'Is God a nigger too?' "—and Joe's conversation with the cruel Negro yardman (named Hamp in the manuscript) who says, "You don't know what you are. . . . You'll live and you'll die and you won't never know" (T 362-63).

Chapter 16 (MS 139-46), as it now stands in the manuscript, has been entirely copied out on the thicker paper so that it

---

[18]Of course, Hines was not actually present during the toothpaste episode and may not have known exactly where Joe Christmas was hiding. Still, there seems no functional reason for Hines's citing a different hiding place; presumably, the discrepancy is the result of careless revision of two versions of the same episode written at different times. Needless to say, beds are not usually placed directly in front of curtained closets or at the corners of rooms.

offers few external clues to help identify its earlier passages. On manuscript page 143 three lines have been scratched out and appear one paragraph later, perhaps to allow for the intercession of a new paragraph in which Bunch interrupts Hines's mad rantings (T 353; beginning: "Its God's abomination of woman flesh"). But one slight factual inconsistency confirms the supposition that Byron took the Hineses to Hightower's in the earlier version, lacking the flashback. When Byron appears at Hightower's with the Hineses in tow, he thinks, "And on Sunday again" (T 342). He tells Hightower that Christmas has been caught: "They caught him yesterday" (T 343). Obviously, yesterday was Saturday, the day on which Christmas's capture was described in those sections retrieved from the previous draft of chapter 15.

One puzzling, short parchment paste-on slip has been affixed to manuscript page 144. It is difficult to discern whether this passage was rewritten and added after the rest of the chapter had been recopied. Faulkner prepares for it by using an extension line on the base page, which would tend to indicate that the base page was written and recopied after the passage inscribed on the pasting, but the paste-on slip itself has a long extension line indicating that it was actually written after the base page passage following it. The extension lines also serve as reminders that the passages they connect are to be typed and printed in a single paragraph, so that it looks as if Faulkner reworked parts of the long paragraph on a separate sheet and then recopied at least manuscript page 144 to accommodate the newer version.

The passage is an extremely important one; it contains Mrs. Hines's words " 'and me trying to get Eupheus to lets move away because it was just that circus man that said he was a nigger and maybe he never knew for certain' " (T 357). If this section had not been added, the statement that precedes it would never have been qualified. Here Mrs. Hines says, " 'And the circus owner come back and said how the man really was a part nigger instead of Mexican.' " The new paste-on slip runs from line 10 (commencing midsentence on page 357 with " 'and all the folks' ") to line 23 (ending " 'and the folks in the church made him quit' "). It also includes the beginning of the scene of Hines at the Negro church that continues on the base page and provides a parallel between Hines and his grandson, Christmas, both of whom profane houses of worship; but its main function seems to be to point out that there is real doubt about Christmas's racial heritage. The revision, therefore, was probably engineered after the flashback had more fully exploited this ambiguity.

The Mysteries of Chapter 19

Further copyings-out of the earlier draft, now submerged in the semifinal version, can be found in chapter 19 (MS 168-74). This chapter not only confirms the supposition that the Hineses were fully developed characters in the shorter version but also adds to the mystification about the previous chronology of the novel.

The opening leaf of chapter 19, the chapter in which Christmas is finally killed, reads, "About the supper tables on that ⟨Wednesday⟩ Monday night, what the town wondered was not so much how Christmas had escaped but why when free, he had taken refuge in the place which he did" (MS 168; T 419). On the same sheet the college professor also arrives on Wednesday (changed to Monday) and sees Stevens putting the Hineses on the train to Mottstown. The shift to Monday suggests that there was some version of Joe Christmas's death in the nearly completed earlier draft and that in that draft he died on Wednesday.

In that version Gavin Stevens may have played a larger role. His sudden appearance in chapter 19 seems somewhat gratuitous as the text now stands. He functions on the plot level only to ship the Hineses and, later, the corpse to Mottstown. But on the thematic level he provides an explanation for Christmas's breaking away from the deputy and seeking out Hightower's house. Stevens's analysis of Christmas's struggle is predicated on a conflict between his white and his alleged black blood: "Because the black blood drove him first to the Negro cabin. And then the white blood drove him out of there, as it was the black blood which snatched up the pistol and the white which would not let him fire it" (T 424). In this passage Stevens loudly echoes the omniscient narrator of the manuscript (but not the text) of chapter 5, who also assumes that Christmas does in fact have black blood. After the omniscient narrator takes over chapter 19, he again refers to Christmas's black blood when he says, "And from out the slashed garments about his hips and loins the pent black blood seemed to rush like a released breath" (T 440). But at no point in the Christmas flashback does the narrator make so positive a statement about the black blood.

As the text now stands, Stevens joins the long line of character-narrators who tell sections of the story of the narrative present and who offer their own analyses of motives and events. He is merely another townsman-observer, not quite as wise in his judgments as his fellow townsman Byron Bunch. His explanation lacks conviction and may even provide irony, appearing as it does after the internal view of Christmas, tired of running and of having to carry his life "like it was a bundle of eggs" (T 319) or thinking of the Negroes in the cabin, "'of their brother afraid'" (T 317).[19]

A comparison between statements of the semiomniscient narrator of the Christmas flashback and those of both the omniscient narrator of chapter 14 and Gavin Stevens illustrates clearly how, as it developed, the tone and intention of the novel changed. The narrator of the flashback frequently qualifies his comments and explores possible motivations that spring from contradictory impulses; he does not presume to know. Although he occasionally speaks in his own voice, he never speculates about Christmas's racial origins.

For that reason, I think it is obvious that Faulkner recopied an earlier draft of the episode of Christmas's death, written before he expanded the Christmas story. It is probable that the previous version lacked the ambiguity now found in the text about Christmas's racial heritage and about his motives for seeking haven in Hightower's house. Gavin Stevens's explanation in that version may indeed have had more veracity and served a different function.

Chapter 19 provides no further clues by way of the physcial appearance of the manuscript. There are frequent changes of

----

[19]It seems to me that Howard Nemerov misses the point when he takes Stevens's explanation literally and claims that Stevens "is perhaps the one man Mr. Faulkner fully trusts..." (*Poetry and Fiction: Essays* [New Brunswick, N.J.: Rutgers Univ. Press, 1963], p. 249).

diction, however, and many paragraphs greatly expanded from manuscript to text, but most of these revisions do not help to verify my assumption that the facts of Joe Christmas's death were changed very little from the previous draft to the Virginia manuscript. Still, one detail should be pointed out regarding Gavin Stevens's discussion of the Hineses. Repeatedly, Stevens reiterated Mrs. Hines's assertion that she has not seen her grandson in thirty years, so that in the text the misconception is forcibly reiterated that Joe Christmas was thirty when he died. This error remains because Faulkner did not adjust his final chapters to include the time span of the new Christmas episodes added to the manuscript.

One additional change of diction provides evidence for the assumption that chapter 19 was written before the Christmas flashback. Gavin Stevens, in attempting to explain Mrs. Hines's motives for trying to save Joe Christmas, says: " 'She had just been with him before they took him back to the courthouse again; she and the grandfather—that little crazed old man who wanted to lynch him, who came up here from Mottstown for that purpose. *Not that she believed that the man was her grandchild*, you understand. Or even hoped much' " (MS 168, my italics). But in the text, in a lengthened version, Stevens explains as follows:

"I don't think that the old lady had any hope of saving him when she came, any actual hope. I believe that all she wanted was that he die 'decent,' as she put it. Decently hung by a Force, a principle; not burned or hacked or dragged dead by a Thing. I think she came here just to watch that old man, lest he be the straw that started the hurricane, because she did not dare let him out of her sight. *Not that she doubted that Christmas was her grandchild*, you understand. She just didn't hope. Didn't know how to begin to hope." (T 421, my italics)

Faulkner in the earlier version seems to have wanted to establish a degree of doubt about the relationship between Joe Christmas and the Hineses—at least in the mind of Mrs. Hines. A line still remaining in the text reinforces that doubt: "Its right hard on that old lady that thinks she is his grandmother" (T 400). But with the addition of the direct view of Christmas in the orphanage and the further expansion of the flashback, there was little reason for maintaining ambiguity about Christmas's relationship to the Hineses, for a new ambiguity had become more tantalizing: the mystery of Christmas's black blood.

The Earlier Shape: Chapters 17, 18, 20, and 21

Four more chapters remain to be discussed; in these chapters, Faulkner resolves the Lena-Bunch and the Hightower stories. In chapter 17, with the assistance of Hightower and in the presence of the Hineses, Lena's baby is born. In chapter 18 Byron Bunch leaves Jefferson and, after having been thoroughly beaten up by Joe Brown, returns; Brown again escapes from Lena.

Certain inconsistencies of narrative fact in chapter 17 again help to validate the assumption that the episode of the birth of Lena's baby had also been written before Faulkner added the long Christmas flashback. For one thing, there are conflicting figures in the text on the length of time Hightower had lived in Jefferson. A careful examination of the manuscript indicates that Faulkner originally thought of Hightower as an older man, who had lived in Jefferson for thirty years instead of the twenty-five years of the published text. The references to Hightower's period of residence in Jefferson have been corrected toward consistency (although not always successfully) from the manuscript to the text of chapters 2 and 3, but they have not been corrected in chapters 16 and 17.

Thus, on manuscript page 19, the omniscient narrator once said that "30 years ago" Hightower was a minister in Jefferson, but the manuscript was corrected to the "twenty-five" of the text (T 43). The townsman of the purple ink manuscript page 24, which was once the opening page of the novel, says that Hightower's wife went bad on him "about twenty years ago"; the text has been corrected to "twenty-five years ago . . . right after he came" (T 54). Manuscript page 25 states in purple ink that no one has been in Hightower's house for twenty years; the text reads "twenty-five" (T 54).

The statistics in the manuscript clearly show that in a previous draft Hightower had lived in Jefferson for a total of thirty years—ten years as a practicing minister and twenty years after losing his pulpit. Faulkner's revisions shorten the thirty years to twenty-five but add more confusion to the manuscript by stating that Hightower bought "the little house on the back street" twenty-five years before the action of the narrative present. The text prefers the more general "where he has lived ever since" (T 65).

A revision inscribed on a 0.003 paste-on slip affixed to the 0.003 manuscript page 29 shows Byron thinking that people forget a lot in twenty-five years. This figure presumably refers to the years in which Hightower had been alone, so that Faulkner has changed it in the text to twenty years (T 67). The revisions, therefore, in the early section, tend to shorten the number of Hightower's years in Jefferson, possibly because some of the episodes relating to those years were either eliminated or compressed.

One needs only the text, however, to observe that in chapters 16 and 17 Hightower had lived alone for twenty-five years. He had needed no watch for twenty-five years (T 346) and still built a fire clumsily after twenty-five years (T 382). Moreover, he had lost his pulpit twenty-five years ago, for he had had nothing to do for twenty-five years (T 383). The repetition of this figure strongly indicates that chapters 16 and 17 were copied from a draft written before Faulkner revised the time structure of the episodes of chapters 2 and 3.

The two time-references of the preceding paragraph occur after Hightower has returned from delivering Lena's baby, and their significance rests heavily upon that event, for Hightower, as a man, changes drastically after he has helped Lena. Thus, Faulkner must have "given birth to the baby" in the draft from which he copied out the several twenty-fives of chapters 16 and 17. Hightower also must have delivered the stillborn Negro child in the earlier draft. Most of the episode is recorded in a paste-on slip in chapter 2, but the careful time references to "four years ago" and "despite fifteen years between them" (the delivery of the child and the K.K.K. episode) are inscribed on the base page (MS 30; T 68). Again, Faulkner has failed to correlate the time periods of chapters 3 and 17, for although he revised chapter 3, he allowed chapter 17 to reveal that more time had elapsed in the previous draft between Hightower's services as a midwife. In a paste-on slip on manuscript page 150, the omniscient narrator explains that the doctor who had arrived too late the first time "was an oldish man now, and fussy" (T 374). Four years seems to be too brief an interval for the doctor to have grown so much older. One can only assume, therefore, that the time signals of chapter 3 were added later than the passages to which they refer.

Thus, the time structure of the LBH story, as well as its shape, was once quite different. Byron Bunch's departure, now in chapter 18, once formed a part of the chapter in which Lena's baby is born because the last manuscript leaf of chapter 17 (MS 156) includes approximately one-fourth of the first leaf of chapter 18 (MS 157). The repetition is deleted on manuscript page 157 and recopied at the beginning of chapter 18, leading into a paste-on slip, midsection. In addition, the first sheet of chapter 18 consists of the tissue-type paper with hand-drawn margins; this generally demonstrates that the chapter divisions have been revised for the semifinal draft.

One puzzling change of diction on the opening leaf of manuscript page 149 (chapter 17) prompts speculation about the earlier order of events. The first line of chapter 17 once read, "The child was born ⟨that night⟩." Instead, the text reads, "That was Sunday night. Lena's child was born the next morning" (T 371). Furthermore, as Hightower is returning to visit Lena after he has delivered her baby, he muses about Joanna Burden, " 'Poor woman . . . to have not lived only a week longer, until luck returned to this place' " (T 385). But in the final version the baby was born not a week but ten days after Joanna's death. This discrepancy in the published text reinforces the assumption that the earlier draft was based on a different time structure but included the events of the present chapters 17 and 18.

The change of day of the birth of Lena's baby was probably made after Faulkner had added the Christmas flashback and the description of Joe's week in the woods, at the same time that he changed the day of Christmas's death from Wednesday to Monday. Obviously, Faulkner wanted to exploit the parallels, and perhaps the antitheses, between the birth of the baby and the death of Christmas.

It is risky to speculate about the remaining chapters, for most of them have been copied out and include few paste-on slips from earlier drafts. What clues there are indicate rearrangements in the order of chapters or illustrate Faulkner's method of writing out an episode or a character study, such as the Hightower musings and memories of chapter 20, before deciding where they would appear in the text. One can deduce, however, from several slight hints that Faulkner composed both the first and the final Hightower chapters (3, 20) at the same time.

Although there are no helpful canceled numbers on the semifinal version of chapter 20 (MS 175-83) because it has been entirely recopied for the Virginia manuscript, there is the small but significant residue of the previous draft that also appeared, although corrected, in chapter 3. In both passages describing Hightower's departure from the church, he held up his hat to hide his face (MS 28, 182). The hat has been changed to a hymnbook in the text, but the manuscript version of chapter 20 has not been altered with respect to that detail (T 63, 463). Apparently the incongruity of the use of a hymnbook to cover "the face of Satan" was a touch of irony that occurred to Faulkner after chapter 20 had been copied out.

In addition, after he had recopied chapter 20, Faulkner added several new passages to remind the reader that directly after the death of Joe Christmas, Hightower, in his study, is remembering many years later the events of his childhood and youth. Textually linked passages have been separated so that Faulkner could add to the base page between paste-on slips a reminder of the narrative present, such as " 'but sanctity is not the word for him,' his son in turn thinks, sitting at the dark window while outside the world hangs" (MS 177; T 448, "the son's son"). Moreover, Faulkner has added to manuscript page 181 a new paste-on slip that forms a complete unit and begins, " 'I admitted that' he thinks" (T 460). This passage also includes a reminder of the narrative present and establishes the fact that Hightower is now wearing a bandage. The second textual reference to his bandaged head does not appear in the manuscript (MS 183; T 467).

Evidently the recopying of chapter 21 (MS 184-87) had already begun before Faulkner made his last revisions of the two leaves of chapter 20, for manuscript page 184 reveals a canceled 182. This slight evidence is all that can be mustered to verify the assumption that some version of the novel's final chapter was also a part of an earlier draft. There are numerous changes of diction from the manuscript to the text, but they are not relevant to the problem of identifying early draft passages.

In sum, I have tried to identify and extract from the semifinal draft those episodes and passages that once formed a part of the nearly completed novel before Faulkner became more interested in the inner workings of Joe Christmas's mind. I have drawn on both internal and external evidence in the attempt to verify my theory that the dramatic action of *Light in August* was once entirely set in the narrative present, with only secondhand reports or memories of Christmas's past. Structurally, the mill hands' description and discussion of Christmas may have been balanced against the townsmen's reports of Hightower's life in Jefferson. In the later chapters Hines's tale of Joe at the orphanage may have served to contrast and parallel Hightower's memories of his own childhood and youth. The two scenes between Byron and Mrs. Beard, now in chapters 4 and 17, underscored the beginning and false end of Byron's romance with Lena. Internal views of both Christmas and Hightower were also provided in the hypothetical shorter version. Many whole episodes and many long passages from previous drafts can still be discovered, buried in the last holograph manuscript at the University of Virginia.

A close study of the manuscript reveals a major change of intention in both the Christmas story and the character of Joe Christmas. The racial theme was always present, as well as the Puritan overtones, but Joe Christmas, as a character, figured no more prominently in the earlier version than Byron Bunch, Gail Hightower, or Lena Grove. Moreover, the narrator at one point in the development of the novel clearly echoed the sentiments of Gavin Stevens in believing that Joe Christmas did, in fact, have Negro blood. At this stage of writing Joanna Burden was merely a name, and there were no McEacherns or a Bobbie Allen.

In the act of composing his narrative, Faulkner must have become deeply interested in the character of Joe Christmas and the social and religious forces that shaped him. Or perhaps the author felt that he lacked a central core and focus for the book. In any event, it appears that he added at some later date the episodes now found in the seven chapters of the Christmas flashback, from chapter 6, which opens with Joe at the orphanage, through chapter 12, in which he kills Joanna Burden.

After Faulkner had written out the new episodes in chronological order, he systematically cut them up so that there would be an interplay between flashforwards and flashbacks—time remembered and events anticipated. He also sought means of compressing the episodes that involved Hightower, Bunch, and Lena Grove, as well as ways of balancing the episodes occurring in the narrative present—the ten days that shook the world of Jefferson, Mississippi—with the major events of Joe Christmas's life.

Originally Faulkner probably unwound the threads of the LBH story in a far looser and more leisurely fashion. But both the need Faulkner felt and the method he employed to tighten these episodes show up clearly in the manuscript in the kinds of revisions he made. Consequently, he changed the narrative point of view, making fuller use of his omniscient narrator to achieve cohesion among the characters and compression of episodes. On numerous occasions he situated his narrator in Byron Bunch's consciousness, employing Bunch as observer, auditor, and judge. Thus, Byron's mind in the first section of the novel becomes almost as useful a glue as that which secures the passages affixed to the base pages of the manuscript. In his skillful manipulation of point of view, Faulkner manages to tell several stories simultaneously, to both describe and present, to combine the pictorial and scenic methods of narration at the same moment in time.

If my assumptions are correct about the creative processes of *Light in August*, what began as a formula chase story involving a series of interacting flights and pursuits, perhaps in the mode of mock-courtly romance in which a chivalric Byron Bunch sets forth to rescue a damsel in distress, was adjusted to accommodate the addition of a long narrative having an element of the Bildungsroman. The newer material, dealing primarily with Christmas, seems to have altered the emphasis of the novel. The shorter version, large sections of which are still present in the published text, had many dark and brooding moments, particularly in the passages devoted to Hightower and Christmas. But because Christmas's character was less fully developed, Lena Grove and Byron Bunch probably figured more prominently, thereby brightening the overall tone of the work. In fact, epithets such as "comic pastoral" or "bucolic idyll" are still occasionally tagged to the novel. But with the fuller development of the Christmas character, the tragic elements seem to have been magnified to such an extent that no reader can forget the proud and baleful figure of Joe Christmas, who ultimately came to dominate the novel.[20]

[20]Samuel A. Yorks refers to the Lena-Brown-Bunch story as a "complex minor plot" ("Faulkner's Women: The Peril of Mankind," *ArQ*, 17 [1961], 127). He is almost the only critic to this date who claims that Christmas is the central character in the novel. Faulkner's massive enlargement of Christmas's story seems to support that view.

III

The Christmas Flashback

WILLIAM FAULKNER was once asked how he shaped his novels. He replied: "There's always a moment in experience—a thought—an incident—that's there. Then all I do is work up to that moment. I figure out what must have happened before to lead people to that particular moment, and I work away from it, finding out how people act after that moment."[1] The incident in the novel that inspired the long Christmas flashback may have been the murder of Joanna Burden, and the moment in Christmas's fictional experience that Faulkner worked up to was probably the instant of Joe's rising and moving toward Miss Burden's house as the clock struck twelve.[2]

Faulkner also said that although Lena Grove inspired the creation of *Light in August*, in telling the story he had to "get more and more into it, but that [the novel] was mainly the story of Lena Grove."[3] I would dispute his statement that *Light in August* is mainly about Lena Grove, but not his comment that he put more and more into it. Actually, he not only put the Christmas flashback into it, but he put more and more into the flashback, so that it too grew in stages and was revised to accommodate the later additions. There are indications in the manuscript that Faulkner probably ended the flashback at least three times: first, after the Negro prostitute scene when Joe contemplated running away from the McEacherns; second, after the addition of the Joanna Burden episodes; and finally, after

---

[1]*Lion in the Garden*, p. 220.

[2]For a description of the possible real-life prototypes of Joe Christmas and Joanna Burden, see John B. Cullen, *Old Times in the Faulkner Country* (Chapel Hill: Univ. of North Carolina Press, 1961), p. 90, et passim.

[3]*Faulkner in the University*, p. 74.

adding the details of the Bobbie Allen affair. The first version presumably included Joe Christmas's first five years at the orphanage, his adoption, and his early life with the McEacherns. These episodes at one time may have been longer and have been compressed when the later episodes were added. But before providing a detailed description of the manuscript version of chapters 6 through 12, I should try to answer a rather pressing question.

A reader well may wonder why I have insisted with such conviction that the Christmas flashback was written *after* the story of the narrative present. How can we be sure that Faulkner had not already written some version of the flashback before he introduced the characters of Gail Hightower, Byron Bunch, and Lena Grove? Of course, unless work sheets and previous drafts—all carefully dated—are someday discovered, we can never be sure. But the external evidence on the leaves of the semifinal draft indicates strongly that Faulkner did not work over the seven chapters of the long flashback as often and as carefully as those of the narrative present. Although most of the base pages and the slips affixed to them are far too clean to be considered first-draft material, there are frequent changes of diction from the manuscript to the typescript and text, paragraphs placed in a very different order, and considerably more deletions on the leaves of the semifinal draft itself. The confusion, moreover, about Christmas's age results from the later addition of the flashback.

Furthermore, the five canceled number-sets appearing on forty-five of these pages (MS 70-75, previously described, are exempted), beginning with the catechism episode when Christmas was eight and ending with the murder of Joanna Burden when Christmas was in his thirties, show that these pages were treated separately as a discrete unit and were as a whole interjected into the story of the narrative present. Actually there are many more instances of revisions of the LBH story made to accommodate the Christmas story than alterations in the reverse direction. The means by which Faulkner joined the two will be discussed in the next chapter. Meanwhile, a careful survey of the physical appearance of the leaves on which the flashback is written is in order.

Although there are many paste-on slips in chapters 6 through 12 (MS 50-109), none consist of the thinner paper weighing 0.003 millimeters. Nor is any such paper found among its sixty base pages. Of the fifty-one leaves that comprise chapters 7 through 12 (MS 59-109), all but six (MS 70-75; T 161.16-177-20) supply the correct number that ultimately results in the five perfectly ordered sets of canceled numbers listed in the Appendix, table 2. Moreover, if six hypothetical numbers are assigned to the pages that have no canceled numbers, the five sets become complete. There are also two numbers scratched out on manuscript page 74 of chapter 8 that indicate a previous arrangement of the scene, as well as margins which reveal that a new chapter was to have begun here, with the episode of the ritualistic killing of the lamb (T 173.3). The base pages 74 and 75, to which the pastings inscribed in black ink have been attached, are written in bright blue ink. Thus, it is apparent that chapter 8 was revised several times and that the six pages that comprise the hiatus in each of the five number-sets were the last to be added to this section of the manuscript, replacing six previous pages. There are also three to six canceled roman numerals on the first page of each of the six chapters. Few chapters before or after the Christmas flashback have so many indications of previous chapter arrangements, and only chapter 13 shows as many as three canceled roman numerals.

In this section, the first and basic ink is the dark blue-black of most of the manuscript; this color frequently attests to a copying-out of a previous draft. Some sequences show even earlier copy stages, and others show paste-on slips brought forward from such copy stages. There are leaves inscribed later at substages, or sub-substeps, and others inscribed when the sequence was first foliated. Thus, the manuscript in general shows that the process of composing was fundamentally a process of expansion, although there is evidence, too, that certain previous episodes were compressed.

In discussing these revisions, I shall try to show by what means Faulkner expanded and lengthened a shorter version of the Christmas flashback, for just as he added to the LBH story the episodes of Christmas's childhood, youth, and final years, the author added new episodes to a previously written truncated version of the Christmas story. Originally he seems to have written out both the older and the newer episodes in chronological order and then systematically cut them up, inserting portions of these episodes into a new base page, carefully inscribed to prepare for them, at a point at which they finally appear as significant flashbacks illustrating what "memory believes before knowing remembers" (T 111). I shall first identify those episodes still remaining in the manuscript that formed a part of the earlier, shorter Christmas flashback. I shall also try to reconstruct the order in which new episodes were added and to cite the ways in which Faulkner wove the newer episodes into the older version. Within the seven chapters under discussion (T chaps. 6-12; MS 50-109), Faulkner shuffled chronology, shifted the point of view, inserted a long flashback that forms a separate story, and made a series of later revisions that link the later episodes of the Christmas flashback to the earlier ones, as well as to the events of the narrative present. In short, he revised the section as a separate discrete unit, adjusting each component to the other components within the section, and he also added passages that serve to connect the final chapter of the long flashback with the events of the LBH story, bringing the tale of Joe Christmas to the moment he commits murder.

It will be necessary in the following analysis to trace in more detail than in my previous chapter alterations within individual chapters of the flashback. I shall be forced here, in the interest of clarity, to combine the methods of chapters 2 and 4 of this study. As the argument proceeds, the reasons for my method will become clearer; meanwhile, I beg the reader's indulgence for what may seem a rather complicated procedure.

As it stands, the Christmas flashback illustrates the working-out of the three forces set forth in chapter 6 that were to shape the pattern of Christmas's future life: sex, race, and religion. The power of these forces and the power struggles among the human beings who respond variously to them are dramatized through the events of Joe Christmas's life. These themes are sounded separately or together throughout the six chapters following the orphanage scenes.

The catechism lesson that opens chapter 7 is followed by the episode of the Negro prostitute, leading into the heifer–new suit mystery that anticipates the Bobbie Allen affair. Thus, chapter 7 also contains the three themes of religion, race, and sex (in that order), although the last two are not as artificially separated as this discussion would imply. In chapter 7 the major influences on Joe Christmas are illustrated as they affect the stages of his development at eight, fourteen or fifteen, and finally eighteen. Despite certain inconsistencies to be discussed later, chapters 8 and 9 focus on Joe from seventeen to eighteen and show both his confusion between sex and love and the development of his rebellion against McEachern's stringent religious training.

In all, there are three major events before Joe takes to the open road, each representative of one aspect of the unholy trinity that governs his fate. They result in Christmas's hatred of prayer and all forms of religion, and his repugnance for Negroes, which he acts out in his compulsive struggles with women. He has been taught his lesson by the rod, and he can therefore express his emotions only through violence. In chapters 7 and 8 he is repeatedly either whipped or beaten up. His own response is to strike out, first at the Negro prostitute, next at Bobbie Allen when his expectations are denied, and finally at McEachern, smashing him with a chair and perhaps killing him. Although Joe attacks McEachern to protect the woman he thinks he loves, he soon learns to despise her too. Thus, hatred and violence become Joe's natural way of life.

He had learned early to deny and distrust maternal love of any sort. Mrs. McEachern can do little to counteract this lesson; in fact, she merely reinforces his distrust and suspicion of women. Throughout the years in which Joe Christmas is known as Joe McEachern, his foster mother, the woman he despises, hovers over him. Both the catechism and the heifer scenes of chapter 7 end with Mrs. McEachern trying to comfort or protect Joe. But he continually resists her affection and finally steals her horde of coins, rudely pushing her out of his life forever.

Chapter 10 frees Joe from the McEachern milieu. It synopsizes the next fifteen years, which consist of a long flight and a series of fights as he wanders north and south across the continent between the two sides of the hard, paved street: the black and the white. At the end of the chapter Joe arrives on a dust road leading into Jefferson, Mississippi. The zigzag street has formed a circle.

This chapter also forms the bridge to the last two chapters (11, 12) of the flashback, in which Joe engages in a three-phased affair with Joanna Burden involving the same three themes of sex, race, and religion, now played in a new key extending into the "darker reaches of the soul."[4] Phase one of the affair is based strictly on sex; phase two combines sex and race, and the last phase combines race and religion.[5] In the last two chapters, it is Joe who administers the beatings and finally commits murder.

Had there been no flashback, there would have been no inconsistency about Joe Christmas's age. Nor would the problem have arisen had Faulkner added to his story of the narrative present only those episodes of Christmas's past that occurred in the orphanage and those concerning the catechism lesson and the Negro prostitute. From the appearance of the manuscript of chapters 6 and 7 and from the contradictions of fact in both the manuscript and the text, Faulkner at one stage may have considered the flashback complete after these episodes. Subsequent revisions in the later chapters of the flashback also provide evidence for this assumption. I shall, therefore, posit the existence of another document, parts of which have been copied out and carried forward to the semifinal manuscript in Virginia. Such a draft probably included some version of Christmas at the orphanage and a more extensive treatment of his life with the McEacherns. But it did not include detailed episodes presenting Joe's life after he left the McEacherns at the age of fourteen or fifteen.

---

[4]This phrase is taken from a description of Faulkner's novels in the *New Yorker*, Nov. 28, 1931, written when he was in New York working on *LIA* and quoted in *Lion in the Garden*, p. 23.

[5]Richard J. Dunn has noted that Joanna Burden combines the misdirected religion and love in Christmas's earlier experience. He relates her three stages to the motherly qualities of Mrs. McEachern, the passion of Bobbie Allen, and the inbred Calvanism of Simon McEachern. However, Dunn's explanation does not sufficiently account for the racial theme ("Faulkner's *Light in August*, Chapter 5," *Expl*, vol. 25 [1966], item 11).

The First Stages: Chapters 6 and 7

The content of chapter 6 (MS 50-58) is, of course, part of the Christmas flashback, but its physical appearance is more closely allied to chapter 5, sections of which I previously identified as having formed part of the earlier version of the nearly completed novel, probably composed before the flashback was conceived.[6] Like chapter 5, the passages in the manuscript of chapter 6 describing Christmas in the orphanage lack any signs of the tissue-type paper. Nor has chapter 6 the canceled number-sets that characterize the rest of the flashback. One can only deduce, therefore, that both chapters 5 and 6 were revised a final time after Faulkner had expanded, copied out, and paginated five successive times the six chapters that succeed them.

Evidently the author was still making revisions within the manuscript of chapter 6 after he had begun to type it, for he seems to have retyped seven of its pages. The series of canceled numbers at the beginning and end of the chapter does not appear from pages 134-40 of the typescript (see Appendix, table 4). The canceled numbers stop on the typescript at approximately the same place as the pastings in the manuscript begin (T 120) and do not reappear until the abduction scene (T 127). These extremely late revisions indicated by the pagination of the type-script may explain why the manuscript of chapter 6 shows no canceled numbers and may mean that Faulkner revised it a final time after he had completed the manuscript's overall revisions and decided on the placement of the Christmas flashback.

Originally, because of its physical resemblance to chapter 5 and because I assumed that Doc Hines's story of Joe's early childhood would have been too incoherent to stand alone, I concluded that some of the material of chapter 6 must have been included in the draft of the novel that was devoted almost entirely to the events of the narrative present. But I now think it more likely that the author depended entirely on Hines's rantings combined with the passages of chapter 5 retrieved from the earlier draft to provide whatever background information he

[6]See also my dissertation, "Faulkner's *Light in August:* Sources and Revisions," Diss. UCLA 1971, pp. 104, 160, et passim.

thought necessary about Joe Christmas. A close reading of those sections reveals that Joe's emotions and memories clearly relate to the story his grandfather tells and that Joe's actions are adequately motivated by the combination of factors that emerge from that story.

Chapter 6 bears the same relationship to Doc Hines's story of chapter 16 as the pursuit-and-flight episodes bear to each other in chapter 14, namely, that both deal with two points of view of the same period in time. But in both instances they refer to entirely different episodes. I have already noted that in the later passages of chapter 14, which focus on Christmas in the woods, he does not seem to remember his violent disruption of the Negro church, although it figures conspicuously in the earlier search episodes of the same chapter. I have also pointed out that Hines, in chapter 16, never mentions that when he worked in the orphanage he kidnapped Joe, an episode fully reported in chapter 6, and that the omniscient narrator of chapter 6 never refers to Joe's dialogue with Hines and the yardman about God and Negroes, conversations reported by Hines in chapter 16. In addition, I noted previously the conflicting statement of chapters 6 and 16 as to whether Hines saw Joe drive off in the buggy after he was adopted and those concerning his hiding place in the dietitian's bedroom. From these observations and additional clues, such as the contradictions in the manuscript version of chapter 14 about the days of the week, I concluded that chapter 16 was part of the earlier draft of the narrative present, composed and copied out in its present form before chapter 6.

The first three leaves of chapter 6 (MS 50-52) have been copied out and show fewer diction changes from manuscript to text than appear on the thirteen paste-on slips of the last six sheets (MS 53-58). The paste-on slips of the next three leaves are textually linked; nothing is written on the base pages to which they are affixed. They contain the passage in which Hines asks the dietitian where Joe will be sent; when she refuses to answer, Hines concludes that Joe will be removed to a Negro orphanage. The paste-on slips also establish the fact that the janitor and the child are missing. But the shift to Joe in the arms of the man who he knows despises him is written on the base page, which carefully prepares for the temporal reorientation of

Joe's memories of Alice. The matron's decision to "place" Joe also appears on the base page that leads up to the adoption scene. Thus, one can assume that the three major episodes of chapter 6—the toothpaste trauma, the abduction, and the adoption—were culled from a previous draft in which they probably did not occur in the same chapter. Moreover, the passage about Alice looks as if it has been retrieved from an earlier and fuller description of Christmas's life in the orphanage because of one further allusion to Alice in chapter 7, after which she completely vanishes from the story (MS 67; T 156).

A more detailed examination of these revisions helps to clarify their meaning and effect. In chapter 6 Joe's misinterpretation of his being carried away from the orphanage by the janitor occurs in a flashback in which he is reminded of a little girl named Alice, whom he had liked two years before, but who had also disappeared from the orphanage. The base page prepares for the flashback with an extension line leading up to it. It is followed by a paste-on slip that begins with a complete sentence and describes Joe's memory of Alice and of her departure. After the flashback the base page continues with the scene of Joe's being carried out in the dead of night (MS 55; T 127-28). It looks, therefore, as if the context of the entire Alice episode has been changed, framed, as it now is, by an event occurring two years later and reported in the form of a memory that absorbed Joe's mind during his abduction (MS 56; T 129). This scene probably once appeared as an episode in its own right, occurring in chronological order and not linked to the abduction scene into which it was later interjected to become only a memory.

Manuscript page 57 also consists entirely of three pastings with nothing whatsoever written on the base page. The sheet begins with the adoption scene: "One evening they came to the school room and got him" (T 132); it ends with McEachern's statement " 'I have no doubt that with us he will grow up to fear God and to ⟨love righteousness⟩ hate vanity despite his origin.' " The last line has been changed to " 'fear God and abhor idleness and vanity despite his origin' " (T 134).

It is entirely possible that the adoption episode was originally placed in a separate chapter that included the scene now found in a paste-on slip in chapter 7 describing Joe's arrival at the farm and Mrs. McEachern's bringing him a basin of hot water in which to soak his feet (T 155-56). Still another pasting contextually linked to the preceding one refers to Alice (T 156). Chronologically, the arrival at the farm in chapter 7 follows the long paste-on slip of manuscript page 58 of chapter 6 which describes Joe riding in the buggy beside McEachern and arriving "home" (T 134). As the book stands, Joe's arrival is followed by a flashforward, supplied on the base page of manuscript page 58, in which the narrator adds something that Joe was not to remember until later, when memory no longer "accepted the surface of remembering." Time levels become so intricate here that the narrator must remind the reader that Joe will not remember until later what McEachern said earlier that morning about his name: " 'Christmas. A heathenish name. Sacrilege. I will change that' " (T 135).

The remainder of chapter 6 completes the adoption scene, although Joe, in the narrative present, is already approaching the McEachern farm. The flashback to the matron's discussion of Joe's name and his reaction to it have all been pasted to the base page, indicating that they have been purposely shifted from the chronological order in which they were originally written to a position that would convey their apparent unimportance to Joe at the age of five, as well as the real significance they were destined to hold in the storehouse of his memory. Having placed it at the very end of the chapter, Faulkner has also alerted the reader to the thematic significance of the changed name. Although Joe "didn't even bother to say to himself *'My name aint McEachern. My name is Christmas,'* " the reader does, or should, bother to remember it (T 136).

I have suggested that the earliest composition of the flashback included a longer, chronological development of Joe's life with the McEacherns. Sections salvaged from what may have been a single, separate chapter can now be found in chapters 5, 6, and 7 of the Virginia manuscript. Among these sections is the adoption scene of chapter 6, described above, and the retrospective passage now in chapter 7, presenting the first night at the farm, which begins, "She had always tried to be kind to him, from that first December evening twelve years ago" (T 155). Most of the description of Christmas's first night with the McEachern's has been inscribed in light blue ink on two paste-on slips attached to manuscript page 67; these passages are introduced and placed into a flashback by means of short lines written in dark blue ink on the base page at the bottom of manuscript page 66 and the top of 67. It is in the second of these paste-on slips that the second reference to Alice occurs (T 156).

An additional passage excised from the text but affixed to manuscript page 45 of chapter 5 reinforces my assumptions concerning the first stage of composition of the Christmas flashback, for it looks very much as if it has been retrieved from the McEachern section of the flashback when that section was first written out in chronological order. The passage occurs just after Joe has left the stable and "emerged in the gray and yellow of dawn, the clean chill, breathing it deep" (T 102). It begins on the base page with "in the home of the people who had adopted him he could lie awake waiting for dawn to come" (MS 45). The adjacent paste-on slip continues as follows:

His bed was in the loft, the attic, there, reached ⟨unreadable⟩ by a narrow stair leading up from the room where the people who had adopted him slept. And he would lie there, on his hard, lumpy, shuck-filled mattress, beneath the close slope of the gable roof, feeling the manhate from himself (Mrs. McEachern he ignored save when he deliberately and coldly cut off the buttons which she sewed on his washed clothes) seemed to increase ⟨unreadable⟩ with each one of the man's snores, until at last it would seem to him that he could feel the floor, swelling and bulging upturned beneath him, lifting him toward the low ceiling, compressing the dark air between him and the ceiling until it was too dense for breathing. And he would lie there rigid, breathing like a man buried in cotton, until at last dawn would begin. The hate, the ceiling, the darkness would begin to flow away, going faster and faster, as though ⟨unreadable⟩ the coming of dawn had broken down a flood gate somewhere, so that (he would be at his single window now; it too facing east) despair and impotence seemed to rush unimpeded as sight itself, through the dark orifice, to ⟨unreadable⟩ itself upon a region, a country without boundary and colored golder than promise or desire. He would stand, leaning there, freed for the moment of the dark, tragic ⟨unreadable⟩ of adolescence, breathing deep and quiet, "'now I can sleep a while,' he would think. 'Now I can get through another day.'"

He quitted the loft, carrying the rolled blankets, the cabin stood sharp now against the increasing east. . . .

The passage continues as it appears in the text (T 102).

This addition to the manuscript of chapter 5 is particularly interesting because it indicates that the McEachern section was indeed compressed and that certain parts of it were deleted entirely. Moreover, the physical appearance of manuscript page 45 reveals that the page was recopied to prepare for this addition. There is the familiar extension line on the base page; the pasting is complete in itself and shows an arrow from a margin where nothing is written. It has obviously been removed from the Christmas flashback and placed in chapter 5 to appear as a vivid memory of a habitual pattern experienced many years before.

Chapter 7 (MS 59-68) has been revised to anticipate the Bobbie Allen romance; its final pages belong to stage three in the composition of the flashback. The semifinal draft shows that it has been altered to include references to the earliest Christmas episodes, once part of preceding chapters, and to those passages that were the last to be inscribed, expanding the flashback to depict Joe's sordid and pathetic affair with Bobbie Allen. The time span is actually about ten years, and at the time of each of the three major episodes Joe is respectively eight, fourteen or fifteen, and seventeen or eighteen. The chapter also includes the previously cited memory flashback of Joe at five, arriving at the McEachern's farm. This memory was probably lifted intact from an earlier chapter, and the episode at seventeen or eighteen was probably added much later.

As Faulkner added more and more to the flashback, his desire seems to have been to show how Joe Christmas became a man. For that reason I noted earlier that the Christmas flashback contains an element of the Bildungsroman. From chapters 7 through 9, the narrator of the manuscript announces on five separate occasions that Joe achieves manhood. But more than likely Joe once took only two steps toward manhood in a short version of the flashback that ended with the beating McEachern administered after Joe returned from the fight over the Negro prostitute.

By looking closely at chapter 7, one can locate the episodes that were probably a part of the earlier, shorter version and can also see the point at which the new material begins. Baldly stated, manuscript pages 59-64, which describe the catechism lesson and the confrontation with the Negro prostitute, recount episodes from the short version that also included the description on manuscript page 67 of Joe Christmas's first arrival at his new home (T 137.1-151.2; T 155.11-156.31). The first six pages of the manuscript now include a catechism and a cataclysm; in each instance Joe becomes a man. Although several codas were later attached to the end of the chapter, its original scheme seems to have consisted of two giant strides toward manhood. The chapter opens as follows: "And memory knows this: not believes. Even 20 years later memory is still to believe 'on this day I became a man.' Since even a child of 8 ⟨memory has already lived as long as the love or the hate of which it is the⟩ love or hate is as old as all the human history, chronicled or not, which in the moment of knowing and remembering is localized" (MS 59). Again, on manuscript page 63, while Joe is fighting with the boys after he has attacked the Negro girl, the narrator says that "it was not only rage: it was actual despair. At that moment he became a man."

These two episodes evidently once completed Joe Christmas's education, for after he had submitted to a beating administered by McEachern for a sin he had not committed, Joe went to bed with his mind made up to run away. "He felt like an eagle: hard, cold sufficient. But that passed, like an eagle *he knew* that his own flesh as well as all space was still a cage" (MS 64, my italics). The text has been altered to read, "But that passed, *though he did not then know* that, like the eagle, his own flesh as well as all space was still a cage" (T 150-51, my italics). The best explanation for the change from the affirmative to the negative seems to be that when he composed this episode for the short version, Faulkner felt that Joe's education was complete. But when he provided Joe with two additional major experiences in the flesh-cage, he realized that the adolescent boy still had more to learn.

Before the new material that anticipates Joe's ill-fated romance is discussed, the time-shifts and flashbacks in the catechism and the sex-initiation scenes should be examined. Chapter 7 now ends with the memory flashback to the night Christmas first arrived at the McEachern farm. Years later Joe thinks, "She was trying to make me cry. Then she thinks they would have had me" (MS 68; T 158).

Apparently, however, this realization once occurred to Joe when he was eight, for it also appears on manuscript page 62 when Joe is lying in his bed in the loft after the catechism lesson, listening to McEachern depart to expiate his own sins at a church three miles away. Mrs. McEachern tries to comfort the boy by bringing him a tray of food, but Joe refuses to eat it and dumps the tray into the corner. Manuscript page 62 continues: "He sat up, then. He didn't know what it was, then. He was too young. It was not until years later, when he was almost a man, that he knew what it was, what knowing had always believed but which it remained for memory to know: 'She's trying to make me cry.'" One paste-on slip ends here. A second slip that forms a complete unit adds that years later Joe remembers that after Mrs. McEachern left the room he knelt on the floor and ate the food with his hands, like a savage or dog (T 144-46).

It would thus appear that at a previous writing the catechism lesson was narrated in a separate, complete chapter, ending with the words "she was trying to make me cry." Conceivably, after Faulkner wrote the scene in which Joe hurls food against the wall of Joanna Burden's kitchen, he composed the parallel action, inserting it at the close of an earlier episode that had occurred when Christmas was eight. He may at the same time have strengthened the similarities between Joanna and Mrs. McEachern, such as their affinity for secrecy, for both manuscript pages 62 and 67 display three large pastings that seem to have been added to develop more fully Mrs. McEachern's character and Christmas's hatred of her. Hence, considering the flashbacks and flashforwards pasted to these pages, one may surmise that as his manuscript grew, the author found the use of postpredictions of what Joe would remember a convenient method of interrelating the parts.[7]

---

[7] Emily K. Izsak has noted that Faulkner made many revisions in the first section of *TSATF* to prepare for the sections to follow. She has also observed other charac-

An inconsistency in tense also attests to changed time sequences, occurring at the beginning of the episode involving the Negro prostitute when Joe is on his way home, knowing full well that he will be whipped. He is thinking of the irony to follow—that he will be whipped just as hard for something he did not do as he would have been had he committed the sin. He thinks: "And he [McEachern] won't ever know I ain't done the sin. It won't even make no difference that he won't know it. Because he couldn't have whipped me no harder" (MS 62; T 146). These words are written on the base page directly following the paste-on slip describing Joe's having eaten the food with his hands like a dog. The narrator continues: "He was 15. He was a virgin." In the published text, however, Joe's ironic musings are transferred to the narrator, who wisely anticipates that when Joe reaches home he will receive the same whipping for the sin he did not commit as for one he may have committed. While supplying the transitional passages between the paste-on slips, Faulkner became somewhat confused between action anticipated and action remembered, as he shifted the relationships between the two. Although he failed to adjust the tense to the new location of the passage in the manuscript, he corrected it in the published text.

Beginning with manuscript page 65, an episode has been added to amplify the Christmas flashback; it was probably not present in the shorter draft of chapter 7 (T 151.3-155.10). Chronologically, manuscript pages 65 and 66 belong to chapter 9 because they record the beginning of an action that occurred on Christmas's last night as Joe McEachern. Consisting almost entirely of two large paste-on slips, these leaves seem to have been inserted long after the preceding episodes of the chapter were written.

---

teristics of the manuscript of *TSATF* that resemble the manuscript of *LIA*. Among these are the addition of links connecting the parts that were added after the completion of the manuscript of the first section, revisions to make images more consistent, and scenes recalled in the first person that are composed of other characters' dialogue, so that their roles can be expanded without affecting the conception of the character recalling these scenes ("The Manuscript of *The Sound and the Fury*," pp. 190, 198, 202).

Manuscript page 65 opens at the moment McEachern realizes
that the heifer is missing (T 151). He forces Joe to admit that
he has sold the heifer and then traps Joe into lying about what
he has done with the money. Mrs. McEachern tries to support
the lie but only succeeds in increasing her husband's wrath. Joe,
"cold and rigid in his bed in the attic," hears their argument in
the bedroom below (T 154-55). Then he remembers that she
had always been kind to him from the evening he had arrived,
twelve years before. The chapter ends with the flashback to the
night of Joe's arrival, which, as noted previously, probably once
followed the adoption scene of chapter 6.

The two pages that found their way into chapter 7 provide an
excellent example of the hook-and-link method by which Faulkner connects the future with the past and welds the chapters
together throughout the novel. Employing a particular motif, in
this instance the heifer so reminiscent of the one on the Keatsean
urn, the author orients the reader in time, while at the same
moment anticipating future action to gain narrative suspense.
The manuscript helps to illustrate the mechanical means whereby
Faulkner achieved his ends. Having begun chapter 7 with Joe's
later recognition that at the age of eight he had become a man,
Faulkner, in his new manuscript page 66, returns to that theme.
Although Joe has lied about the heifer, McEachern does not
beat him with his leather strap; instead, acknowledging that
Joe is now a man, he strikes him with his fist (MS 66; T 154).

But the heifer motif that was inserted into chapter 7 to link
it to chapter 8 was not the springboard for Joe's escape from
the McEacherns in the first treatment of the flashback. Joe's
motivation for escape was probably the whipping administered
for his previous escapade, the episode of the Negro prostitute,
which completes the short manuscript page 65 and may once
have completed the chapter as well. Additional evidence is provided by certain changes of diction from manuscript to text in
the passages describing Joe's first sexual encounters.

The manuscript version of Joe's attack on the Negro girl
reports that "the falsetto voices of children" come to him at
that very moment and that "in time and space somewhere still
undissolved" they shrilly shout, " 'Nigger; nigger!' " All that he
"ever knew clicked into pattern" (MS 63). Such a shock of

recognition might well have sufficed for the shorter version, harmonizing with the portrait of Christmas of the early chapter 5. But since his sexual adventures were later expanded, Faulkner deleted all mention of the children's voices and of Joe's sudden self-understanding, revising the text to read: "But none of them knew why he had fought. And he could not have told them" (T 148).

The shape of the novel, then, may have been a shorter Christmas flashback that touched more briefly but with great power on the racial, religious, and sexual problems that beset the orphan Joe Christmas. The details of the Burden affair leading up to the murder may have been left completely to the reader's imagination.

Had Christmas, as he originally determined, run away after his experience with the Negro girl, there would have been no problem about his age at the time of his death. And had the Christmas flashback ended with that episode, Mrs. Hines's use of the figure thirty in the later chapters would have been perfectly accurate, for it would not have had to be reconciled with the three years that included the Bobbie Allen affair, the fifteen years on the black-and-white street, and the years in Jefferson with Joanna Burden. In fact, Joe's age when he fled from the McEacherns would be completely irrelevant.

From the diction of the manuscript, the confusion in the chronology of the Bobbie Allen episode, the inconsistencies about Joe Christmas's age and the length of time he spent with the McEacherns, it seems that Faulkner wrote the Burden story before the Bobbie Allen affair and that the discrepancies crept in when he expanded the flashback a final time. The conflicting figures in chapters 7 through 10 are listed below:

The Negro Prostitute Scene

Chapter 7

1. Paste-on slip, MS 62;	"He was 15."
Same paragraph, T 146:	No age given
2. Base page, MS 63:	No age given
Same paragraph, T 146:	"Since to fourteen . . ."

Chapter 8

3. Base page, MS 71:   "Negro girl 2 years ago . . ."
    Same paragraph, T 165-66: "Negro girl three years ago . . ."
4. From margin, MS 79:   "He told her about the Negro
                                girl three years ago."

    Text 184:   The same.

The Bobbie Allen Affair

Chapter 7

1. Paste-on slip, MS 66:   "and then he acknowledged
                                that Joe was a man."

    Same paragraph, T 154:   "And then he acknowledged
                                that the child whom he had
                                adopted twelve years ago was
                                a man." (Joe is *seventeen* here,
                                on the evening he leaves the
                                McEacherns.)

2. Base page, MS 66:   "On that December evening
                                twelve years ago . . ."

    Same paragraph, T 155:   "from that first December eve-
                                ning twelve years ago . . ." (Joe
                                is *seventeen* on the evening he
                                leaves the McEacherns.)

3. Base page, MS 67   "At seventeen, looking back . . ."
    Text 157:   The same. (Joe is *seventeen*
                                on the evening he leaves the
                                McEacherns.)

Chapter 8

4. Base page, MS 69:   "Now with more than a year
                                of practice . . ." (Joe is nine-
                                teen on the evening he leaves
                                the McEacherns because he first
                                climbed out the window when
                                he was *eighteen*. See T 166).

    Text 159:   The same.

Chapter 8 (cont.)

5. Paste-on slip, MS 69:	⟨"If, however, 18 can be in love . . ."⟩
Text 161:	"But to Joe she probably did not look more than seventeen, too . . ."
6. Base page, MS 70:	"⟨It happened during the summer that he was 17⟩ It began in the fall of his 17th year."
Same paragraph, T 162:	"It began in the fall when he was seventeen."
7. Base page, MS 71:	"It was on Saturday this time, in the spring now. He had turned eighteen."
Text 166:	The same.
8. Paste-on slip, MS 73:	No time mentioned.
Same paragraph, T 171:	"It was one month later."
9. Base page, MS 76:	"He was not running . . . the three years, the solitude . . ."
Same paragraph, T 177:	No time given.

Chapter 9

10. Base page, MS 82:	"the old wearying woman who had been one of his enemies for thirteen years . . ."
Text 194:	(Joe is *eighteen* on the evening he leaves the McEacherns.)
11. Base page, MS 84:	"which he at eighteen should have known . . ."
Text 200:	"which he at eighteen knew. . ."

Chapter 10

12. Base page, MS 88:	"he entered the road, the street . . ."
Same paragraph, T 210:	"he entered the street which was to run for fifteen years . . ."
13. Base page, MS 88:	"It [the street] was fifteen years long:"

Chapter 10 (cont.)

Same paragraph, T 211:	"It [the street] was fifteen years long:"
14. Base page, MS 88:	"He was 30 years old."
Same paragraph, T 213:	"He was thirty-three years old."

(Joe arrives in Jefferson at *thirty* in the manuscript and at *thirty-three* in the text.)

The Second Stage: Chapters 11 and 12

The first problem about Christmas's age results from the first expansion of the Christmas flashback, which was designed to include the episodes relating to Joe's arrival in Jefferson and his affair with Joanna Burden. As usual, several stages of revision are apparent in the manuscript of chapters 10, 11, and 12, which contain these episodes, and parts of at least one previous draft remain affixed to their pages. I shall try to retrace the stages through which the three chapters evolved and then, because of its significance for the reconstruction of the manuscript's earlier shape, return to the question of Joe Christmas's age.

Chapters 11 (MS 91-98) and 12 (MS 99-109) relate the details of the strange love affair between Joe Christmas and Joanna Burden. Into the midst of these events occurring in the recent past, Faulkner has inserted an extended flashback which serves as a genealogy for Joanna Burden and which she ostensibly narrates to Joe Christmas. But it is fairly obvious that the tale of Joanna's blighted family tree was written separately from the story of her tortured romance and was revised to provide a motivation for her otherwise incomprehensible behavior. It is difficult, perhaps even impossible, to determine whether Faulkner had a very early version of the Burden chronicle that he much later included in chapter 11 of *Light in August* when he added the Christmas flashback. Joanna's grandfather and half-brother, Calvin I and Calvin II, are referred to in *Sartoris* (1929) but not by name; they both appear in "Skirmish at Sartoris" (1935), which was revised and reprinted in *The Unvanquished* (1938). The date on which Faulkner actually started to write

"Skirmish at Sartoris" is unknown, but the fact that the shooting of the Burdens is mentioned in *Sartoris* suggests that the idea for part of their story antedates the frame story of the Joanna-Joe romance into which it has been placed.[8]

That the story of Joanna's forebears was composed independently can be deduced from the physical appearance of the manuscript into which it was thrust, directly before the second stage of the Burden-Christmas romance.[9] The paste-on slips that run from manuscript page 93 through 97 in chapter 11 record the bulk of the story. Not once in any of these sections is there a single reference to Joe Christmas or the fact that Joanna is telling the story to him one September evening in the cabin he occupies on her property. Every reminder of Christmas and each fragment of dialogue between him and Joanna have been written on the base pages of the manuscript. The insertions not only interrupt the flow of Joanna's recital but are carefully interspersed between the ten large paste-on slips affixed to the five manuscript leaves (T 227-40). This method is reminiscent of the technique used in chapter 3 to engage Byron Bunch as auditor of the Hightower history.

A strange shift in point of view also suggests that once the major story had been written, additional embellishments were added to the Burden chronicle. A third-person narrator begins the family history: "Calvin Burden was the son of a minister

---

[8]James B. Meriwether, commenting on Faulkner's unpublished short stories, says: "We know from the sending schedule that Faulkner tried twice to place 'Evangeline' in July 1931. What happened to it thereafter? In *Light in August*, which apparently was begun in August 1931,. . . when Calvin Burden sees the woman his son is to marry, he says 'Evangeline!' Apparently this was the name of his own dead wife; and the broader significance of the title would certainly be appropriate to the story of Joanna Burden's family, which is told in chapter 11. Did Faulkner stop sending out the story when he decided to use it in the novel?" ("The Short Fiction of William Faulkner: A Bibliography," p. 318).

[9]Leon Howard has observed a similar phenomenon in the "Quentin" section of *TSATF*. He notes that "the original core story was woven into the frame story and the major episodes were composed independently and then woven into the two to create a complex fabric which could be enriched by additions but which did not invite merely impressionistic or decorative insertions" ("The Creation of a Novel: William Faulkner's *The Sound and the Fury*," unpublished lecture notes [1969], p. 8). The weaving-in of the Burden genealogy in *LIA* is somewhat less dextrous.

named Nathaniel Burrington" (T 228). But after the dialogue between Christmas and Joanna on page 234 of the text, Joanna, in the first person, continues the narrative. From that point to the end of her reminiscences, she refers to "father" and "grandfather" and "our kin" and "my mother." The second section of her narrative includes the description of her father's first wedding and the comparison of that ceremony with his quick, businesslike marriage to her mother. These passages lead into Joanna's single, vivid memory of her father on the day he took her to the family burial grounds and terrified her with the "curse which God put on a whole race." The manuscript reads "on the sons of Ham."[10] It continues, "a race doomed and cursed to be forever and ever a part of the white race's doom and curse for its sins" (MS 91; T 239).

The Burden flashback within the Christmas flashback is similar in style to Hightower's memories in chapter 20. In both instances, a third-person omniscient narrator refers to "the father" or "the son." Since there is evidence in the Texas manuscript that Faulkner wrote a preliminary sketch in the third person of Hightower's history, it is probable that he worked out Joanna Burden's background in the same way.[11] But it looks very much

---

[10]Henry F. Pommer wrote to Faulkner in 1954 to ask to whom or what the "Him" refers in the sentence: "But the curse of the white race is the black man who will be forever God's chosen own because He once cursed Him" (T 240). He offered Faulkner three possible readings. Faulkner chose the third, which was the word *Ham*, and claimed that "Him" was a printer's error. Pommer then examined the typescript and the manuscript and found that both showed "Him." He wondered whether Faulkner was confused, or just had no curiosity about the past, or even if he had been deliberately lying. He concluded that Robert Linscott was right in suggesting that Faulkner "agreed to any theory about his writing you happened to advance not caring in the least what ideas were attributed to him" (*Esquire*, July 1963, p. 36). Pommer's article is entitled "*Light in August*: A Letter by Faulkner," *ELN*, 4 (1966), 47-48. The manuscript shows that Linscott and subsequently Pommer were wrong in this instance, for MS 97 shows the phrase "The sons of Ham" a few lines before the questionable "Him" on MS 98. "Ham" has been changed to "a whole race" in the text (T 239). Evidently Faulkner was confused rather than indifferent and actually reveals an amazing memory for a single detail that he ultimately did not use in the novel. Perhaps he consulted the manuscript and forgot that he had eliminated "Ham" from the text. In addition, "him" is not capitalized in the manuscript.

[11]Faulkner's habit of writing sections of his works separately is one of the major points of Edward M. Holmes's *Faulkner's Twice Told Tales: His Re-Use of His*

as if parts of a copying-out of the original sketch have been affixed to the semifinal draft, whereas Hightower's story seems to have passed through more transformations.

The story of Joanna's youthful trauma that became an obsession is written on the base page of the manuscript, suggesting that it was not a part of the original Burden history. In keeping with this addition, in the margin Faulkner has added the details of Joanna's career as mentor to the Negro women, who, in coming to her for advice and help over the years, have worn a circle of paths radiating from her home (MS 99; T 243). The author has greatly enlarged this passage in the text, and even in the manuscript he has inserted from the margin the description of Joanna at her desk writing to offer "the practical advice of a combined priest and banker and trained nurse" (MS 99; T 244). Joanna apparently performs these duties in order "to rise and raise the shadow" of the cursed race with her, as her father had ordered her to do when she was only four years old. Thematically, these insertions provide "foreshadows" of the total eclipse to follow when she attempts to save Joe Christmas's soul.

Another significant passage can be found on the base page in which Joanna's grandfather says of his son's wife, "'Damn low-built black folks: low built because of the wrath of God, black because of the sin of human bondage straining their blood and flesh.'" He adds: "'They'll bleach out now. In a hundred years they will be white folks again'" (MS 96; T 234). The comparison between Lincoln and Moses on the next page is also written on the base page of the manuscript (MS 97; T 238).

I have singled out these passages to demonstrate that there is a consistent theme running through the additions that can be seen on the pages of the manuscript proper, for while the earlier material emphasizes the fanatic religiosity and abolitionist sentiments of the New England family, the newer contributions stress

---

Material (The Hague: Mouton, 1966). Robert A. Wiggins comments that Holmes's study "pretty much documents a point made by other critics that characteristically Faulkner composed in discrete units which he later combined into novels" (*American Literary Scholarship*, ed. James Woodress [Durham, N.C.: Duke Univ. Press, 1969], p. 83).

their hatred of the black race. Such additions must have been the author's way of suggesting thematic relationships between the Burden and Christmas flashbacks.

There are numerous inconsistencies of detail in the manuscript and several still remaining in the published text that bear witness to the yoking together of disparate parts. On the base page of manuscript page 93, Joanna is forty-one years old on the September evening she comes to talk to Joe. In a paste-on slip a few lines later she is forty (T 227). In the manuscript, the family history begins: "Her father, Calvin Burden, was a stocky, dark man with black eyes and hair and a pale beak of a nose . . . his father, *Calvin* too" (MS 93, my italics). Somehow the confusion is adjusted so that the first Calvin becomes her grandfather, but the manuscript develops three generations of Calvins, so that her father is named Calvin and her half brother is Calvin III. In the text, however, Joanna's father is finally named after his grandfather, Nathaniel, and the brother is just plain Calvin.[12] Twice, the original family name of Burrington is contracted to Budden but is corrected to Burden only once (MS 94, 95). The manuscript's repeated use of the name *Calvin* leaves little doubt of the author's view of these New England interlopers as they illustrate one aspect of the novel's theme, but in the interest of clarity Faulkner was forced to change one of the Calvins into a Nathaniel, thereby paying an ambiguous tribute to one of his literary progenitors. Faulkner did, however, relegate to the manuscript alone certain of his more overtly hostile descriptions of the Northerners, and he eschewed the temptation to inform the reader of the published text that Joanna's father in respect to

---

[12] In "Faulkner's One Ring Circus," Richard Pearce attempts to show that *LIA* is comic in form and that an understanding of its structure and unity depends upon seeing the comic elements of the novel. Among his examples is what he calls the calculated confusion of identities in the Burden and Hightower genealogies in which the reader cannot distinguish between the fathers and grandfathers among the oft-repeated "the father," "the son" (*ConL*, 7 [1966], 270-83). Pearce may be quite right in finding that the end result of this confusion in the novel is ultimately comic. A glance at the manuscript readily reveals how Faulkner achieved this "comic" confusion. When the first part of the Burden story was written (the section told in the third person), it did not extend to the fourth generation, and the first Calvin Burden was actually Joanna's father, not her grandfather. Pearce's argument does not depend solely on this example, and his reading of the novel makes some interesting points.

"thought, mind, temperament and behavior—was New England down to and through the very impulse (fanaticism and greed) which had sent him into the South" (MS 93).

Actually, only the first two and one-half and the last one-half manuscript pages of chapter 11 are concerned with the Joe-Joanna story. Accordingly, it appears that in adding to the flashback the episodes of Christmas's final love-hate romance, Faulkner probably first wrote them out, too, in chronological order, then rearranged them to occur in retrospect, and finally interjected the full-scale Burden genealogy into the Joe-Joanna affair. It seems unlikely that the details of the actual affair originally filled two separate chapters.

Whether Faulkner wrote the passages in chapter 10 (MS 87-90) describing Joe's life on the street and his arrival in Jefferson before or after he expanded the Christmas flashback to include the years with Miss Burden it is impossible to determine, but he obviously revised them extensively in order to use the street as the link between the episodes of Joe's adolescence and those of his last years. Once Joe, at fourteen or fifteen, had escaped from the McEacherns in the short version of the flashback, Faulkner somehow had to get him to Jefferson, so that a version of Joe's demonic travels on the paved street may have been written before the story of Joe's years with Joanna.

But the eloquent passages describing Joe's fifteen-year flight on the hard, paved street must certainly have been composed before the Bobbie Allen tale, for the manuscript announces that when Christmas arrived in Jefferson, "he was 30 years old." The text has been corrected to read "thirty-three years old" (MS 88; T 213). The manuscript also provides the information that the street was fifteen years long, which further corroborates the hypothesis that Joe Christmas originally entered the street at fifteen, before Faulkner expanded the flashback to include Joe's infatuation at eighteen with Bobbie, thereby making him no longer the thirty of the manuscript, but the thirty-three of the text (MS 88; T211).

If Faulkner had begun the Burden story with the first words of manuscript page 89, "one afternoon the street had become a Mississippi country road," there would still be no problem about Joe's age (T 213). But when Faulkner supplied the information on the preceding leaf (MS 88) that Christmas was thirty years old and then altered it in the text to thirty-three, he introduced the conflict with his earlier version of the LBH story, in which Mrs. Hines bewails her misery at not having seen her grandson in thirty years. He also added to the text in the field-pea episode the words "and thinking fled for twentyfive years back" in the attempt to refer to Joe's memories of the catechism at the age of eight, again corroborating the statement that he was thirty-three when he arrived in Jefferson (T 217).[13]

On a pasting on manuscript page 102 of chapter 12 in which Joe visits Joanna in September two years or more after they had met, the figure *thirty* appears again. After Joanna has discussed the possibility of their having a child, Joe thinks briefly that it would mean ease and security for the rest of his life. In the manuscript he thinks of the street, which means freedom: "He thought that was it. He did not realize that it was pride: a threat against that which he had spent 30 years in building [?]: the edifice of the self-made pariah." The text reads, "I will deny all the thirty years I have lived to make me what I am" (T 250-51).[14]

This passage is truly baffling. It can be read to exclude the years with Joanna, not lived on the cold, hard pavement, and to refer back to the unrevised manuscript sentence that announced Joe to be thirty years old when he arrived in Jefferson. But it can also refer to the revision that made Joe thirty-three on that afternoon when "the street had become a Mississippi country road," thereby including the two years or more that he had known Joanna, but excluding his five years in the orphanage (T 213). It does suggest that the paste-on slip on manuscript page 102 of chapter 12 was written before Faulkner added the vital statistics to chapter 10 concerning Christmas's age when he arrived in Jefferson and the number of years he spent on the

---

[13]The phrase "and thinking fled for twentyfive years back" does not appear on MS 90; the phrase "where he used to wait in that terribly early time of love, for someone whose name he had forgot" appears on MS 90 as "where he used to wait for someone whose name he had forgotten" (T 217). The manuscript is not specific about Bobbie Allen, but it has unmistakable references to McEachern.

[14]Cleanth Brooks has entitled the chapter on *LIA* "The Community and the Pariah" in his book *William Faulkner: The Yoknapatawpha Country* (New Haven: Yale Univ. Press, 1963). His designation of Christmas as pariah is certainly apt.

street. The frequent repetitions throughout the text of the figure *thirty* and the occasional attempts to adjust it also show that Faulkner added new episodes to the Christmas flashback, as well as indicating the probable order of these accretions.

The Third Stage: Chapters 8, 9, and 10

Despite the flashforwards inserted into chapter 7, chapters 8, 9, and the early part of chapter 10 provide the beginning, middle, and end of the Bobbie Allen story. The addition of this miserable love affair, which perverted Christmas's youthful idealism, enhances immeasurably the reader's understanding of Joe Christmas and, though unintentionally on the author's part, provides many helpful hints to confirm the supposition that the story of this romance comprises the last major series of episodes contributed to the manuscript. It constitutes the third stage in the development of the flashback.

References to the affair, as I pointed out earlier, begin at the end of chapter 7 with "McEachern did not actually miss the heifer for two days" (T 151). Since this sentence appears in a long paste-on slip at the top of manuscript page 65 and since the preceding manuscript page 64 is a "short" one, it is possible either that the heifer motif that introduces the Bobbie Allen affair was added to the end of an already completed chapter or that Faulkner purposely failed to inscribe it to the bottom of the sheet to indicate a printing space designating the passage of time.

Again, Faulkner probably wrote out in chronological order the Bobbie Allen episodes of chapter 8 (MS 69-80) before combining them with the preceding events of Joe Christmas's years with the McEacherns. The distribution of the ten paste-on slips of chapter 8 shows the now familiar signs of a chronological draft cut up and reapportioned throughout the chapter. The first episode in which Joe Christmas is taken into town and sees the waitress, Bobbie Allen, and all the ensuing meetings between Joe and Bobbie are told in the form of a year-long flashback. This flashback is introduced when Joe is waiting in the lane, one year later, to go to the dance on the night that McEachern discovers that the heifer is missing. In the chapter's first paragraph, inscribed on the base page, Faulkner has provided the structural link to the previous chapter (MS 69; T 159). The first leaf is also a short one, probably written later than most of the leaves following it, for it carries the confusing implication that Christmas is now nineteen. From manuscript page 70 to the end of the chapter, Faulkner develops a series of encounters between Bobbie and Joe, ending just a few days before the confrontation with McEachern over the missing heifer, reported at the end of chapter 7. Chapter 9 takes up the narrative at the same moment in time at which chapter 7 ended and chapter 8 began. One can follow this skillful juggling of the narrative present and the more recent past of the Bobbie Allen story by carefully observing what Faulkner has added to the base pages of the manuscript.

The shifting of time levels required frequent signals to the reader, certain of which have been provided only in the text. One such reminder on the base page of manuscript page 71 states that "it was Saturday this time, in the spring now. He had turned eighteen" (T 166). Coming events are foreshadowed by such observations as "Joe was to acquire one of his [Max's] mannerisms. But not yet. That was to come later, when life had begun to go so fast that accepting would take the place of knowing and believing. Now he just looked at the man who leaned upon the counter" (T 167). The text reminds the reader that Joe's killing of the lamb had occurred three or four years ago (T 174), and from the margins of manuscript page 79 Faulkner has inserted "he told her about the Negro girl in the mill shed on that afternoon three years ago" (T 184). To recall the narrative present, in which Joe is waiting for Bobbie to call for him in Max's car, and to anticipate the following chapter, Faulkner has also inserted from the margin "now and then in Max's car he took her to dances in the country, always careful that McEachern should not hear about it. 'I don't know which he would be madder at,' he told her; 'at you or at the dancing'" (T 187).

This résumé serves to point out how, once the Bobbie Allen story has been revised to appear in flashback, Faulkner deftly directs, by means of additions on the base pages, the reader's attention to the concurrent action of the narrative present. But although these additions show an attempt to adjust disparities and confusions about the passage of time, they are not entirely successful, as witnessed by the list on pages 83-86.

Faulkner also uses the heifer motif to guide the reader through his time maze and to link this chapter to the preceding one. But in the manuscript Joe receives the heifer on two separate and distinct occasions. In a slip pasted to manuscript page 73, he is given the heifer directly after the humiliation of the nickel episode. It helps to restore his self-respect "because a month after that day, again on Saturday, he turned into that street, walking fast, and entered the restaurant" (MS 73). Yet on the base page of manuscript page 80, after Joe has spent his first night with Bobbie in her bedroom at Max and Mame's house, Faulkner has written that on the "next Saturday he earned two dollars chopping wood for a neighbor. He gave it to the waitress. A month later McEachern gave him the heifer calf." This discrepancy has been removed from the published text (T 185), but it remains in the manuscript on the base page, indicating that this material was indeed rearranged, probably several times. The repetition also appears in the typescript on page 205: "A month afterward, McEachern gave Joe the heifer calf." Faulkner has deleted it here in blue-black ink.

The heifer, of course, is transformed into the suit that McEachern discovers at the end of chapter 7 (MS 65; T 151); the suit also serves as a link between chapters 7, 8, and 9. In the paste-on slip at the top of manuscript page 65 of chapter 7, it is a new suit, but it has already been worn. For the text Faulkner has added that it has "never" been worn (T 151). The next reference to the new suit appears on manuscript pages 69 and 70 of chapter 8, where, although it is still a new suit, there is no mention of its having been worn (T 159, 160). Finally, in manuscript page 81, which begins chapter 9, McEachern is lying in bed firmly convinced that the suit has been worn. It is this conviction that leads him to follow Joe to the country dance (T 188).

In the matter of whether the new suit has been worn, the manuscript is more accurate than the text. Faulkner apparently added the "never" to the earlier chapter while typing the manuscript. Perhaps he himself became confused by the time shifts and compressions he had made, or perhaps he was remembering deleted material from a previous draft. These inconstancies of fact and the contradictions of time, such as the number of years Joe spent with the McEacherns, his age when he left, his age when he encountered the Negro prostitute and when he met Bobbie Allen—all seem to be the result of Faulkner's methods of composing and revising, his continuous process of expansion and compression.

Of the twenty-one chapters in the novel, chapter 8 (MS 69-81) provides the best example of Faulkner's creative techniques. It is the roughest and most incomplete in the whole manuscript. The six of its pages (MS 70-75) that lack the five canceled number-sets of the rest of the chapter have already been described; table 1 of the Appendix shows the scattered canceled numbers appearing on certain of its pages. The missing number-sets, the bright blue ink of manuscript pages 74 and 75, and the corrections in bright blue on manuscript page 71 attest to the assumption that these pages were the last to have been added to the manuscript version of the Christmas flashback, replacing six previous pages before the final pagination of the manuscript. Certain passages on leaves 74 and 75 appear to have been inscribed for the first time on these sheets. There are, however, paste-on slips carried forward from the six pages that the newer ones replaced.

The two pages written in bright blue ink dip briefly into the past, to the time when Joe Christmas learned the disillusioning facts about women's menstrual cycles (MS 74, 75; T 173.3-177.20). They are not inscribed to the bottom of the page and have been inserted into the manuscript at the point immediately preceding Joe Christmas's first assignation with Bobbie Allen. Since these pages describe the sacrificial killing of the sheep, they have been strategically placed directly before Joe's second attempt at sexual intercourse, doomed like the first to be frustrated, although this tryst is with the object of his boyish adulation. Although the short flashback to the time when Christmas learned about menstruation and the two scenes following it illustrate clearly the process of memory's believing before knowing remembers, the sheep scene was the last episode to be added to the manuscript of chapter 8. To accommodate it, six leaves have been rearranged (MS 70-75).

Manuscript page 70 has been rewritten and now begins, "It began in the fall" (T 162). Manuscript page 74, a short page, was once to have been the beginning of a new chapter, for it shows the double top margin generally used for chapter headings. It was originally numbered 71, and its opening line is inscribed in dark blue or black ink: "On Saturday afternoons" (T 173). From that point on, the page is written in bright blue ink and describes the killing of the sheep. The bright blue continues to the beginning of the dialogue between Bobbie Allen and Joe Christmas, which occurs in a paste-on slip, again written in dark blue or black ink (T 175, "here you are."). The short manuscript page 75 completes the episode and blends into the text that follows on manuscript page 76 beginning with "he was not running"; manuscript page 76 continues the five series of canceled numbers (T 177). There are two short lines missing, however, between manuscript pages 74 and 75, turning the opening line of manuscript page 75 into a non sequitur: "I made a mistake tonight. I forgot something." These words do not appear in the manuscript, although manuscript page 75 still begins, "Perhaps she was waiting for him to ask her what it was" (T 175).

Obviously manuscript page 76 was inscribed before the leaves recording the killing of the sheep because it is corrected in bright blue ink. Here, Joe runs into the woods and seems to see "a diminishing row of suavely shaped urns. . . . Each one was cracked and from each crack there issued something liquid, death-colored and foul" (T 177-78).

Evidently Faulkner originally planned to present the sacrifice of the lamb at the beginning of a new chapter before introducing Bobbie Allen. But he changed his mind, took up the first of six new sheets, numbered it 70, and wrote, "It began in the fall when he was seventeen" (MS 70; T 162). Next, the author seems to have decided to use the sheep episode in a different place, relating it more directly to Joe's first rendezvous with Bobbie Allen. He cut up the previous draft of that first meeting, wrote the bright blue passages on the base pages of the present 74 and 75 to prepare for the dark ink paste-on slips retrieved from the earlier draft, describing that meeting. In so doing, he incorporated some of the material scratched out on the following page, the present manuscript page 76, leaving both 74 and 75 short pages, and changing the number of the previous manuscript page 71 to 73.

Next, Faulkner was forced to revise manuscript pages 70 through 73, cutting up his previous draft and pasting sections of it to his new, as yet unnumbered, pages. All these leaves excepting manuscript page 70 show large paste-on slips. Manuscript page 70 begins with the deleted words "she was a waitress in a small dingy backstreet restaurant in town. It happened during the summer that he was 17." The following superb passage describing the grotesque, spiritually maimed Bobbie Allen is not in the manuscript, but Faulkner must have had a version of it which he later added to the text (T 161-62) and which he began to copy out on the present manuscript page 70. In so doing, he eliminated the passage on the preceding leaf (MS 69), which once began the Bobbie Allen story: "⟨If however 18 can be in love then he was. 18 is so quick to confuse sex and love: she who satisfied one, regardless of⟩."

In the revising and recopying of manuscript pages 70 through 73, Faulkner may have added to his earlier draft such passages as the previously cited flashforward to the time when Joe would acquire Max's habits, now found on the base page of manuscript page 71 (T 167). In fact, the author probably expanded his earlier version, thereby raising the previous manuscript 73 to its final number, 74, at the same time as he paginated manuscript pages 70-75.

This step-by-step tracing of Faulkner's revisions in chapter 8 is, of course, speculative, but it does illustrate a late revision that may explain why there are no canceled number-sets on six of the manuscript leaves of chapter 8. The six leaves under discussion must, therefore, have been altered after Faulkner had decided at what point in the novel to introduce the Christmas flashback.

There are other rough spots and diction changes that help to confirm that the Bobbie Allen affair of chapter 8 was the last material to be added to the Christmas flashback. For instance, Joe reaches manhood twice again among the leaves of this chapter. At the close of the lamb episode Joe says to himself, " 'I am a man. I have killed a woman.' " This musing has been eliminated from the text as has the narrator's unnecessary explanation that Joe reacted to Bobbie's sickness as he did because the last three years, the "solitude and ceremonial blood," had been too much for him (MS 76).

Faulkner also thought better of including in the published novel still another description of Joe's reaching manhood, as well as the inflated language he formerly employed to describe Joe's disillusionment on discovering that Bobbie was a prostitute: "He didn't even lie, who saw now in the distant [?] far [?] cosmos the dead [?] ghosts of all youths who ever died. . . . But he got over it. He grew to a man that night (or maybe died, with the pale ghosts of all dead youth) (MS 80)." Note that this quotation represents the fifth time in the manuscript that Joe grows to a man after learning a new, stinging truth.

Only two references to Christmas's achieving manhood remain in the text. The first occurs at the opening of chapter 7 and refers to the fateful catechism lesson Joe is taught at the age of eight that "twenty years later memory is still to believe" turned him into a man. The second is McEachern's acknowledgment nine years later of Joe's manhood by striking him with his fist instead of whipping him with a strap (T 154). There is no inconsistency in these two references because the evaluation is made from two different viewpoints.

Of the three manuscript references to Joe's attainment of manhood not carried over to the text, two are directly contributed by the narrator and the third reports what Joe thinks after killing the sheep. It would have been possible, of course, for Joe to have had several initiations into manhood, but apparently the author chose to delete all but the two overt statements remaining in the text. It seems, therefore, that when Faulkner integrated the newer, separately written episodes into the material composed earlier, he sought to unify the McEachern years by imposing a time frame on them and by opening and closing that period in Joe's life with the coming-of-age theme.

Characteristically, Faulkner salvaged and pasted to the leaves of the semifinal draft many of the passages of what may have been his first version of the Bobbie Allen affair. Thus one can see that in the paste-on slip at the end of manuscript page 71, Bobbie was named Jack, but on the base page immediately preceding this slip she was called Bobbie (T 168). She is also called Jack, but the name has been changed to Bobbie, in the paste-on slip attached to manuscript page 73 (T 171). Some corrections are made in the bright blue of the two latest sheets in the chapter, and on manuscript page 73 there are long arrows from former margins that no longer show the words to be inserted.

The number of manuscript revisions Faulkner made in just the structure of chapter 8 indicate that he was struggling with the problems of integrating the new episodes. The first page, 69, is a new one, linking the chapter to the preceding one in time and setting the stage for the flashback. The following six pages contain passages from an earlier draft of the third stage of the flashback that adds Bobbie Allen to Christmas's misadventures. There is also the insertion of the flashback of the lamb episode to occur at the most significant moment, directly before the scene of Joe and Bobbie's first tryst. Finally, there are the innumerable additions of new passages that have been cited above.

In sum, Faulkner took episodes out of chronological order, compressed time, inserted flashbacks, and used the heifer-new suit motif to ring out the hours of the last night Joe Christmas spent as Joe McEachern. It is on this motif that he proceeded to chapters 9 and 10.

The next two chapters of the Christmas flashback, chapter 9 (MS 81-86) and 10 (MS 87-90), taken together, comprise only ten manuscript pages. Bobbie disappears forever from Joe's life at the beginning of chapter 10, and the rest of the chapter provides the bridge that spans fifteen years and transports Joe to the point at which he begins his affair with Joanna Burden. The major action of the two chapters consists of the scene at the dance where Joe may or may not have killed McEachern, his plan to take Bobbie away, which ends unexpectedly in his being severely beaten up, and the summary of his life on the street that ran for fifteen years and ultimately led him to the Mississippi country road and the dark house of Joanna Burden.

The ten leaves of the semifinal draft are exceptionally clean, indicating that they have been copied out from earlier versions.

Although there are a great many changes of diction from the manuscript to the text, none are very revealing about the stages of the work's composition. One can, however, observe structural changes that were made after Faulkner had copied out most of the leaves of both chapters.

Chapter 10 (MS 87-90) is in two parts. Its first two pages form a complete narrative unit that describes Christmas's departure from the house where he last saw Bobbie Allen, and his life on the paved street (MS 87, 88; T 207.1-213.9). In fact, Faulkner has pasted a previously inscribed complete sheet to a new sheet, ruled to designate the beginning of the new chapter. As the text illustrates, this leaf continues and completes the episode of the previous chapter in which Joe, after having been beaten up by Max and the stranger, lies in a semiconscious state listening to the dialogue of Bobbie and the others as they make their hasty departure (MS 87; T 207.1-209.18, midsentence, ending "that he was"). Obviously, when this scene was written and recopied, there was no chapter division where one now occurs. The last two leaves of the chapter form a complete unit, and, as pointed out above, take Joe to Jefferson (MS 89, 90; T 213.10-218.9). These leaves were either written or revised after the composition of the Bobbie Allen episodes, for as Joe contemplates Joanna's open window the narrator speculates as to whether he thought of that "other window of his childhood" (MS 90; T 216, "other window which he had used to use").

There has also been some alteration in the preceding chapter, which begins with McEachern lying awake trying to solve the mystery of when and where Joe had worn the new suit. The first leaf, manuscript page 81, tells in its entirety the episode of McEachern's arrival at the dance, his behavior there, and Joe's retaliation (T 188.1-192.4). The next leaf, which shows a stray canceled number 74, shifts immediately to Christmas. The episode of his return to the farm where he sees his thirteen-year enemy and steals her hidden horde of money is continued from manuscript page 82 through the paste-on slip at the beginning of manuscript page 83, which has a canceled 88. This passage, which completes the episode, is the only one pasted to any of the leaves of chapter 9; the base page of manuscript page 83 begins a new episode with the words "a clock was striking one when Joe urged the flagging old horse through the main street of town" (T 196).

Examining the clues, one can see that the description of McEachern at the dance and Christmas's last encounter with him and later with Mrs. McEachern were once placed earlier in the narrative and were not part of the chapter in which Joe returned for Bobbie. This last episode, as is indicated by the canceled 88 (a stray number in excess of, and not relating to, the five number-sets), must once have been separated by fourteen leaves from the scene with Mrs. McEachern, which now directly precedes it.

One leaf of chapter 9, manuscript page 85, may have been copied out a second time after the others were completed. Beginning in midsentence with the words "center of an African village," the sheet is not fully inscribed to the bottom, but the empty space does not appear in the text (T 201.7-203.16. "See" does not appear in the manuscript.)

Since there are no paste-on slips from previous drafts, this leaf must have been composed at a later stage. Because it displays the five canceled number-sets, it was obviously added before the author combined the Christmas flashback with his earlier LBH story, but he may have copied it out again only to accommodate the addition of the paste-on slip to manuscript page 83. Still, one normal-length page intervenes, making it likely that the "short" page contains some new material.

It is on this leaf that the author makes it perfectly clear that Joe Christmas does not know whether he killed Simon McEachern. The point should be noted during this description of the manuscript because it has an important bearing on the discussion of textual ambiguities in chapter 5 of this study. It should also be noted that although Joe does not know, he believes that he killed, for he thinks, *"Why, I committed murder for her"* (T 204).

Only manuscript page 87, the first of chapter 10, shows hesitancy on Faulkner's part. Here he has crossed out several lines of dialogue that originally appeared between quotation marks and rewritten and underlined them to indicate italics instead. Although there is no consistency in either the manuscript or the text in the use of single and double quotation marks or italics, Faulkner seems to have wanted to change the point of view so that the dialogue between Bobbie, Mame, Max, and the stranger would look as if it were being filtered through Joe's semiconscious mind. Ultimately, in the published novel Faulkner used italics for the same purpose in chapter 9 too. Perhaps when the first sheet of chapter 10 was part of the previous chapter, Faulkner purposely switched to italics mid-chapter in order to focus more closely on Joe and to prepare for the swift montage of his next fifteen years.

It is notable that Faulkner ends chapter 9 with Joe's being brutally beaten up just as he had been whipped in each of the three McEachern episodes of chapter 7. The punishment theme persists throughout these portions of the novel. The rhythm, though, is completely reversed. With respect to McEachern, Joe is the victim who finally rebels and, perhaps, kills his victimizer. In dealing with Bobbie Allen, Joe is the first to attack. When he realizes that she is incapacitated on the night of their first meeting, and when he learns later that she is a prostitute, he strikes her remorselessly. But this behavior seems only to increase her masochistic desire for sex. After McEachern has insulted her, she in turn attacks Joe both physically and verbally; later, her sadistic companions delight in smashing at him. In each instance, Joe is not only physically assaulted, but his youthful innocence is also abused. Ultimately, his body recovers, but his spirit, his hopes and dreams, have completely collapsed. Thus chapters 7 through 10 are linked by the repeated rhythm of the violent punishment and reprisals that close each major episode. Chapters 9 and 10 are further linked by the author's use of the responses of Joe's semiconscious mind to the brutal beating he receives before he enters the street of violence.

Just as Joe has circled back to the South, where he began, the novel, at this point, is beginning to circle back to the recent past. The next two chapters fill in the two or three years that lead up to the night of the murder in chapter 5, where Joe is seen for the last time on that savage, lonely street from which he ultimately escapes, first in the woods and, finally, in death.

While showing the process through which Joe became what he was, Faulkner has left in the text some of the crudities and inconsistencies that are always a part of the creative process.

Such inconsistencies are trivial and would not be worth mentioning were they not examples of the sorts of revisions under discussion. Taken together, these contradictions of narrative fact seem to indicate that the episodes concerning Joe's affair with Bobbie Allen were added after the rest of the flashback was written. Most of these episodes were first composed in chronological order, either ignoring the matter of a time span or referring to one of longer duration. When combined with previous material, they were rearranged to occur in flashback, and the time period was either compressed or otherwise changed in some parts of the manuscript but not others. Thus, assuming that Joe was five when he was adopted by the McEacherns and that he lived with them for twelve years, as chapter 8 indicates, one can conclude that he was seventeen when he left, but if one assumes that he lived with the McEacherns for the thirteen years that chapter 9 reports, he was eighteen. The latter figure seems to have been supplied as an afterthought for the purpose of providing consistency in the published version of chapter 10, in which Christmas is described as being thirty-three after having been on the road for fifteen years.

The Next Step: Chapter 5 Altered Again

In trying to follow Faulkner's steps, one must take as he did, a circuitous route that leads back to chapter 5. After providing a long and checkered past for Joe Christmas, Faulkner evidently took up again his earlier draft of chapter 5 and revised it to include Joe's memories of that past. Certain of the base pages of the manuscript reveal that new material was added to refer to the new characters Faulkner created in the Christmas flashback. I have already identified (chap. 2 of this study) the older passages of chapter 5 that were carried forward from the shorter version of the novel, a version that was set almost entirely in the narrative present. Most of the new passages can be found on the base pages of manuscript pages 42 and 43.[15]

---

[15]This statement does not refer to the loft-bedroom passage that was discussed earlier in this chapter. That passage, not carried over to the text, was pasted to MS page 45 when the previous draft of the McEachern section was compressed.

The longest section on any base page (MS 43) includes references to Christmas's memories of Bobbie Allen, who is mentioned by name, and also memories of "himself 18 years old, lying on the floor of a cheap room and the ⟨unreadable⟩ of 3 people stooping above him." He hears the "voice of the woman for whom he had stolen money and bought what he believed was love. He was bleeding but quite conscious." Joe also remembers "the woman with her lips drawn bare and her face heaped with bitter fury, cursing him, calling him a black son of a bitch." He sees himself "lying there, ⟨unreadable⟩ quietly, peacefully almost" and thinks, *"Why, I stole for her."*

Other rooms and other voices introduced in the Christmas flashback echo through Joe's mind:

[the] orphanage which he scarcely remembered; ⟨McEachern and Mrs. McEachern, the voice of another woman whom he had known⟩ the voice of ⟨two⟩ the two people who had adopted him; the voice of the nameless woman whom he had known as Bobbie, from whom he believed that he had learned love and from whom he knew that he had learned betrayal and despair ⟨unreadable⟩ which he had been conscious of all his life without knowing it, which were his life, or perhaps God and he did not know that too. It was in his mind like a printed sentence quiet and dead *God loves me too*. Like the faded and weathered letters on a last years billboard *God loves me too* (MS 42)

Allusions to these memories can still be found in the text as they drift through Joe Christmas's memory, blurred and blended into "the myriad sound . . . voices, murmurs, whispers: of trees, darkness, earth; people: his own voice; other voices evocative of names and times and places—which he had been conscious of all his life without knowing it, which were his life" (T 98). But the explicit references are missing from the final version, as is a passage on the base page of manuscript page 43 in which Joe Christmas tries to understand his homicidal rage against Joanna Burden. The narrator says that "perhaps" it was not the physical betrayal of her body or the lies, nor even her trying to force him to "assume responsibility for his actions and to make him alter his behavior." But, the narrator states explicitly, "It was because he believed that the love and the prayers were on the black blood in him and not the man." This passage describes Joe in the half-light trying to see the black blood in his body and culminates with "'you prayed on the nigger,'" he said. "'Now listen to the nigger pray on you.'" It is at this point that Joe stands outside Joanna's window and curses her (T 99).

Three times, on the base page, references occur to Joe's furious resentment at Joanna's having prayed over him. Once he says, "'Because she started praying over me'" (MS 42; T 98) and later, on two more occasions, "'She ought not have started praying over me'" (MS 43, T 99; MS 46, T 104). The last reference to praying is on the base page wedged between two large paste-on slips that were obviously cut up and separated for this insertion.

This particular addition not only anticipates the last few meetings between Joanna and Joe at the end of chapter 12 but also introduces a major theme that runs through most of the Christmas flashback, starting with the janitor in chapter 6, his Bible on his knee, and continuing with McEachern in chapters 7, 8, and 9. It reaches back too to Hightower, the former man of God, whom the reader met in chapters 3 and 4. But all these references to Joanna's praying over Joe must certainly have been written after the scene at the end of the long flashback in which she implores him to join her in prayer, because they appear only in the newer revisions of the chapter.

Thus, by examining the passages on the base pages, one can observe that the references to Bobbie Allen and to the explicit details of the relationship with Joanna Burden occur only in this position, and never in the paste-on slips retrieved from the earlier draft. It can be assumed, therefore, that they were never a part of the version of the novel that lacked the extended flashback.

Approaching the Narrative Present

Up to this point I have been citing evidence to verify the thesis that the Christmas flashback was written separately from the rest of the book and that Faulkner kept adding episodes to the Christmas story that necessitated the compression of previously written material. I have drawn heavily on the inconsistencies of

narrative fact in both the manuscript and the text to show that
Faulkner wrote the Christmas story *after* he had written and
copied out most of the events occurring in the narrative present.
I will return to a further discussion of chapters 5 and 6 and also
take up the three and one-half manuscript pages of chapter 14
in my next chapter when I discuss the revisions Faulkner made
when he combined the flashback with the rest of the novel.
Meanwhile, before completing the description of the flashback,
I would like to point out two types of revisions Faulkner made
in the flashback in anticipation of integrating it with the LBH
story and the previously written Christmas episodes of the narrative present. In handling these particular revisions, I shall limit
the discussion to chapters 7 through 12 because those six
chapters (with the exception of manuscript pages 70-75) were
apparently completed before Faulkner took up the task of fusing
his two plots. Had they not been completed, their pagination
would not have formed the five long closed sets that still appear
on their leaves.

The revisions to which I refer are, first, those in which
Faulkner carefully adjusted his tale of Joe Christmas's life in
Jefferson in chapters 11 and 12 to the external view of those
same years provided in chapter 2. Since in both instances there
are few paste-on slips from previous drafts, the two versions
may have been written and copied out at the same time. The
second type concerns the Negro theme, which changed direction
as the Christmas flashback developed. Most of these revisions
are found on the base pages of chapters 11 and 12 and appear
to have been made for the purpose of supplying thematic or
plot connections to the rest of the novel after the basic details
of Joanna and Joe's romance had been worked out.

The first base page of chapter 11 (MS 91) provides the link
to the previous chapter by repeating that Joanna looked no
more than thirty in the soft candlelight; the action then leaps
ahead one year to recount in flashback the first phase of the
affair. In the paste-on slips of manuscript pages 91 and 92 are
found the actual accounts of Joe's first night with Joanna, of
the following day, and the second night. The base page of manuscript page 92 describes the second day and adds the scene in
which, on the third night, Joe goes first to Joanna's locked door,

then enters through the unlocked kitchen door and finds the food *"set out for the nigger"* (T 224). This leaf also provides the reverse side of chapter 2 in the statement "the next day he went to work at the planing mill. He went to work on Friday. He had eaten nothing now since Wednesday night" (T 225). These two sentences recall both the opening of chapter 2 of the novel ("Byron Bunch knows this: it was one Friday morning three years ago") and the lunch pail that Byron offered to share with the hungry Christmas, which was so coldly rejected (T 27, 31).

Other notations involving time are provided in the base page of both manuscript pages 92 and 93. A three-line overlapping crossed out at the top of the base sheet of manuscript page 93 indicates that this sheet once directly followed the paste-on slip at the top of manuscript page 92 because the deleted sentences continue the episode of Joe Christmas's second night with Joanna. All these factors lead to the conclusion that the passages on the base pages of the manuscript have been added after the fundamental elements of the Christmas-Burden relationship were written, in order to carefully integrate and balance the story of Joe Christmas's life in Jefferson with the earlier sections of the LBH narrative.

Not only has the author arranged to present his two parallel stories in the same diurnal rhythm, but he has added on the base page several episodes that reintroduce an earlier theme of the Christmas story, which he places in counterpoint to the LBH story. The first is the scene in which Joe hurls against the kitchen wall the food laid out for him by Miss Burden (T 225). The precedent for this action can also be found on a base page of chapter 7 where Joe upsets the tray of food Mrs. McEachern had brought him (MS 62; T 145). Turning back still further, to chapters 1 and 2, one sees the converse attitudes of Lena Grove and Byron Bunch in respect to the offering and accepting of food. These episodes too, I have suggested, were missing in the very earliest drafts of the novel.

I shall not summarize the implications of the revisions of chapter 11 until I have discussed chapter 12 more fully because the two chapters include the progressive stages of development of a single story within a larger narrative. In fact, as stated above, it seems almost certain that when it was composed, the story of the affair was not divided into two chapters at all. It was probably separated after having been written out chronologically, in order to accommodate the inclusion of the Burden flashback.

Chapter 12 (MS 99-109) has six sections pasted to three of its eleven pages. Again, the opening page has been revised to refer back to the previous chapter (beginning "thus the second phase began"), almost as if it were a continuation of the scene that terminated chapter 11 (MS 99; T 242). The next line, ultimately deleted from the book, continues, "This too was something outside his experience, outside his very imagination." The referent can be found twenty pages earlier in " 'my God. How little I know about women, when I thought I knew so much' " (T 222). But before the addition of the Burden flashback, the two lines were probably more logically related.

Most of manuscript page 100 consists of two large sections affixed to the base page; they supply the details of the furious second phase of the romance. The new material on the base page is particularly significant, for the one line that separates the long paste-on slips stresses Joanna's need to think of Joe as a Negro: "She would be wild then,. . . her wild hands and her breathing: 'Negro! Negro! Negro!' " (T 245). And at the bottom of the base page is a short section that includes " 'she wants to pray, but she don't know how.' " These revisions immediately call to mind the new material added to chapter 5, heightening and emphasizing Joe's memories of the racial and religious aspects of his affair with Joanna.

Nothing is affixed to manuscript page 101. The entire sheet seems to have been inserted to perform various summarizing services, as well as to adjust the time periods to the information already provided in chapter 2 (T 247.9-350.23). Discounting the passages that provide narrative transitions between what precedes and follows this leaf, one finds references to Mrs. McEachern and to the waitress, at this point unnamed, and to the fact that Joe is still working at the mill and has begun to sell whiskey illegally. Summer is turning into fall and Joe has begun his Memphis trips, during which he betrays Joanna with other women. The manuscript proper leads into the discussion between Joanna and Joe about having a child, which is completed in the dialogue of the first slip pasted to manuscript page 102 (T 250).

On the following sheet, manuscript page 103, the base page also establishes the duration of the elapsed time and contains the information that Brown had appeared in the early spring and had become Christmas's partner. This passage prepares for the recollection on the base page of Joe's meeting with Joanna to tell her that Brown is also now living in the cabin.

From manuscript page 104 to the end of the chapter, there are no pastings (T 257.1-270.31). Most of the revisions consist of additions to the text. Various guidelines are provided in the text to help the reader find his way between time present and time past, including a "glanceback" to chapter 5, in the text but not the manuscript, that reiterates that "he had not been to the cabin since early morning" (T 266).

Unquestionably, these pages have been copied out from a previous draft, and since they are free of any passages affixed to them it is hard to isolate the newer material added. Nevertheless, I suspect that they have been rewritten several times to incorporate allusions to Christmas's earlier experiences, which were actually composed after the Burden affair, and to lead up accurately to the exact moment at which Joe Christmas is sitting in the garden just before entering Joanna's bedroom on the night of the murder. It is here that the previously cited overlapping of a single detail is found, for Joe rises and approaches the house on both manuscript pages 49 and 107. Since the first of these can be observed on the paste-on slip that terminates chapter 5, its position would tend to substantiate my theory that the paste-on slips of chapter 5 (identified in my chap. 2) were written before the details of the affair with Joanna Burden were conceived (T 110, 266).

Faulkner also used a motif to link chapter 12 to chapters 2 and 4 in the repeated references to Christmas's trips to Memphis. As noted previously, an ominous episode on the road to Memphis is mentioned four times in the earlier chapters, hinting at some act of violence on Christmas's part that Brown witnessed (MS 22, T 50; MS 32, T 74; MS 34, T 81; MS 39, T 92). The trips to Memphis are also mentioned in a different context in chapter 12 (MS 101; T 249). The frequent references to this episode in chapters 2 and 4 were interpreted in my earlier discussion to mean that the episode at one time held a more prominent position in the book. But the fact that only the allusions to it, not the episode itself, remain in the novel indicates that it was retained to supply time signals and cross references between the two large sections of the novel in the same way that the heifer–new suit motif was used to link chapters 7, 8, and 9.

Throughout the six chapters under discussion, Faulkner has returned over and over again to the ambiguous matter of Joe Christmas's alleged Negro blood. He had dramatized the effect on all Christmas's relationships of his fear and anxiety that he may be a Negro. Although many of the manuscript's more overt statements of Joe's dilemma have been muted in the text, both documents carefully chronicle the development of his ambivalence on the subject. Sometimes he thinks of himself as a white man; at other times he seems convinced he is a Negro. Always, until his transformation and release in the woods, he fears that he may be a Negro, and this fear grows into outrage when he realizes that Joanna is trying to make him identify as one.

The earlier discussion of chapter 7 noted that in the manuscript Faulkner directly related Christmas's attack on the Negro prostitute to his memories of the children in the orphanage calling him "nigger, nigger" (MS 63). For the text Faulkner left these memories more deeply buried in Joe's psyche. He also removed a more explicit description of Christmas's appearance in which Joe is described as having rust-colored hair, hazel eyes, and a thick, smooth pallor (MS 63). Perhaps Faulkner felt that these visual details would conflict with the ambiguity he preferred not to resolve. On the preceding sheet Joe thinks of himself as a white man, musing ironically, "Here I ain't going to do the one thing he says a white man can [*sic*] do and I'll get the same whipping I'd get for doing it" (MS 62). But only a few pages later, at the point at which Joe is thinking about Mrs. McEachern, whom he hates more than the hard work, the punishment, or the injustice, Joe longs to tell her that he is a Negro. He would like to dare her to tell McEachern "that he has nursed a nigger beneath his own roof, with his own food at his own table." This passage occurs on a paste-on slip that begins "sometimes he thought" and ends "at his own table" (MS 67; T 157). It forms a complete unit and could be eliminated with no loss whatsoever of narrative coherence. It may have been composed and added later or clipped from an earlier draft and placed in a new position for the purpose of reminding the reader, before beginning the next chapter, of Joe's confusion about his identity and his shifting and ambivalent attitude toward his possible Negro blood.

In chapter 8 Joe tells Bobbie that he thinks he has "nigger blood" in him, that he doesn't know, but that he believes he has (MS 79; T 184). From the margin Faulkner added that Joe told Bobbie on the same night about the Negro girl in the mill shed, thereby linking Joe's racial dilemma to his sexual activities in a far subtler manner than he had originally done in chapter 7.

In chapter 10 Joe starts on the fifteen-year street with the voice of the woman he had loved following him, shouting "Bastard! Son of a bitch! Getting me into a jam, that always treated you like you were a white man. A white man!" (T 205). And he hears the stranger who had thrashed him say, *"We'll see if his blood is black"* (T 204). In this chapter, on one single sheet, manuscript page 88, Faulkner gathers up the themes that express the experiences of Joe Christmas's formative years and presents them in a powerful objective correlative: the savage and lonely street. It is a street of sex and violence, of punishment sought, of flight from self and pursuits of self. But always it is a street of color polarities.[16] Faulkner has added in the margin of the manuscript and from the manuscript to the text several explicit statements of the color split. He has made sure that Joe teases "white" men into calling him a Negro and that he did not know until he had almost killed a white prostitute for her indifference to his announcement that he was a Negro that "there were white women who would take a man with black skin" (T 212).

The author has also made sure that when Joe arrives in Mississippi he is still a white man to the Negroes he meets. After

---

[16]The street is described in the manuscript as "a thousand grieving streets" (p. 87). In the typescript it was once "a thousand proud streets" (p. 228). Ultimately, in the text, it becomes a "thousand savage and lonely streets" (p. 207). The street can be seen as an objective correlative not only for Joe's life during that period but also for Joe himself.

Joe's question directed to the Negro boy about the woman in the dark house beyond (" 'colored folks look after her?' "), the following description has been added to the text: "At once it was as if the boy had closed a door between himself and the man who questioned him" (MS 89; T 214).

In his relationship with Joanna Burden, Christmas moves from the uncertainty he first expresses to an angry, reluctant near-acceptance of his possible Negro blood. The first reference occurs on the base page of manuscript page 92 in chapter 11, in the scene already described in which Joe hurls at the wall the food Joanna has laid out for him. Before doing so he thinks, "Set out for the nigger. For the nigger" (T 224). At this moment he painfully resents being treated, or even thought of, as a Negro. At the end of the chapter, again on the base page, Joe first tells Joanna that one of his parents was "a nigger" and then adds that he doesn't know for certain. He muses, " 'If I'm not, damned if I haven't wasted a lot of time' " (MS 98; T 240-41).

Near the end of the following chapter, one slight revision from manuscript to text indicates how effective Joanna's influence has been. When she is urging him to attend a Negro school and to learn law in the office of a Negro lawyer, Christmas incredulously replies, "Tell niggers that I am a nigger too?" The "too" has been added to the text, reinforcing Christmas's gradual assumption, along with Joanna's, that he is a Negro (MS 105; T 262). He seems to agree, but it is clear that Joanna has forced him into that position. Moreover, Faulkner has added a short passage to the base pages to accentuate Joanna's insistent determination to force Christmas into the racial role she prefers. It is the passage noted above, which appears between two large pastings on manuscript page 100 and in which Joanna "in the wild throes of her nymphomania" cries " 'Negro! Negro! Negro!' " (T 245). Faulkner also added to the text of chapter 11, at the point at which Joanna tells Joe about her traumatic memory of her father's taking her to see the graves of her forebears, that she not only felt that Negroes had become a shadow but that *she and all white people lived in their shadow* and that she must get away from *under* the shadow *or she would die* (MS 97; T 239). I have paraphrased (and italicized for emphasis) the new ideas included in the published novel's version of Joanna's tor-

mented vision. They are highly suggestive of her true plight and
provide a far more striking image of the sexual interrelationship
of the two races as she imagined them.

If it is Joanna who, in the flashback, forces Joe into the role
of a Negro, it is also Joanna who is responsible for his final loss
of innocence. Throughout the flashback Faulkner has pictured
the gradual loss of Joe's youthful idealism. There is one relevant
passage that does not appear in the text. It occurs in chapter 8
when Joe returns to the restaurant with the dime McEachern
had given him "clutched hot and small in his palm as a child"
might carry it (T 166): "Then he entered the street. When he
did so he walked completely out of that place of quiet and
exalted passion in which he and the woman had dwelt without
any compulsion whatever. He realized that he had been thinking
of her as just a face without body: his face without his body
thinking of her face without body, as he might think of a
flower" (MS 71).

Although Christmas's disembodied fantasies did not find their
way into the printed version, other passages that describe Joe's
youth and innocence remain. On the page preceding the passage
just quoted, Joe thinks that he now understands why he re-
frained from intercourse with the Negro prostitute and assumes
that Bobbie will be proud of him for waiting (T 165-66). And
after Joe's self-purgation by killing the sheep, Faulkner has
added to the text *"all right. It is so then. But not to me. Not in
my life and my love"* (T 174). When he and Joanna discuss the
duel in which her grandfather and brother were killed, a line
appears on the base page in which Christmas asks, "Just when
do men that have different blood in them stop hating one
another?" (MS 96; T 236). Such passages illustrate Faulkner's
attempt to make Joe into a more sympathetic character in the
flashback, hoping, perhaps, that the reader, understanding Joe's
boyhood struggle to keep his life and love untainted, would
have more compassion toward the cold, cruel man Joe later
becomes.[17]

---

[17]Jerome Gavin alludes to Christmas's early idealism and ability to love. He gives
several examples, such as Joe's responsiveness to Alice, his shock at discovering
menstruation, and his love for Bobbie Allen (*"Light in August:* The Act of Involve-

Earlier I cited a line in which Joe Christmas found himself thoroughly confounded by the sexual behavior of Joanna Burden. Once he thought, " 'My God. How little I know about women, when I thought I knew so much' " (T 222). And the narrator of the manuscript had commented that "this [Joanna's sexuality] was something outside his experience, outside his very imagination" (MS 99). As the remaining line stands, it reinforces the impression that it was Joanna Burden who finally corrupted Joe Christmas. This point is clarified by Faulkner's revisions of the diction from the manuscript to the text of the passages in which Joanna, having become as fanatic a religious zealot as she had been a sexual libertine, tries to shoot herself and Christmas in order to save their souls. In the manuscript Faulkner wrote of Joanna's right hand: "It held an old style, single action, cap-and-ball ⟨pistol⟩ revolver almost as long and heavier than a small rifle. But the shadow of it and of her arm and hand which the lamp cast did not waver at all, and her eyes did not waver at all" (MS 107). To the text he added a powerful and richly evocative image that elevates the single instant to the level of myth: "It held an old style, single action, cap-and-ball revolver almost as long and heavier than a small rifle. But the shadow of it and of her arm and hand on the wall did not waver at all, the shadow of both monstrous, the cocked hammer monstrous, backhooked and viciously poised like the arched head of a snake; it did not waver at all. And her eyes did not waver at all" (T 267).

Thus, the snake image now includes both the revolver and Joanna's arm; her unwavering, calm, still eyes become identified with the unblinking eyes of a snake. The imagery of the whole scene reflects man's primal loss of innocence, even to the later detail of the final disposition of the pistol that crashes "once through the undergrowth" where Joe has flung it away (T 270). Joanna, merging with the pistol, becomes the snake in the garden, exemplifying the Puritan perversion of the new Eden. It is

---

ment," *Harvard Advocate*, 135 [Nov. 1951], 15). Robert Penn Warren was one of the first critics to realize that Christmas, "though he is sometimes spoken of as a villain, is a mixture of heroism and pathos" ("William Faulkner," in *Forms of Modern Fiction*, ed. William Van O'Connor [1946; rpt. Minneapolis: Univ. of Minnesota Press, 1948], p. 140).

not, ironically, Joanna and all white people who, as her father
had instructed her, must live under the shadow of the Negro
until he is elevated by the white race, but, in this final image,
Joanna, the white woman, who casts the shadow and forces Joe
Christmas to become a Negro and to enact, as her father predicted, the curse that finally dooms her for her sins. Joanna sees
Negroes, "not as people, but as a thing, a shadow"; to her the
shadow is evil, the doom and curse of the white man (T 239).
Twisted by such fear and guilt, she plays the final part in de-
stroying what little hope or humanity Christmas has preserved.[18]
But to the author, neither the shadow nor Joe Christmas is evil.
After Christmas's spiritual renewal in the woods, he dies "with
something, a shadow, about his mouth as though he were
inwardly smiling" (MS 174). His eyes, as he looks at those who
witness his death, are "peaceful and unfathomable and unbear-
able" (T 439).

When Faulkner was asked if Popeye of *Sanctuary* and Joe
Christmas were not similar people, sharing the same problem of
being outcasts from society, he replied: "Not at all. Popeye was
a monster. Joe Christmas, to me, is the most tragic figure I can
think of because he himself didn't know who he was—didn't
know whether he was part Negro or not and would never
know. . . . Now I don't understand Popeye. He, to me, was a
monster. He was just there."[19]

Perhaps without the long flashback Christmas and Popeye
would indeed have been more closely allied. But with the fuller
development of Christmas's character, the series of brutal disil-
lusionments that made him a man, and the purposeful ambiguity
about his racial heritage, Faulkner has tried to achieve for this
tragic figure the compassion he himself felt.

In sum, in the analysis of the flashback I have tried to identify
the three stages of its growth: (1) the orphanage, the adoption,
and the McEachern episodes up to Christmas's fourteenth or
fifteenth year; (2) the years in Jefferson with Joanna Burden,

---

[18]Samuel A. Yorks notes that "Joe Christmas is betrayed by fate, by man's evil
condition, and, primarily by women" ("Faulkner's Women," p. 120).

[19]*Faulkner at West Point*, ed. Joseph L. Fant III and Robert Ashley (New York:
Random House, 1964), p. 83.

and (3) the Bobbie Allen affair. I have demonstrated how the McEachern episodes were compressed when the Bobbie Allen romance was added and how Faulkner developed the details of Christmas's involvement with Joanna separately from the chronicle of her long family history. In order to relate the past and the present levels of the narrative and to motivate more clearly the behavior of both Joe and Joanna, Faulkner amplified the Negro and the Puritan themes. In addition, he carefully adjusted the time span of the close-up of approximately the last three years of the Christmas flashback to the long shot provided in chapter 2, and he also linked the later sections of the Joe Christmas story to both the earlier chapters of the same story and the LBH narrative by providing significant parallel and antithetical scenes involving the commonplace ritual of the offering of food. Moreover, he added to or revised some of the diction so that Joe Christmas's character could appear more sympathetic and so that his pitiful lack of self-knowledge, resulting from the mystery of his birth, would lead to his painful ambivalence and self-torment. In the next chapter, I shall point out the ways in which Faulkner joined the pages of the Christmas flashback to those of the narrative present and balanced the disparate time levels and the many characters who participate in the two stories.

HAVING COMPLETED THE major structural revisions of chapters 7 through 12, Faulkner truned back to his draft of the narrative present. He returned to Lena, Bunch, and Hightower, to the aftermath of the murder, and to the murderer's grandparents, the Hineses. In order to introduce the long Christmas flashback, Faulkner had held in a long suspension the events of the narnative present, turning away from the murder to the story of the murderer himself. Next he sought the most significant means of integrating the two.

As the published text stands, the action of the narrative present begins on the Friday before the murder; it continues chronologically through the Sunday following the murder, then moves back in time to the Thursday night preceding the Friday midnight murder, focusing directly on Joe Christmas's activities during the twenty-four hour period that led up to the murder. With the exception of Lucas Burch, alias Joe Brown, Faulkner ignores all the Jefferson characters he had so carefully established and turns his penetrating lens on the history and development of Joe Christmas. To this investigation the author devotes seven chapters, covering a period of approximately thirty years and filling in the intimate details of Christmas's past life, which is totally unknown to the inhabitants of Jefferson.

But Faulkner made many revisions before he achieved this final pattern. Four out of five of the canceled arabic numbersets and all the canceled roman numerals in chapters 7 through 12 are higher than the final pagination, indicating that more manuscript sheets once preceded the present chapter 7. These numbers do not refer to discarded episodes nor even in all instances to abandoned leaves of the manuscript, for the low canceled numbers on pages 110, 111, 120, 121, and 122 show that these same leaves once preceded the flashback, contributing to the higher pagination of the canceled number-sets. In addition, the higher canceled numbers in chapter 13 on manuscript pages 110, 111, 119, 120, 121, and 122 confirm the suspicion that more episodes of the narrative present and more manuscript leaves devoted to those episodes were placed at the beginning of the novel at various times in the process of combining the two stories.

Still, without further evidence one could not completely dispose of the possibility that the canceled number-sets on the pages of the Christmas flashback could refer to episodes that were ultimately eliminated from the manuscript were it not for an additional factor that seems to indicate that Faulkner indeed experimented with using some of the same leaves both before and after the flashback. It is not coincidental that there are six series of numbers visible in chapters 7 through 12, for six stages of revisions are apparent, not on the leaves of the Christmas flashback, but on the leaves on which Faulkner inscribed the story of the narrative present. The six number-sets, therefore, must refer not to the flashback but to the passages and chapters that precede and follow it. The six stages can be found in the arrangement of the two types of paper Faulkner used for the revisions. These papers have already been mentioned; table 5 of the Appendix charts the distribution of the two different weights. In all, it records six separate transactions by which Faulkner expanded, compressed, or otherwise altered the arrangement of the Virginia manuscript. It looks very much as if these particular revisions were made when Faulkner combined the flashback with his draft of the action of the narrative present. Table 1, which lists the types of paste-on slips as they appear on the two weights of paper, may be helpful.[1]

---

[1] The revisions under discussion here apply only to chaps. 1 through 4, 13 through 18, and 20. The order in which I have arranged the list is purely conjectural, for I cannot determine the precise order of Faulkner's revising.

Table 1. Types of paste-on slips

	Before Chapter 5			*After Chapter 12*		
1.	*Only 0.004 pastings affixed to 0.004 leaves*					
	Ch. 1:	MS	2	Ch. 15:	MS	133
		MS	3	Ch. 16:	MS	144
	Ch. 2:	MS	17	Ch. 17:	MS	149
				Ch. 18:	MS	158
				Ch. 20:	MS	177
					MS	181
2.	*Only 0.004 pastings affixed to 0.003 leaves*					
	Ch. 2:	MS	20	Ch. 13:	MS	112
		MS	21		MS	113
		MS	22		MS	116
	Ch. 3:	MS	26		MS	117
		MS	27		MS	119
		MS	28	Ch. 14:	MS	129
	Ch. 4:	MS	36		MS	130
		MS	37	Ch. 15:	MS	132
		MS	38	Ch. 18:	MS	157
3.	*Both 0.004 and 0.003 pastings affixed to 0.003 leaves*					
	Ch. 3:	MS	29	Ch. 13:	MS	118
		MS	30	Ch. 14:	MS	126
	Ch. 4:	MS	34		MS	128
		MS	39	Ch. 17:	MS	150
					MS	151
4.	*Only 0.003 pastings affixed to 0.003 leaves*					
				Ch. 14:	MS	127
5.	*Only 0.003 pastings affixed to 0.004 leaves*					
				Ch. 14:	MS	124
6.	*Both 0.003 and 0.004 pastings affixed to 0.004 leaves*					
				Ch. 14:	MS	123
					MS	125
				Ch. 17:	MS	152

Obviously, Faulkner salvaged large quantities of his earlier draft of the LBH story by affixing sections of it to new leaves of the Virginia manuscript. Each transaction involved copying out transitional material and repaginating the Christmas flash-back. New passages may also have been supplied both in new paste-on slips and on the base pages. Of the chapters before and after the flashback, only the twenty-one leaves showing canceled numbers seem to have been carried forward intact from at least one previous ordering of the manuscript. For that reason it is probably impossible to ascertain the time order of these revisions.

Unfortunately, the five canceled number-sets in the manuscript version of the flashback (recorded in table 2 of the Appendix) provide little aid in trying to establish a time order, for it cannot be assumed that Faulkner began with the figure at the top of the column (62) on his first manuscript page on which the series appears and proceeded in order to the bottom figure (69). But the numbers, together with the types of paper, do supply clues that help to illuminate the structural problems Faulkner was trying to solve and the artistic impulses behind these revisions.

The major problem seems to have been to decide how much of the action of the dramatic present to record before introducing the flashback. The author quite feasibly could have chosen either of two points in the narrative to turn away from the LBH story to the Christmas flashback: the moment before the murder, which Faulkner chose, or the period after the murder, while Christmas is hiding in the woods. It is most unlikely that any of the episodes after the present chapter 14 ever preceded the flashback, for that chapter carries the narrator to the point of Christmas's decision to go to Mottstown, and the action from chapter 15 to the end of the novel is dependent on his previously having arrived there. Perhaps, therefore, the author experimented with narrating some or all of the episodes of the week following the murder before he began the history of Joe Christmas. Accordingly, the difference between the lowest (47) and the highest (72) canceled number-sets may bear some relationship to the twenty-five tissue-type leaves added to the manuscript in front of chapter 15 in which Christmas appears in Mottstown.[2]

---

[2]Only one of these tissue-type leaves, MS 23, the last of chap. 2, has nothing affixed to it; the page completes the scene inscribed on the paste-on slips preceding it.

Again, it should be noted that the six number-sets (five canceled and one remaining) of chapters 7 through 12 demonstrate that Faulkner was concerned with the point at which the flashback should be inserted into the manuscript and that, leaving these chapters intact, he revised the episodes preceding and following them. Each time he changed the arrangement of the other chapters he renumbered manuscript pages 59 through 109.[3] At each stage Faulkner was forced to recopy certain leaves of the LBH story to accommodate the rearrangement of earlier, and the introduction of later, material. He also made many alterations both within individual chapters and in the overall chapter order. While each alteration does not indicate a major step in rewriting the novel, taken together, these revisions illustrate the new shape into which Faulkner was molding his earlier material. The six number-sets record six stages of revision; the arrangement of the two types of paper illustrates the procedure by which he made those six revisions and further confirms the statement that this set of revisions was engineered only on the draft of the story of the narrative present.

It is tempting to speculate that Faulkner pasted his parchment slips to his parchment leaves before taking up his tissue-type sheets. But this assumption cannot be substantiated, for in many cases several stages of revision are shown to have been made on a single sheet that bears both the thinner and the thicker paste-on slips. Moreover, the fact that textually linked passages follow each other on both weights of paper would tend to disprove such a theory. Therefore, in order to illustrate how Faulkner assembled his composite manuscript, I must anatomize the key chapters and repeat some of the descriptions of passages discussed for a different purpose earlier (chap. 2).

By examining the collation of papers provided in table 1, one can readily see that the highest concentration of salvaged passages occurs on the thinner leaves and that the leaves that clearly show passages from three stages of revision appear most frequently in chapters 3, 4, 13, 14, and 17. These three stages include the passages inscribed on the base page, those on 0.003

---

[3]MS 70-75 are, of course, excepted; they were rewritten after the two stories were joined. See chap. 3 of this study.

paste-on slips, and those on 0.004 paste-on slips. The clues to
the problem Faulkner was trying to resolve can be found in the
manuscript version of chapters 4, 13, and 14. A careful analysis
of these three chapters throws light on the author's methods of
joining the extended flashback to the earlier version of the
novel, as well as on the ways in which he constructed individual
chapters.

Interlacing the Two Tales: Chapters 4, 13, and 14

By now it should be apparent that many of the episodes of
chapter 13 were composed before the long Christmas flashback.
In assembling the semifinal draft, Faulkner shifted the position
of these passages at least four times, as witnessed by the four,
and in some instances five, sets of canceled numbers on the
thicker leaves still remaining in the manuscript. These revisions
were made primarily in connection with the present chapters 4,
13, and 14, all of which describe the week of the search for
Christmas before he appears on the streets of Mottstown. With
the exception of the three and one-half sheets in the manuscript
version of chapter 14 in which the narrator relates his story
through Christmas's consciousness, the whole of chapters 13
and 14 concern the search for Christmas and Lena's closing in
on Brown. These chapters include many short episodes, several
shifts of narrative perspective, and a certain duplication of
events already related in chapter 4 but recorded here from a
different angle.

Chapter 4 and the beginning of chapter 13 deal with events
that occur at approximately the same period of the narrative
present, the Saturday and Sunday following the fire and murder.
Chapter 13 continues the story through Wednesday of the following week, and chapter 14 concludes with Joe Christmas's
arrival in Mottstown on Friday.

In the first part of chapter 4 (MS 31-40), Byron Bunch tells
Gail Hightower about his first meeting with Lena Grove at the
lumber mill and his taking her afterward to Mrs. Beard's boarding house. He also repeats the information already reported in

chapter 2, that Christmas and Brown were engaged in bootlegging activities and that they were living together in a cabin on Miss Burden's property when the fire and murder occurred. The only new aspect of this report is not the link between Brown and Lena, which has actually been established in chapter 2, but Bunch's continued involvement with Lena. On the tissue-type manuscript page 36, Byron begins to tell Hightower the details of the discovery of Miss Burden's death, the sheriff's first attempts to investigate, and Brown's appearance to give testimony, to accuse Christmas, and to claim the reward. Five of the chapter's ten pages consist of this tissue-type paper; each of the five displays parchment paste-on slips, and two also show tissue-type pastings. It is this material that Faulkner takes up again in chapter 13. The revisions of these two chapters show a similar pattern, not only in the assortment of papers, but also in narrative technique.

Written at the top of the first leaf of chapter 13 (MS 110) but deleted from the text is the headnote quoted earlier: "The week of the hunt for Christmas from the fire to his disappearance at the cotton house." Faulkner has also deleted on the same page the opening transitional passage: "He threw the pistol away and walked from the dark road into the dark woods and vanished from the knowing sight and hearing of man for 4 days. That was Friday night or Saturday A.M. And the next forenoon the countryman found the fire and spread the word."

This leaf and the following one were actually taken from an earlier draft, as were the textually linked paste-on slips on the two tissue-type leaves that succeed them. Furthermore, as table 3 of the Appendix shows, they were at first part of the sixth chapter of the draft and then part of the seventh. On these four pages the narrative is carried forward to the Monday morning following the murder. After the final paste-on slip of manuscript page 113, the author establishes on the base page the fact that the first meeting of chapter 13 between Byron and Hightower occurs on Tuesday of the same week (T 282).

A glance at the canceled numbers on manuscript pages 110 and 111, as well as at their content, shows that they could easily have followed the present chapter 5 during several of Faulkner's experiments with finding what he considered the best point to begin the long flashback. And although I do not think that the rest of the chapter was originally combined with its first four pages, all the episodes in chapter 13 could quite logically have preceded the flashback. As the chapter now stands, it seems to have been culled from various parts of the earlier draft, expanded, and rearranged to anticipate chapter 14.

From manuscript page 114 almost to the end of page 117, Hightower and Byron discuss the advisability of moving Lena Grove to the cabin which Christmas and Brown had formerly occupied on Miss Burden's farm and which Brown ostensibly had been preparing for Lena. Hightower tries to dissuade Bunch from arranging for the move. After a space in manuscript page 117, the author takes up Hightower alone, returning from market, where he has just learned that Christmas has been seen at the Negro church. Hightower suffers intense anguish, meanwhile silently determining that he will not become involved because he has already paid enough in human suffering. This scene continues to the space on manuscript page 119, after which a completely changed Byron Bunch arrives at Hightower's house but does not stumble "heavily on the dark bottom step" (T 294). This passage, written on the last paste-on slip of manuscript page 119, introduces the final event of the chapter, the scene in which Byron informs Hightower that he has already moved Lena to the cabin (MS 120-22). Thus, chapter 13 tells two stories. The first part of the chapter (MS 110-13) deals with the search for Christmas, and the second part concentrates on Hightower and Bunch as they argue over the propriety of Byron's relationship with Lena.

The Tuesday-night meeting between Byron and Hightower, described on manuscript pages 114 through 117 (T 282-91), seems to have been expanded when it was placed in chapter 13, for it is obvious that the canceled 116 at the top of page 117 indicates that a new leaf has been added. The leaf begins with the unattached suffix "ing," which connects with nothing preceding it. In fact, the last line of manuscript page 113 and the first line of manuscript page 114 duplicate each other with the words "they sit again" (T 282). In addition, manuscript pages 114 and 115 are written in the bright blue ink of the single-set leaves 70-75, which were added very late to the Christmas flashback, and manuscript page 115 is a short page, textually linked to the paste-on slip that begins and continues through most of manuscript page 116. Both pages 115 and 116 are inscribed on thick paper, but the subsequent two dark-ink leaves are thinner, having affixed to them passages contextually linked to the preceding leaf and inscribed on thick paper. The author, moreover, has changed his tenses to convey the impression of present action.

It is quite likely that this meeting on Tuesday night between Bunch and Hightower once concluded a chapter of a previous draft because the few new lines on the base page at the end of manuscript page 117 effect the transition to the scene of Hightower returning from market and also lead into manuscript page 118 (0.003 mm.), which includes three paste-on slips that alternate between the two different types of paper. Manuscript page 118 consists of the dialogue between Hightower and the proprietor (called merchant in the manuscript), who reports that the sheriff has taken the dogs out to the church before daylight "this morning" (T 291-92). But the day of the week on which the posse follows the church clue is not known until the reader reaches chapter 14. Actually, because of the facts stated, Hightower's excursion to market must be on Wednesday, the day named in chapter 14 on which the posse tried to pick up Christmas's scent at the Negro church. But since the day is not named in chapter 13, it is possible that this episode was once placed directly after the Wednesday pursuit of Christmas. The manuscript proper is inscribed with newer material to stress the action-and-reaction relationship between the two stories in such lines as " 'well, they found that nigger's trail at last' " and, in a separate pasting of tissue paper, the information that Hightower's hands felt like ice (T 291, 293).

The last three pages of chapter 13 were identified previously as part of the earlier, shorter version, written before the extension of the Christmas story (MS 120-22). But manuscript page 119, which precedes them, is a new page added to conclude the newer scene in which Hightower reiterates his determination not to become involved. The base page performs this function.[4]

[4]MS 119 shows the canceled number 122, which begins the highest canceled series on the last four leaves of chap. 13. Because MS 19 lacks any other canceled

After a space to indicate the passage of time, the narrative continues in the next pasting with Hightower's musing about Byron's changed demeanor as Byron approaches the study (T 293-94). It is not stated on which night of the week this meeting occurs, but because one normally thinks in terms of an orderly progression of events in time, the reader assumes that it is the Wednesday night following Hightower's trip to the grocery store.

Perhaps before the last three leaves were tacked on, Faulkner, having already expanded the Tuesday-night meeting and added the Wednesday trip to the grocer's, contemplated ending the chapter on manuscript page 119 with the same line that was to begin a new chapter: " 'That sounds like it may be either hope or threat, Byron,' Hightower said" (T 295).[5] It is a technique Faulkner employed to link chapters 10 and 11; he also ended chapter 3 with Byron's arrival at Hightower's house and began chapter 4 with "they sit facing one another," the line that recurs in similar form on manuscript pages 113 and 114 (T 71, 282). As the hope-threat line stands in the manuscript, it represents a vestigial remnant of an earlier stage of the novel's evolution.

It is clear that manuscript pages 120-22, which now form the end of the chapter, were actually placed in five different slots of previous arrangements, for they display five sets of canceled numbers. One can be sure that they were not originally created for the particular niche to which they were ultimately assigned because they contain the odd anachronism discussed earlier (chap. 2) about Hightower's comment that Byron did not seek his advice when he moved Lena to the cabin. The anachronism, as well as the low numbers, mark manuscript pages 120-23 as part of the preflashback draft; they were also written before the extended debate about Lena's move, inscribed in bright blue ink on manuscript pages 114 and 115. In addition, manuscript page 120 contains Byron's confusing statement that Lena had already been in Jefferson for one week when he moved her to

---

numbers, it seems probable that it was added when Faulkner first joined MS 120-22 to the preceding leaves of the chapter.

[5]This repetition was discussed in my chap. 2. The text reads: " 'Is that a hope, or is it a threat, Byron?' "

the cabin (T 297). This schedule of events conflicts with the day of the sheriff's discovery in chapter 14 of Lena in the cabin, which must occur before Christmas appears in Mottstown. The confusion, therefore, probably results from the author's having used intact a leaf from a draft composed before he reordered his plot and his manuscript. In chapter 17, however, the author confirms Wednesday as the day of the move by saying that on the Monday of its birth, Byron had been expecting the birth of the baby for five nights (T 377).

Moreover, in the manuscript of chapter 13 there is an interesting pattern in the changes of tense. In the posse episode at the beginning of the chapter, Faulkner changed the tenses from present to past, and in the sections involving Hightower and Byron he changed them from the past to the present. On these leaves there are several marginal notes in which Faulkner has written "present tense", although he has not always followed his instructions to himself in the manuscript.[6]

The shifting of tense is consistent with the abrupt termination of the Christmas flashback. After being in the world of Joe Christmas for eight chapters, the reader is suddenly thrust into the world that exists outside and around the murderer. For that reason, Faulkner's having put details of the search for Christmas in the past tense instead of the present makes the Christmas story the minor action of chapter 13, pushing it into the background as a sort of accompaniment to the present action involving Bunch and Hightower. Using the present tense for their meetings gives their story a sense of urgency. To underscore this effect, Faulkner includes two successive meetings in the same chapter. The two meetings carry the narrative through at least Wednesday following the murder and give the impression of building to a crisis in the LBH story. Actually, though, very little new plot action occurs in this chapter, which functions more to define character and theme. Hightower and the reader learn that Lena has been moved to the cabin, but the basic plot would have been little changed had Lena's baby been born elsewhere.

---

[6]There are several instances in chap. 4 in which Faulkner scratched out both the past and present tenses in the manuscript.

In addition, Faulkner has revised the chapter to balance and reinforce chapter 14. Although the direct description of the search for Christmas in chapter 13 progresses only to the point of Monday morning, the scene at the Negro church early Wednesday morning is foreshadowed, and the dialogue between Bunch and Hightower constantly reminds the reader of the major action of chapter 14, the concurrent search for Christmas. In fact, the last page added to the chapter, 115, consists almost entirely of Byron's report to Hightower of the progress of the posse from Sunday through Monday and of Brown's frantic impatience during the pursuit of Christmas (T approx. 286.3-287.22). Both manuscript pages 114 and 115 have an enormous number of deleted lines that nonetheless appear in the text.

Chapter 14 (MS 123-30) begins with the sheriff's discovery of Lena at the cabin. The day is not specified. Next, after a space on manuscript page 124, a Negro rides into Jefferson on a saddleless mule at three o'clock Wednesday morning and tells the sheriff of Joe's appearance at the Negro church (T 304). The omniscient narrator then continues the tale beyond what the Negro could know, describing Christmas outside the church and the third foray of the posse in search of the fugitive. This last pursuit, inspired by the Negro's story, begins on manuscript page 125, after a space not carried over to the printed page (T 308.29). It continues through manuscript page 126, ending with the discovery that a Negro woman is now wearing Christmas's shoes. The sheriff in disgust kicks the dogs, "once each, heavily" (T 312).

Manuscript page 127 begins with one large paste-on slip that extends the description of the energetic but futile activities of the dogs. After a space, a second pasting has been added that shifts the focus to Joe Christmas in the woods. From this point to the end of the chapter, the narrator uses Joe as the center of consciousness, thus concentrating on Joe's growing self-awareness, and ultimate acceptance, of his alleged Negro blood. Hence, chapter 14, after a brief reference to Lena and Bunch, deals entirely with the pursuit-and-flight, the search-and-escape motifs of the narrative.

My listing of the distribution of papers (table 1, p. 120) shows that chapter 14 prominently features five of the six methods of revision indicated by the arrangement of the two types of paper. The stage conspicuously missing is the one represented by only the 0.004 paste-on slips attached to 0.004 paper. The first three leaves are parchment, and the last five are tissue. Significantly, at the point at which the narrator turns from the search for Christmas to the fugitive himself, the transition is accomplished in a tissue-type paste-on slip, complete in itself (MS 127; T 313.6-29). From that point to the end of the chapter, all but one of the paste-on slips measure 0.004 millimeters. Thus, it looks very much as if Joe's sojourn in the woods was not originally linked to the last fruitless attempt of the posse to capture him.

In fact, evidence in chapter 15 indicates that at one stage of revision there were no chapters 13 and 14 as such, for one can observe on the pages of the present chapter 15 a canceled number-set (123-30) that continues the highest series found on chapters 7 through 12 (72-122). Furthermore, the opening page of the present chapter 12 displays a canceled 15 (MS 99), the first page of the chapter ultimately numbered 15 contains a blotched numeral that looks very much like 16. These factors tend to bear out the theory that Faulkner tried various arrangements of the episodes of the week following the murder before he settled on the final one and that many of the episodes now following the flashback once preceded it. In the version indicated by this high number-set, chapter 15 would have directly followed the present chapter 12, and many of the episodes in chapter 13 and 14 would have preceded the long flashback.

The last three and one-half pages of chapter 14 (MS 127-30) seem to have been revised three times, combining passages from two separate drafts, the first one possibly composed before the addition of the flashback and the second one after the flashback was extended to include the episodes concerning Christmas's affair with Joanna Burden. The three stages of revision are apparent in the arrangement of papers and the confusions of time and age, which indicate that Faulkner incorporated parts of disparate drafts composed at different periods.

The final page of the chapter (MS 130; T 321) conveys the impression that Christmas is thirty years old. References to thirty years occur here in both a parchment paste-on slip and on the newer, tissue base page. First, the narrator says that Joe is "entering it again, the street which ran for thirty years." Again, the narrator says, "Yet he has travelled further than in all the thirty years before," and Joe verifies the figure with " 'and I have been further in these seven days than in all the thirty years' " (MS 130; T 321). This reiteration of thirty years is reminiscent of the use of that figure in chapters 5 and 12 and so far as the published text is concerned can be interpreted as in the previous chapters to refer to the years after Christmas left the orphanage. But the use of thirty in this place makes it difficult to discover in what order the fourteenth chapter was combined from previous versions.

Actually, the problem of Christmas's age in the narrative present arose when Faulkner protracted Joe's McEachern years in the second expansion of the flashback and provided the information that the street with imperceptible corners ran for fifteen years. Consequently, without that information we might assume that he was thirty, as Mrs. Hines insists in the next chapter (15), throughout all the stages of the composition of the novel except the second (and last) expansion of the flashback. These passages, then, could have been written at any of those earlier stages.

But one passage of manuscript page 128 was definitely composed after Christmas's affair with Miss Burden. It is inscribed on a parchment paste-on slip and describes Joe's memories, while he is gathering food in the woods, of the meal set out for him three years before and the dishes he had hurled against the wall of Joanna's kitchen (T 316). Because this leaf contains both parchment and tissue paste-on slips, it is safe to assume that it incorporates material from two separate drafts. Since this leaf contains the reference to Joanna and also the error in the day of the week (Wednesday instead of the Tuesday of T 315), it was probably the last to be added to chapter 14 of the manuscript. There is no reference on manuscript page 128 to Christmas's age.

Two Christmas passages of manuscript page 127 may have been taken from an earlier draft because they refer back to chapter 5. One is a reminder of the dinner Joe ate in Jefferson on the Friday night of the murder (T 314). The second echoes the diction of chapter 5: "It seemed to him that he could see himself hunted by white men at last into the black abyss which had been waiting, trying, for thirty years to drown him" (T 313). The same passage includes Christmas's longing for peace and his thoughts: "That didn't seem to be a whole lot to ask in thirty years." Almost the same words can be found in the manuscript of page 129, but the passage has not been carried forward to the text.

Moreover, the scenes in the woods, if not all of chapter 14, were once placed in the manuscript to occur earlier in the narrative. This last, intimate glimpse of Joe Christmas once appeared eight or nine pages earlier in the manuscript, as indicated by the stray canceled number 121 found on the present manuscript page 133 of chapter 15. On that sheet, under a slip affixed to the base page, a passage can still be deciphered to read "he has lurked and crept among its secret places, yet they were strange to him, the very physical and immutable laws whereby they who used the earth must obey were strange to him." An almost identical passage can now be found at the end of manuscript page 129 and the beginning of manuscript page 130 (T 320). The previous pagination of the sheet on which this passage is written would tend to verify the supposition that material has been added to chapter 13 and that the search-and-flight episodes of chapter 14 may have been reordered when the passage was copied out for its final positioning.

The only tissue-type paste-on slip other than the one that links the two sections of chapter 14 can be found on manuscript page 128. In that passage Faulkner has included the words that express Joe Christmas's most positive statement of self-identification with Negroes: "Of their brother afraid" (T 317). He has also written on the tissue-type base page of manuscript page 129: *"Here I am I am tired I am tired of running of having to carry my life like it was a basket of eggs"* (T 319). Both these passages, because they are not written on the thicker paper identified as that used in the earliest drafts, could well have been written after Faulkner completed the Christmas flashback. There too revisions were effected to increase the reader's sympathy for Christmas and to indicate that Christmas was beginning to think of himself as a Negro. But the last parchment paste-on slip of chapter 14, in which Christmas enters the street that ran for thirty years, must have been taken from an earlier draft, for it perpetuates the confusion about Christmas's age (T 321).

In the last paragraph, Christmas, wearing "the black shoes smelling of Negro", becomes Negro (T 321). "That mark . . . definite and ineradicable of the black tide creeping up his legs, moving from his feet upward as death moves" is consistent with the "pent black blood" that rushes out of his "pale body" like "a released breath" when he dies at the end of chapter 19 (T 321, 440).[7] Although these passages may have been written

[7]Cleanth Brooks says that "we are never given any firm proof that Joe Christmas possesses Negro blood for the sufficient reason that Joe would have become what he became whether he had an infusion of Negro blood or not" (*Yoknapatawpha Country*, p. 50). In the introduction to the Modern Library College Edition of *LIA*, 1968, Brooks denies that Joe Christmas chose to die as a Negro and quotes the Mottstown resident who describes Joe's capture. This narrator says he acted as if he were neither white, black, nor murderer.

Since this particular narrator is describing his own view of Joe's manner and can know nothing of Joe's spiritual or emotional condition, his judgment is not very reliable. However, the omniscient narrator provides a more direct internal view of Christmas that leads us to believe that he did achieve the serenity in the woods that led him to accept his reputed Negro blood. But Brooks may be right, despite his evidence drawn from an unreliable narrator, if Christmas in death represents not only the victimized black man but also the alienated white man and therefore does not die as a Negro solely. Irene C. Edmonds states that Joe Christmas was unquestionably a Negro. She feels that there was a definite connection in Faulkner's mind between Christmas and Christ. But she finds that "the vagueness with which he [Faulkner] establishes the connection suggests that the magnitude of his theme was too great for the limits of his imaginative powers to assimilate" ("Faulkner and the Black Shadow," in *Southern Renascence*, ed. Louis D. Rubin, Jr., and Robert D. Jacobs [Baltimore: Johns Hopkins Press, 1953], p. 196). Edmonds lists the analogies between Christmas's life and Christ's, but her theory is weakened by the error in her reading of Christmas's age as thirty-three at his death. She concludes that "Faulkner, a Southerner, when confronted by the enormity of his attempt to liken a man with Negro blood in his veins to Christ could not find the moral courage to make the analogy inescapably clear" (ibid.). This statement sounds as if Faulkner failed to achieve what he set out to do, namely, to write an analogy to the Christ story. This assumption of Faulkner's goal is, I think, a false one. Scott Greer sees "Negroism" as the center of *LIA* and says that "Faulkner ironically underlines the relation of Negroism to the conditioned values of Southerners, rather than the empirical nature of Negroes. Of Joe Christmas we can only say 'he was a man who thought he was a Negro.' (This is probably the most precise possible definition of a Negro.)." Greer adds that his genetic background is irrelevant; it is the social definition that kills him ("Joe Christmas and the 'Social Self,'" *MissQ*, 11 [1958], 160-66; the quotation is on page 165). The list of critics who assume that Christmas is part Negro is far too long to enumerate.

at the time the narrator actually thought of Joe Christmas as a Negro, the author's revisions throughout the published text place them in a far richer and more complex context. They serve to show that Christmas gradually came to accept the possibility of his Negro blood and that he was killed because the members of the white society readily assumed he was a Negro. The pursuit becomes in Joe's mind a symbol of his whole life in which he sees himself "hunted by white men at last into the black abyss which had been waiting, trying for thirty years to drown him" (T 313). To Joe, the black tide is identified with death; in accepting one, he accepts the other.

The purpose of summarizing the above episodes is to emphasize that they fall into two categories and that there is considerable overlapping of detail when they are recounted by the various narrators or in direct dialogue. There is the discovery of the murder followed by the search for Christmas, and there is Lena's move from Mrs. Beard's boarding house to the cabin. Chapter 4 begins the unfolding of both stories; chapter 13 retraces the preliminary steps and then moves forward; chapter 14 concludes the search-and-pursuit story, shows Joe Christmas riding toward Mottstown on Friday, and presents the picture of Lena waiting at the cabin to give birth to her baby. Taken together, these three chapters form a complete unit, and many of their parts form small independent units. In all, they describe the major events in the lives of all the major characters during the week following the fire and the murder of the preceding Friday.

Faulkner has left many provocative clues to the stages and kinds of revisions he made on the twenty-one manuscript leaves of chapters 13 and 14. There are the low canceled numbers on certain of the sheets of chapter 13 and the sections affixed to the new thinner pages that complete the episodes of the first two sheets. These serve to confirm the supposition that the episodes they recount were once placed far earlier in the narrative. There are also the thirty pastings on the sheets without canceled numbers found in both chapters. Moreover, there are the two kinds of paper used for both the base pages and the paste-on slips, to say nothing of the bright blue ink of manuscript pages 114 and 115. Finally, there are certain changes and inconsistencies of fact that illustrate Faulkner's problems in revising and shifting his material.

These multiple revisions indicate not only the author's attempt to place the Christmas flashback at the most significant juncture of the story but also the effort to blend the actions of his two parallel stories into the same chapters, as he did in chapters 2 and 4. There are signs, too, of his struggle to add up and relate the developments of both stories on a day-by-day basis. The result is a mosaic of material combined from various drafts and subdrafts and culled from different locations to form chapters 13 and 14.

In sum, by shifting the position of various episodes to form chapters 13 and 14, Faulkner has designed an intricately balanced pattern that correlates his flight-and-pursuit plots. At the beginning of each chapter the sheriff makes a discovery. The first placed in the Bunch-Lena-Hightower chapter, concerns Christmas; the second, placed in the Christmas chapter, concerns Lena and Bunch. Next, the author allocates individual episodes of the hunt to each of the two chapters, and, finally, he provides in chapter 13 enlarged insights into the psyches of both Hightower and Bunch and, in chapter 14, into the mind of Joe Christmas. Significantly, Hightower's inner fears in chapter 13 are revealed as a result of information concerning an episode connected with the pursuit of Christmas, more fully detailed in chapter 14. Joe Christmas's thoughts and feelings are, in turn, revealed to show a diminishing fear and a growing acceptance of his fate.[8]

---

[8]Various critics have referred to Faulkner's structure as a counterpoint of stories. James Linn and Houghton Taylor defined early Faulkner's form as contrapuntal. Linn uses *LIA* as an example of the contrapuntal novel and analyzes the structure from that point of view (*A Foreword to Fiction* [New York: Appleton-Century-Crofts, 1935]). Olga W. Vickery also calls *LIA* a counterpoint novel in which separateness is deliberately stressed (*The Novels of William Faulkner* [Baton Rouge: Louisiana State Univ. Press, 1964], p. 307). Richard P. Adams also finds that Faulkner's structure is often contrapuntal, juxtaposing apparently unrelated matters to build aesthetic tension between them, or arising from varying points of view (*Faulkner: Myth and Motion* [Princeton, N.J.: Princeton Univ. Press, 1968], p. 7, et passim). These critics seem to define and use the concept of counterpoint in different ways. Henry Campbell and Ruel Foster, for example, distinghish between the

The Order of Chapters 17, 18, 19, and 20

The remainder of the manuscript provides further indications of
Faulkner's greater concern with the order of chapters than with
structural revisions within individual chapters. Except for the
coda of the last chapter, chapter 15 through 20 deal with the
three days beginning with "that Friday when Christmas was
captured in Mottstown" and ending with the Monday of his
death (T 322). These chapters, including the final one, resolve
the Christmas story through death, the Lena-Bunch story in a
commitment to life and love, perhaps conjugal love but surely
maternal, and the Hightower story in the attainment of self-
understanding.

Many of the details of these six chapters I have already
discussed (chap. 2). I have also noted the additional closed
canceled number-set on the leaves of chapter 15, which may at
one time have been intended to be chapter 16. There is also an
indication that the episode in which Bunch again calls on Hightower, this time with the Hineses in tow, once directly followed
Bunch's previous visit at the end of chapter 13, for the first leaf
of chapter 16 shows a canceled number 126 that may have
followed the last page of chapter 13 when it was numbered 125.
Moreover, chapter 16 once ended before Hightower's stern determination not to help Christmas, because manuscript page 147
shows a canceled XVII above the first line (T 365.22). Perhaps
Faulkner was copying out a draft of that order of events when
he wrote at the beginning of the present chapter 17, "The child
was born ⟨that night⟩." For the text he wrote, "That was Sunday night. Lena's child was born the next morning" (MS 149;
T 371).

Again, in chapters 17 and 18 one sees evidence of Faulkner's
methods of composing, his habit of completing a series of epi-

---

kind of counterpoint employed by Faulkner in *LIA* and that used by Huxley and
Gide, to whose technique Linn and Taylor compare Faulkner's. The two critics find
in *LIA* more plot and thematic unity and a more symphonic structure (*William
Faulkner* [Norman: Univ. of Oklahoma Press, 1951], pp. 82-83).

sodes dealing with a single individual or a particular group before
he decided how to separate the story into chapters and exactly
where in the manuscript to place those chapters. On the last
sheet of chapter 17, Faulkner has written and then deleted the
first four lines of the following chapter (MS 156; T 392). When
he decided to open a new chapter with Byron's search for the
sheriff to arrange Brown's visit to Lena, the author pasted almost
the whole 0.004 page of a previous copying-out to the present
0.003 manuscript page 157, with only the first few lines of the
story written on the base page (T 393). This maneuver explains
why he had to cut up and paste sections of that copying-out to
the next leaf, a thick one, on which he must have had to recopy
the transitional passages before he added the paste-on slip.

In chapter 19 Joe Christmas dies. Signs of indecision about
the placement of that chapter are likewise visible, as indicated
by the canceled XVII on its first leaf. As the text now stands,
Byron learns of Christmas's death at the end of chapter 18,
before the reader discovers how and why it occurred. But perhaps in this instance Faulkner too had already completed the
Christmas story before determining exactly where he would
place its last episode. Considering his penchant for weaving back
and forth in time, one can perfectly well imagine that the author
tried a version of the novel in which Joe Christmas's death was
narrated before the birth of Lena's baby. Chronologically, chapters 18 and 19 occur on the same day, Monday (although in an
earlier version Christmas died on a Wednesday), and involve two
parallel actions in the two parallel stories. Had the present chapter 19 followed chapter 15 and 16, in which the Hineses tell
Hightower the details of Joe Christmas's parentage, birth, and
first few weeks of life, the novel would have contained a second,
complete, unified Christmas section that explained both his
beginnings and his end.

Instead, Faulkner chose to interrupt this sequence with the
Lena-Bunch story, now related in chapters 17 and 18, which
also reached its climax on the day of Christmas's death. Both
stories are immediately followed by the probing internal view
of Gail Hightower, who had participated in each of the preceding actions. The final Hightower chapter, 20, describes the details
of Hightower's birth, childhood, marriage, his achievement of

self-understanding and, according to some critics, his death.[9] Although there is no statement of the day on which Hightower communes with the ghosts of his past, the immediate juxta-position of chapters 18, 19, and 20 implies that all three relate events of the same day. Thus, Faulkner has finally interwoven the various episodes affecting the various characters so that each climax and resolution occurs on the same Monday.

Only chapters 17 (MS 149-56) and 18 (MS 157-67) reveal structural revisions within individual chapters at the end of the novel; they follow the familiar patterns of the revisions of some of the earlier chapters.[10] Chapter 17 shows two new pages with a total of seven sections of varying weights affixed to them (MS 150, 151). The first page has one paste-on slip and the fourth page has two.

Thus, in chapter 17 a parchment first page (MS 149) was recopied with new material added to accommodate the re-arrangement of the episodes in the last section of the book, so that the birth of Lena's baby directly followed the Hineses' visit to Hightower. This sheet prepares for Byron Bunch's second intrusion on Hightower on Sunday night or, more accurately, before dawn on Monday morning. Three of the sections affixed to these pages and one on the following page have been taken from a later draft, written on the tissue-type paper. All but one of these sheets deal with Byron's disturbed reaction to the birth of the baby, his attempt to find a doctor, and his evaluation of his own role in the affair. With these additions, Faulkner breaks up linear time to show the reader before the baby's birth how Byron learns later what earlier had seemed "to lurk clawed and waiting" within him (T 377). His decision to leave Jefferson is included in one of these tissue-type pastings, as is Hightower's later discovery that Byron has taken the mule, leaving Hightower to walk home after the exhausting experience of delivering Lena's baby.

[9]Critics disagree as to whether Hightower dies at the end of the novel. Faulkner stated unequivocally, but long after the book was written, that Hightower did not die (*Faulkner in the University*, p. 75). However, his comment seems to refer more logically to the manuscript than to the book. This ambiguity will be more fully dis-cussed in the next chapter.

[10]The revisions in chap. 15 were discussed in chap. 2 of this study.

As is true of other episodes in the novel, there are in chapter 17 two versions of Byron's trip to the doctor, one reported by the narrator (T 374-75) and one remembered by Byron outside the cabin door, "where he had stopped as the doctor entered" (T 376-79). The repetition records the progressive stages of Byron's reluctant awareness that Lena has borne another man's child. The first four pages show that the chapter was revised several times, with the chronology rearranged to record mental time, as Byron's troubled mind shifts back and forth over the events of the morning, then leaps ahead to anticipate the loathsome duty he must perform in notifying Lucas Burch. Three periods of composition are recorded by the papers and also by the royal blue ink, the light blue-black and the dark blue.

The short tissue-type paste-on slip in which Hightower discovers the missing mule was probably added to accentuate the fact of Byron's departure and also to negotiate the shift to Hightower as center of consciousness (MS 152; T 381.28-382.4). The base page prepares for this insertion. After Byron rides off, leaving Hightower to walk home, the remainder of the chapter focuses on Hightower. He visits Lena and afterwards tries but fails to find Byron in town (MS 152; T 380.22-392.23). The significance of the duplication of the last manuscript page (156) of the chapter has been discussed above; it shows that the leaf at one time continued on, changing the focus back to Byron.

The revision Faulkner evidently made in the structure of this chapter was aimed at conveying two contrasting responses to the birth of Lena's baby. Possibly the earlier sections focusing on Byron, now in chapter 17, were once placed with the passages of chapter 18 in which Byron leaves Jefferson, fights Brown, and returns to Jefferson. And perhaps the passages that focus on Hightower were attached to the last two manuscript pages of the present chapter 16. But, as in chapters 2, 3, and 4, Faulkner has avoided the neat packaging of the experience of each character in its own separate box, although many of the episodes dealing with a single character were probably first written out as complete units.

The thinner paste-on slips of chapter 17 all refer in some curious way to Byron Bunch. This phenomenon is true also of five of the seven 0.003 slips affixed to the leaves of chapters 3 and 4. It is tempting to generalize from this observation that one of the purposes of the revisions made on the tissue-type pastings was to enhance Bunch's role and characterization. For example, in chapter 17 two such paste-on slips are concerned with Byron and the mule. On one slip, Byron gallops furiously to demand Hightower's help in delivering Lena's baby; on the other, Hightower discovers that Byron has taken the mule, leaving Hightower to walk home.

In chapter 4 two of the 0.003 paste-on slips in which Byron is present also show evidence of having been added after the Christmas flashback was written. Both appear on manuscript page 39; on the first Byron tells Hightower that Brown said that Christmas was a Negro, and on the second Hightower muses, "Poor mankind" (T 91, 93). These passages also serve to underscore the Negro question of the Christmas flashback and to illustrate Hightower's compassion, which grows to a fuller understanding in chapter 20 when he sees the blended vision of Christmas and Grimm on the wheel of thinking. The revisions of chapter 4 are consistent with an addition from the margin of chapter 19, in which Faulkner has added Grimm's parting words to Christmas: " 'Now you'll let white women alone' " (MS 174; T 439, "even in hell" added).

The Final Manuscript Revisions
of Chapters 5 and 6

In discussing the revisions Faulkner executed when he added the extended flashback to the nearly complete draft of the narrative present, I have drawn on whatever clues seem to shed even a dim light. The alterations of chapter 5 have, at each stage of my argument, proved helpful. Here, again, this same chapter offers material for further speculation.

There are three kinds of revisions in chapter 5 (MS 41-49) that are apparent in the new material written on the base pages of the chapter (some of which has not been included in the published novel) and in the changes of diction from the manuscript to the text. The first type includes all the new passages added to accommodate and refer to the episodes of the Christmas flashback. The second testifies to the efforts made to adjust and balance the newly revised chapter 5 with the chapters that precede it. These involve transitional passages, some of which are ultimately missing from the novel, and also some new material that underscores the theme. Finally, there are changes that provide for the new direction in which Christmas's character moved after Faulkner had worked out the later episodes. This shift in character can be observed in the previously cited diction changes from the manuscript to the book.

In the published novel, the reader encounters Joe Christmas face to face for the first time in chapter 5. He is immediately caught up in Christmas's torment and agony without understanding anything beyond the fact that Christmas despises Negroes, has an aversion to prayer, is brutal to his partner Brown, is obsessed by some act he feels compelled to perform, and is a lonely, baleful man who is haunted by strange memories. The reader learns nothing in this chapter that concerns the plot development of the novel. In fact, narrative coherence would in no way be affected if the account of Joe Christmas's twenty-four hours preceding the murder were completely missing from the novel.

One may speculate, therefore, as to why, after extending the Christmas story to so great a length, Faulkner permitted the chapter to remain in the completed novel. True, it contains some of the finest writing in the novel and many memorable tableaux, such as the picture of Joe in the woods quietly reading a magazine from beginning to end, or standing outside the barbershop, "so cold so baleful," or walking down the "wide, empty, shadow-brooded street" like a "phantom, a spirit, strayed out of its own world, and lost" (T 105-6). Perhaps Faulkner clung to the chapter for passages such as these.

But it is more likely that the author thought a transition was needed between the narrative present of the first four chapters and the leap into the past of the sixth chapter. For as chapter 5 now stands it is Janus-faced as it pivots, first toward the LBH story of the present and then toward the orphanage-McEachern-Burden story of the past. It seems to belong equally to each.

Thus, although chapter 5 appears to serve no precise plot function, it bears a heavy load in the narrative structure of the novel as a whole. And in respect to the exercise of analyzing the revisions of the manuscript, to say nothing of the power it achieves in presenting the protagonist of the work, it is fortunate that the chapter remains.

Earlier (chap. 3) I noted the newer passages written on the base page of chapter 5 to accommodate the addition of the McEacherns and Bobbie Allen and the more explicit details of the Burden affair. I also discussed the paste-on slip taken from the previous version of the McEachern flashback. In the present analysis, I will try to point out Faulkner's various experiments with methods of introducing Joe Christmas and attempting to link the chapter with the material preceding it, which is a part of the LBH story of the narrative present.

To link chapter 5 to the first four chapters, Faulkner, naturally, started with the opening page. Here he tried a favorite device. He set the episode of Christmas's attack on Brown into a flashback by beginning the chapter a few hours after the fight had occurred. The manuscript version, therefore, has a slightly different time structure. The base page of manuscript page 41 begins as follows: "Brown told the sheriff that he saw Christmas leave the cabin and go up to Miss Burden's house before daylight on Saturday AM. But Christmas did not return to the cabin at all on Friday night. In fact, he saw Brown but once after he left the cabin early Friday AM—"[11] That the quotation above is a later passage than the paste-on slip that follows it is obvious not only because of the suspension lines but because of the deleted syllable of the first passage affixed to manuscript page 41: "⟨ing.⟩ That was about 9: o'clock in the evening. He was passing the barbershop, wearing a cap now instead of the stiff straw hat, and he was walking slowly, with an air not purposeless so much as that of a man killing time, and as he passed the barbershop he looked in through the plate glass window and saw the first and last serious mistake he had ever made; ⟨He saw

---

[11]This extension line and all subsequent ones in the quoted material in this chapter are shortened versions of the lines Faulkner drew from the end of his sentence to the edge of the page. They appear on both the base pages and in the paste-on slips. Apparently Faulkner used these lines to remind himself when typing to begin a new paragraph. They also indicate in some instances that new material has been added.

at once that Brown was drunk⟩ and, as usual, the mistake was drunk."

The base page starts the short flashback with "Brown came in drunk Thursday night. It was after midnight and though Christmas had been in bed for 2 hours, he was not asleep. Lying on the cot his hands behind his head,——" The next paste-on slip continues as follows: "Christmas watched the other in silhouette propping himself in the door way; he could hear Brown breathing short and heavy and loud. Standing there between his propped arms, Brown began to sing in a saccharine nasal tenor. 'Shut it,' Christmas said." The passage, still a part of a paste-on slip, continues in somewhat different language the description of the same episode that appears in the published text. It records Christmas's brutal attack on Brown, while thinking, *"Something is going to happen to me. I am going to do something"* and includes *"this is not the right one"* (T 95). After the scene with Brown, the base page records Joe's activities until he departs from the cabin and rips off his clothing in the fresh, cool, night air (MS 43; T 100).

That Faulkner suffered through many revisions and indecisions about the plunge into the Christmas story is further evidenced by one of the two covered-over sections found in the manuscript (MS 72). This particular leaf has a canceled number 41 above its final pagination, and under the paste-on slip at the top of the page can be seen a roman numeral V and four lines of writing.[12] A few words can be discerned, such as "lying on his cot in the dark cabin, his hands beneath his head" and "stroke of more than midnight—Christmas heard ⟨Brown as he approached⟩ his drunken approach." The words "Brown's silhouette" are also legible. Moreover, the margin at the top of manuscript page 72 has been bisected to indicate the beginning of a new chapter. Although the sheet now forms the fourth page of chapter 8, the partially hidden words obviously represent a different beginning

[12]That the beginning of chap. 5 was already numbered 41 when the manuscript leaf was inscribed with the now covered-over passage provides further evidence that Faulkner added MS 72, now part of the flashback, as well as the others lacking the canceled number-sets, after he had copied out and rearranged the rest of the manuscripts.

of chapter 5. This beginning was discarded in favor of the opening that heralds the Christmas flashback in the manuscript: "Brown told the sheriff that he saw Christmas leave the cabin and go up to Miss Burden's house before daylight on Saturday AM." Faulkner probably thought at one time during the composition of the novel that some such link with the previous chapter was necessary. By the time he reached the typing stage he changed his mind again and made the final revision of the opening paragraph, beginning with "it was after midnight" (T 95), thus reverting back to something that more closely resembles the covered passage on manuscript page 72. It would seem, therefore, that Faulkner had a definite purpose in abruptly taking up the Christmas story without a transition. Ultimately, he provided the reader with no such guideposts as the trail of smoke from the burning house that leads from chapter 1 to the action of the narrative present at the end of chapter 2, or as the convenient figure of Byron Bunch, telling, being told, and knowing in chapters 2 through 4.

One passage on the base page of chapter 5 appears to have been added to echo Brown's climactic accusation, reported by Bunch to Hightower near the end of chapter 4. It begins, "Brown struggled again. 'Take your black hand off of me, you damn nigger-blooded—'" and continues through the final "'let me breathe'" (T 96-97). This passage forms a complete section written on the base page between two pastings. It has obviously been added to give Christmas an additional motive for "thinking quietly *Something is going to happen to me. I am going to do something*" (T 97). It also reminds the reader of Brown's statement in chapter 4 that Christmas had admitted to him that he was part Negro (T 91).

A summary of the various revisions of this pivotal chapter shows that certain changes were obviously made after Faulkner added the Christmas flashback. Such alterations involve the addition of specific references to such characters as the McEacherns, Bobbie Allen, Max and Mame to Christmas's gallery of memories. The changes also include the more explicit memory of the love affair with Joanna Burden and the allusions to her praying over Christmas. Moreover, the reference to Joe Brown as Christmas's only mistake has been eliminated from the published novel, possibly because with the addition of Bobbie Allen, Faulkner provided an example of a more serious mistake.

In the manuscript as it now stands, there are more explicit references to Joe's Negro blood and his motives for killing Joanna Burden, as well as to the hatred Joe still feels for McEachern and the contempt for his wife. But between the manuscript and the book Faulkner decided to make Joe's motives, background, and past experiences far more subtle and ambiguous, perhaps realizing that having told the story backwards he could gain more mystery or suspense by subduing the more overt statements. Apparently he chose to accentuate the level at which one asks *why* Joe committed the murder instead of "and then what happened?"[13] As for the matter of changed intent as it is revealed in the character of Joe Christmas, one receives from the manuscript of chapter 5 the definite impression that Joe indeed had Negro blood. But the published text of the chapter leaves the reader with a sense of bewilderment.

In the course of trying to determine when and why Faulkner added so many of Joe's explicit memories to the manuscript of chapter 5 and why he did not transfer them into the novel, I have speculated on the possibility that at one time he contemplated placing the chapter in chronological order at the end of the flashback, just before Joe's final meeting with Joanna Burden. Perhaps it was once intended to occur immediately before the scene in which Joe sits in the dense shadow of the

---

[13]Norman Holmes Pearson says that Faulkner uses the structure of a detective story and carefully arranges his clues, giving scattered information while withholding other information ("Lena Grove," *Shenandoah*, 3 [Spring 1952], 3). George Palmer Garrett claims that Faulkner deliberately breaks the rules of slick fiction, one of which is to state clearly the basic problems and relationships at the outset, although his first inclination is to follow these rules ("Some Revisions in *As I Lay Dying*," *MLN*, 73 [1958], 416). Linton Massey notes that Faulkner handles pure suspense, ironic suspense, and dramatic emphasis by manipulating the time element and by using syntactic idiosyncrasies, abrupt transitions, and deliberate procrastinations ("Notes on the Unrevised Galleys of Faulkner's *Sanctuary*," p. 119). B. R. McElderry, Jr., points out that we know about the murder before it is committed so that the suspense that carries through the flashback comes from our desire to know why it was committed ("The Narrative Structure of *Light in August*," *MissQ*, 11 [1958], 179). Robert Hilton Knox says of *Light in August* that the reader must grope through time dislocations and causal relationships toward the meaning of events ("William Faulkner's *Absalom, Absalom!*" p. 54).

shrubbery thinking "'so now it's all done, all finished'" (T 265). Had the chapter been located after the flashback, the reader would have recognized the references Faulkner added to the manuscript but removed from the published text. In any event, the explicit names were ultimately removed and Faulkner again deleted the transitional reference to Brown, choosing instead a sharp turn from one story to the other.

The typescript shows that Faulkner was still reworking chapter 5 after he had begun to type the manuscript. The final pagination of the typed chapter is pages 105 to 122/23. Its last page bears both numbers, the higher having been written in pencil after the final numerical corrections were made on the rest of the typescript in ink. The last six pages of the typescript have two series of canceled numbers (T 105.26-110.32). The first set runs from number 119 to number 124 and was typed at the same time as the text. This version may have included the transitional material, later deleted, and the section describing Joe Christmas in his loft bedroom at the McEacherns. The six typed numbers have been canceled in blue ink.

A second set of hand-written canceled numbers in blue ink runs from number 118 to number 123. It too has been scratched out by hand to accommodate the final hand-numbering in ink of these last six typed pages. Which of the two sections mentioned above was the last to have been deleted it is impossible to say. But the changed pagination in the typescript could not indicate that the passage describing Joe in the commandeered car and later disposing of the gun was once in the typed version of this chapter, for the section in its present form seems far too long.[14] (Faulkner's typed pages generally have twenty-seven lines.) What the canceled numbers do indicate is that the earlier part of the chapter was retyped twice, for it lacks the two canceled number-sets; they also demonstrate that both typings were done after the beginning of chapter 6 was typed because of the

[14]Since I do not know when Faulkner began the typescript, I cannot be sure of what he deleted from chap. 5. It seems unlikely that he began it before effecting the revisions represented by the five canceled number-sets, because those revisions changed the opening chapters drastically. I doubt, therefore, that chap. 5 included the final two leaves of chap. 12 at any stage of the typing, for those two leaves (MS 108, 109) carry the five canceled number-sets.

disparity between the final pagination of the last page of chapter 5 and the first of chapter 6.

I have already discussed (chap. 3) the revisions of chapter 6 that pertain to the reordering of an earlier time structure and those made to link the chapter more closely to the McEachern matter of the following chapter. That it was not written in direct conjunction with Doc Hines's description in chapter 16 of Joe's life in the orphanage is quite apparent in the contradictions of fact found in the two versions of the story. But the Virginia manuscript plainly shows that chapter 6 was revised a second time in conjunction with a revision of the manuscript of chapter 5 and that both chapter 5 and 6 were revised once more after Faulkner began to type the manuscript.

The three episodes of chapter 6 (MS 50-58) are causally linked. Joe Christmas at the age of five is discovered hiding in the dietitian's bedroom closet at the orphanage in which he has been placed. Although he is squatting behind the curtain among the "soft woman-garments," first savoring and then being sickened by the sweet, sticky toothpaste, he is utterly unaware that he is witnessing the dietitian's clandestine lovemaking. As a result of being discovered, Joe becomes the target of the woman's fear, fury, and hatred. She determines to have the little "nigger spy" removed from the orphanage by one means or another. She tries to make an ally of the janitor because he seems to possess hidden knowledge about Christmas. But the janitor refuses to cooperate with the dietitian's "womanfilth," "bitchery," and "damnation." Instead, fearing that Christmas will be placed in a Negro orphanage, he abducts the child and tries to put him into a second orphanage for white children in Little Rock. The janitor is apprehended and the child brought back to the original orphanage in Memphis; the janitor subsequently disappears. Almost immediately the child pays for his harmless peccadillo by being put up for adoption and delivered into the hands of the stern, harsh McEachern, who vows to teach him " 'to fear God and abhor idleness and vanity.' " "Thus the promissory note which he [Christmas] had signed with a tube of toothpaste on that afternoon two months ago, was recalled" (T 134).

Despite the shattering of linear time, the three episodes of this chapter—the toothpaste scene, Joe's abduction, and his adoption—are organized in a completely different way from the more random association of episodes in the previous chapters. Although Faulkner has a penchant for delayed nemeses, he has energized the events of the sixth chapter with the force of brutal necessity.

In chapter 6 Faulkner delves into the deep past, to the time when Joe Christmas was five years old. As the novel stands, the transition is accomplished in a single paragraph beginning "memory believes before knowing remembers." The corridor of memory leads back to the "big long garbled cold echoing building of dark red brick" (T 111). These memories occur sporadically throughout the Christmas flashback but are more frequent and specific in the manuscript than in the text. Structurally, the memories alluded to in chapter 5 open the door to the long corridor that the reader enters when he meets Joe Christmas in chapter 6 at the age of five. But the corridor represents more than memory. It is the link between the first and last sections of the book. It provides a series of complications leading into the situation of the narrative present, as well as the motivations for the murder that resolves the Christmas story. The flashback is as palpable a part of the action as the rest of the book. It is linked to the earlier section by means of the memory, but the entire section is not simply one all-embracing memory, as at least one critic has asserted.[15]

The first three sheets of the manuscript of chapter 6 have been copied out for the semifinal draft and show none of the paste-on slips that characterize the remaining six sheets. The same characteristic was observed in chapters 2 and 4, which was identified in each case as a copying-out of new material or possibly older material resituated to effect a transition between chapters.[16] The first leaf illustrates one of the major changes in

---

[15]In a perceptive article Sister Kristen Morrison propounds the theory that the entire Christmas flashback is part of Joe's memory while he is committing the murder of Joanna Burden. Although she fails to explain the scenes in this section that Joe could not possibly remember because he was not present, she makes many interesting distinctions about the uses of the narrator's several voices ("Faulkner's Joe Christmas: Character through Voice," *TSLL*, 2 [1961], 431, 325, et passim).

[16]The fused words and italicized sections in the book have also been fused and italicized on the base page of the manuscript of these pages but not on the sections

the direction of the work (MS 50; T 111). It begins precisely as the book begins. After the first paragraph, though, there are several sentences which do not appear in the book and which have also been deleted in the manuscript: "Knowing remembers later [?] how the other children had been calling him nigger longer than memory even at 5 years recollected or knowing even at only 5 wondered. At 5 he did not know the reason why they called him nigger. But calling him nigger was reason for escape. He escaped into a corridor. . . . It would be in the early P.M." The passage continues almost as in the text: "In the ⟨corridor⟩ quiet and empty corridor during the quiet hour of early afternoon, he was like a shadow, small even for five years, sober and quiet as a shadow" (T 111).

In deleting this explicit statement of Christmas's having become accustomed to being called a Negro at the early age of five, and also in removing from chapter 5 any mention of the orphanage, Faulkner has achieved two ends toward which he seems to have been working. He has certainly made his work more ambiguous, since a reader coming to the novel for the first time does not know positively, however much he might suspect, that the child in this chapter is Joe Christmas until the point, many pages later, at which the dietitian tells the matron, " 'That child, that Christmas boy, is a nigger' " (T 124).

In addition, in the final version the toothpaste episode builds up gradually to a horrifying climax when the dietitian discovers the child hiding in her closet and hisses furiously at him, " 'You little rat! Spying on me! You little nigger bastard!' " (T 114). In the published text, this outburst marks the first mention in the chapter of the Negro theme and comes as the kind of shock of recognition that involves the reader's memory of the previous chapters and the believing without yet knowing that so absorbs Faulkner in this novel. In fact, directly after the scene, Faulkner wrote and then crossed out the following passage: "Memory knows first, long before knowing catches it. . . . He was not whipped. He was permitted to leave the room—with the vomit

---

affixed to their later leaves, a practice which often indicates that the base-page passages were written after the sections attached to them.

on the floor, ⟨unreadable⟩ the spoiled shoes, the emptied tube"
(MS 51).

Here, again, Faulkner deletes an obvious statement of theme,
to the effect that Joe was not punished immediately for what
he thought was the heinous sin of stealing the toothpaste; he
remembers instead without understanding the escape from the
expected whipping. Somewhat later, after Joe has been abducted
by the janitor and returned to the orphanage and after the
janitor has disappeared, the narrator says, "He was so busy
avoiding her [the dietitian] that he had long since forgot the
reason for it; soon he had forgotten the trip too" (MS 56). In
the novel the narrator adds, "Since he was never to know that
there was any connection between them" (T 132). In this
instance Faulkner demonstrates the significance of the action
before he explains it. He always hesitates to overexplain. For
example, the last paragraph of page 134 of the published text
begins in the manuscript: "Thus he got at last the whipping he
expected. The promissory note which he had signed with a tube
of toothpaste on that afternoon two months ago was recalled"
(MS 58). That reference to the whipping has been omitted. It
will be dramatized instead in chapter 7.

Even more important is the fact that Faulkner no longer
opens on the Negro theme and at no point in the chapter shows
Christmas's response to being called a Negro. (In the next chapter he has also eliminated the explicit references found in the
manuscript to Joe's memories of having been called Negro.) The
discussion of Joe's alleged Negro blood is relegated to the dietitian, the matron, and the janitor. The double effect of this
subtle change is to show that Joe's feelings on the Negro subject
are buried beneath his bewilderment at having escaped punishment for the forbidden sensory pleasure in which he had
overindulged. The author thus prepares for Joe's martyrlike
enjoyment of the beatings he receives from McEachern in the
next chapters.[17]

[17]Several critics have noted the effect on Joe Christmas of the punishment
manqué. Jerome Gavin attributes the later developments in Christmas's life to the
episode with the dietitian in chap. 6. Here sex, food, and race are linked. Joe expected punishment and was bribed instead. Gavin also notes that both of Joe's
murders occur when a sexual adjustment is threatened by religious fanaticism (*"Light*

The reader on first meeting Christmas in chapter 5 does not know why he seems to despise Negroes so passionately, connecting the "fecund mellow voices" of the women of Freedman Town with the return to the "lightless hot wet primogenitive Female" (T 107). Nor does chapter 6 provide explicit information. But throughout the flashback the reader observes Joe responding to the impulses generated by these feelings, which he himself does not fully understand. Faulkner's deletions, therefore, purposefully eliminate overly simple, pat explanations of Christmas's psychological responses and motivations.[18]

In general, then, chapter 6 has been arranged to present in a series of vivid scenes the early events that form Christmas's character. They begin with his first encounter with a woman, which ends in guilt, nausea, vomiting, and finally bribery instead of the feared and almost hoped-for punishment. Next, Joe experiences the shock of the epithet "nigger," which is to haunt him fatally all his life, and also the apparently motiveless hatred of a mad religious fanatic who teaches him the pattern of flight that he later follows. Finally, he is put into the hands of a

---

in August: The Act of Involvement," p. 14). Robert D. Jacobs points out that Joe "accumulates unpunished crimes waiting for eventual reckoning at some awful and deferred Judgment" ("Faulkner and the Tragedy of Isolation," *Hopkins Review,* 6 [Spring 1953], 162-83; rpt. in *Southern Renascence,* p. 176). William Van O'Connor also refers to Joe's wanting to be rejected (*William Faulkner* [Minneapolis: Univ. of Minnesota Press, 1959], p. 22). Edward Kimbrough, after an interview with Faulkner in 1951, writes: "Maybe, he thinks, this urge to purify the flesh belongs to the Protestant tradition he senses among his own folk: the deep-founded belief that man in this life must pay, somehow and somewhere, for whatever pleasure he allows himself" (*Lion in the Garden,* p. 65).

[18]It seems to me that Richard Chase errs in finding a flaw in this chapter in Faulkner's not relating the meeting between the dietitian and the janitor through the mind of Joe Christmas ("The Stone and the Crucifixion: Faulkner's *Light in August,*" *Kenyon Review,* 10 [1948], 539-51; rpt. in *Two Decades of Faulkner Criticism,* ed. Frederick J. Hoffman and Olga W. Vickery [East Lansing: Michigan State College Press, 1954], p. 214). Actually, Faulkner was doing something quite different, having already used the consciousness of a childish mind in *TSATF* and *As I Lay Dying.* He was establishing episodes that later became symbolic. He was concentrating on the genesis of the guilt feelings, confusion, hopes, and fears of a child of five, of which the child himself is unaware but which direct much of his behavior in later years. Had he used Joe's psyche as the center of consciousness here, it would have oversimplified Faulkner's view of how man responds to, and comprehends, his experience.

rigorous religious bigot who forces a false identity and a false name on him, one that he later violently rejects. But he cannot cast off the deep impression of his early experience, for memory believes before knowing remembers. In the chapters that follow, each of the themes established in chapter 6 is fully dramatized in the events of Joe Christmas-McEachern's later life.

The technique Faulkner used to heighten these themes and to present them as dramatically as possible becomes brilliantly clear when his careful revisions are observed. By paring down overt explanations, by juxtaposing significant memories, and by anticipating the events to come that grow out of these memories, Faulkner has succeeded in expressing through plot action how the believing and knowing that grow out of memory interact and form the matrix of experience that shapes future events.

Revisions within Chapters 1, 2, 3, and 4

In chapter 2 of this anatomy of a manuscript, I alluded to the possibility that Faulkner did not write the opening chapter of *Light in August* until he had completed the major Jefferson episodes of the LBH story. Both the diction changes from manuscript to text at the end of chapter 2 at the point where Lena and Byron meet for the first time and the insertion of a scene between Lena, Bunch, and Mrs. Beard into chapter 4, which seems to have been moved in toto from the earlier draft, suggest that chapter 1 was a second and greatly expanded version of the basic facts of Lena's short biography. However, there is no real proof of such a conjecture nor any indication of when Faulkner wrote the extraordinary description of Lena's early life and journey to Jefferson.[19] All that can actually be proved is that a former draft of the novel began with Hightower in his study.

The present chapter 1 of the Virginia manuscript is a copying-out, inscribed almost entirely in the same blue-black ink used

---

[19]The twelve-digit difference between the lowest canceled number-set and the final pagination of chap. 12 may have some bearing on the period of composition of chap. 1, which is numbered 2-12.

for most of the manuscript (MS 2-12). It is distinguished by having two leaves numbered 3, to which I shall refer as 3A and 3B. Only pages 2 and 3A carry paste-on slips from a previous draft; two of these slips refer to Lena's climbing out of the window of her lean-to bedroom and the third to her waiting for the wagon to mount the hill (T 3, 4, 5). These revisions must have been made after the rest of the chapter was copied out because there are many fewer lines inscribed on page 3A than on page 3B, which follows it, and the ink of the base page 3A is different from that of the two paste-on slips attached to it. The first page 3, therefore, must have been the last to have been added to the chapter (T 4, from "anyway were even fewer," to 5.25).

In examining the manuscript to discover why the new page 3 was added, one sees that its base page carries the first references to Lucas Burch by name. Still, it would hardly have been necessary to add a new leaf for that purpose alone, for Lucas's name is inserted from the margin elsewhere in the chapter. Reading on, one can locate fairly easily the passages that carry the narrative forward and are necessary to the sense. Only one such passage is unnecessary to the progress of the action, although it adds volumes to the thematic meaning of the work. It begins with a short flashback: "She had been doing that now for almost four weeks" (T 4). It continues with the description of the peaceful corridor that Lena traveled, peopled with kind and nameless faces, and ends with the various identical wagons, the "succession of creakwheeled and limpeared avatars, like something moving forever and without progress across an urn" (T 5).

This particular revision is extremely useful in analyzing how Faulkner attempted to contrast the life-styles and the responses to experience of Joe Christmas and Lena Grove, for he wrote the passages in which Lena's journey is compared to the figures on Keats's artifice of eternity *after* manuscript page 76, in which Joe Christmas seemed to see the diminishing row of suavely shaped but cracked urns, from each of which "there issued something liquid, deathcolored and foul" (T 177-78).

It is clear that the urn passage of chapter 1 postdates that of chapter 8, for manuscript page 76 displays the canceled number-sets characteristic of most of the Christmas flashback. These numbers do not accommodate the new page 3; in fact, none of the pagination of the manuscript has been altered to adjust to the additional leaf. But the pagination of the typescript has been raised two digits from chapters 2 through 4, indicating that chapter 1 was revised after one typing of the first four chapters had been completed. One can conclude, therefore, that the addition to chapter 1 of the famous Keatsean allusion was one of Faulkner's last revisions of the semifinal draft and that he did not wish to renumber again the entire manuscript from page 3 to the end.

It should also be noted that Faulkner has introduced a second parallel between Lena and Christmas; both have the habit of climbing out of windows when pursuing their romantic affairs. In the manuscript Christmas was originally associated with windows more frequently. In the loft passage cited previously he welcomed the dawn at his single window after a sleepless night of "manhate" for McEachern. In addition, chapter 7 once began with "in the window the boy acquired his springboard for hatred soon enough." This sentence has been crossed out and changed to the following: "And memory knows this; not believes. Even 20 years later memory is still to believe 'On this day I became a man.' Since even a child of 8 ⟨memory has already lived as long as the love or hate of which it is the⟩ love or hate is as old as all the human history, chronicled or not, which in the moment of knowing and remembering is localized" (MS 59). The whole passage is compressed in the published text into the now familiar "and memory knows this: twenty years later memory is still to believe *on this day I became a man*" (T 137).

The line beginning "and memory knows this" seems to be almost a continuation of the more famous passage at the opening of chapter 6: "Memory believes before knowing remembers." Both are late revisions of diction, but they also serve to repeat the memory theme of the Christmas flashback and to link chapters 6 and 7. The image of Joe in the window, however, which immediately calls to mind Hightower, also pictured in a window, has been deleted. Perhaps such an image was too static for Christmas's characterization; perhaps Faulkner preferred to heighten the parallels between Lena and the adolescent Joe Christmas. As the text reads now, Joe's only connection with windows is in climbing out of them, an observation that might serve to strengthen the suspicion that chapter 1 was written with the Christmas parallel in mind after Faulkner had completed the flashback.

In trying to follow Faulkner's steps as he combined his two stories, I have had to shift as he did from one chapter to another often separated by many intervening ones. In so doing, I have tried to pick up the loose ends of my theory and weave them into as complete a pattern as possible to present a final picture of the successive stages of the manuscript's growth. At this point, only a few pages of chapter 2 and certain later revisions to chapter 3 and 4 remain to be discussed.

The first seven leaves of chapter 2 have been recopied in blue-black ink; most of them are fairly clean (MS 13-19; T 27.1-45.1). The episodes describing Christmas's and Brown's activities and behavior at the Jefferson planing mill have been reset on the first leaf to occur in a three-year flashback of what Byron Bunch now knows (T 27). Faulkner had originally introduced Bunch into the manuscript version of chapter 3 with the words "Byron Bunch knows this" (MS 25), but he chose instead to use Byron as observer in chapter 2, where the same words now introduce him (T 27). That some version of the same episodes were recounted in at least one previous draft can be inferred from the paste-on slip (discussed in chap. 2) of manuscript page 17, the only one found among the first seven leaves of the chapter. In the passage inscribed on this slip, Mooney, formerly called Ad, says that he saw Christmas and Brown driving around in a new car. The episode was once repeated as a dialogue within a dialogue because both double and single quotation marks for each new speaker remain in the manuscript (T 38.3-17).

Although one cannot assign a time order to the composition of the episodes dealing with Christmas and Brown at the mill, it is fairly clear that these episodes were revised to accomplish several ends: to employ Bunch as reflector of the action, to join his memories of Christmas and Brown to the episode at the end of the chapter in which he first meets Lena Grove, and to provide a brief background for Byron Bunch, as well as for Joanna Burden and Gail Hightower.

A reading of the published novel amply indicates the techniques Faulkner used both to foreshorten the dimension of time and to effect the introduction of Byron Bunch, not only to Lena Grove, but to Joe Christmas, Joe Brown, and the reader as well. But an example drawn from the manuscript illustrates even more clearly how skillfully these ends were achieved. At the point where Joe Christmas first appears, the published text reads, "And Byron watched him standing there," whereas the manuscript shows the correction in "and ⟨he stood there⟩ Byron watched him standing there" (MS 13; T 27). Evidently Faulkner transferred a story that was previously told by one of the characters in the novel who spoke in colloquial diction to his omniscient narrator who, using Byron as center of consciousness, could remind the reader that Byron Bunch is remembering these events three years later, on the day he meets Lena Grove.

In reconstructing the order of the revisions of chapter 2, I have speculated that Faulkner first combined into a single chapter earlier draft sheets in which the men at the mill describe and discuss both the arrival and departure of Brown and Christmas. After writing the shorter Christmas flashback, Faulkner revised certain of those sheets, compressing them and altering the narrative point of view. Since, however, he had not yet worked out the details of the Christmas-Burden affair nor shortened the time span of the Hightower story, the manuscript is at variance with the text about certain statistics. On manuscript page 19 Miss Burden's grandfather and brother are said to have been killed fifty years previous to the present action; the text reads "sixty years" (T 42). On the same leaf Hightower was a minister in Jefferson "30 years ago," but the thirty has been changed in the text to twenty-five (T 43); on manuscript page 13 Christmas appeared at the mill "three years ago," and on manuscript page 14 he had been living on Miss Burden's place for "about 3 years." The later time period has been revised in the text to "more than two years" (T 32). Perhaps at this time, in order to prepare for chapter 4, Faulkner, again employing his omniscient narrator, added the expository passages found on the base page about Bunch and Hightower's weekly meetings (MS 19; T 43-44).

There are other indications too that the bulk of the mill hands' dialogue about Christmas and Brown was composed before chapters 11 and 12. For example, there is no indication in chapter 12 that Christmas ever quit his job at the mill. In fact, he considers leaving Jefferson after payday, which implies that he is still employed (T 252). Of course, he never manages to extricate himself, and there is every indication that he continues his daily routine (T 254). The only day on which he quite obviously does not report for work is the Friday of the murder, which fact bears no relationship at all to the information that Christmas "quit one Saturday night, without warning, after almost three years" (T 36).

After lengthening and revising the Christmas flashback, Faulkner seems to have made additional revisions to the structure of chapter 2. He apparently rewrote and recopied the first two leaves of the chapter to include the scene in which Byron offers Joe Christmas his lunch pail and Joe replies, "I ain't hungry. Keep your muck." Manuscript page 14 reveals two long extension lines following "he had lived on cigarettes for 2 or 3 days" (T 31). Since manuscript page 15 begins with a complete sentence, "Then one day about six months ago . . .," it is clear that Faulkner recopied and perhaps revised the earlier leaves of the chapter, supplying the extension lines so that the new sheets would fit neatly with what followed (T 32). The food scene may have been added in order to parallel the two scenes in the flashback in which Joe Christmas violently rejects food; these episodes are also inscribed on the base pages of the manuscript and are the newer passages of those sheets (T 145, 225). Or perhaps after the addition of chapter 1, Faulkner added Christmas's refusal to share Byron's lunch in order to contrast Joe's responses with the more sociable behavior of Lena Grove.

Lena's and Bunch's meeting obviously was the last episode to be included in chapter 2, although it represents, along with the purple ink pages of chapter 3, the earliest material in the manuscript. The parchment purple ink passages affixed to the four tissue-type pages are textually linked; only one or two lines are written on the base pages to complete a sentence or passage (MS 20-23). But the first tissue-type sheet (MS 20) shows a recopying in dark blue ink of several paragraphs that may have been executed in order to link Lena's arrival to the preceding passages that supply the information about the fire at Miss

Burden's (T 45). The dark blue ink is also used to change some of the tenses of the purple slips. The changes in diction from manuscript to text in the passages telling of Bunch and Lena's meeting at the mill are the most radical in the chapter.

Chapter 3 (MS 24-30) shows two stages of revision. Briefly, it records the events of Hightower's life in Jefferson from the beginning of his wife's strange behavior to her death. It continues with the loss of his pulpit and his determination to remain in Jefferson despite the persecution he endures from some of the community's less admirable members. The account of those years ends with the story of the stillborn Negro child whom Hightower had delivered four years previous to the narrative present. This passage is followed by Byron's musings, in the narrative present, upon the sad and strange events of Hightower's life (T 56-58).

There are many paste-on slips of the parchment paper affixed to the tissue-type paper on manuscript pages 26-28. In certain of these passages the previous narrator is still in evidence. A second stage of revision is also apparent, beginning on manuscript page 29 with the second paste-on slip; this pasting consists of the same thinner paper as the base page to which it is affixed. In this section Byron is present, listening to the story, and the narrator's voice and diction are the same as in the published version. This revision seems to have been made for the purpose of recording Byron's reactions to the story, his thoughts and philosophic observations. In addition, the second stage of revision prepares for a return to the narrative present as well as incorporating into the chapter Hightower's reaction to the townspeople. On page 69 of the text, in the passage beginning "and Hightower said" and ending " 'I don't know,' Byron said, 'I reckon that's just my life,' " the careful shifting of time levels can be observed in such a phrase as "that was soon after Byron had heard the story, shortly after the evening visits to Hightower's study began . . ." Since the entire section is found on one of the thinner paste-on slips and written in a lighter ink, it seems to represent a second reorganization of this chapter. It blends into the base page of 30, which leads up to the final paste-on slip, written in royal blue ink on parchment paper and taken from the earlier draft in which Hightower on the Sunday night of the narrative present observes Byron Bunch approaching his study and stumbling on the dark bottom step. This last paragraph of the chapter prepares for the protracted dialogue of the succeeding chapter (T 70).

While revising chapter 3, Faulkner used the base page to reorder the time structure of Hightower's delivery of the Negro child. A passage from the previous draft, narrated by the semi-literate voice, has been pasted to the base page after the words "one day about four years ago . . ." (MS 29; T 68). The paste-on slip is followed by a second time notation, again inscribed on the base page: " 'Even despite the fifteen years . . .' " (MS 30; T 68). Obviously the episode was retrieved from the previous draft and inserted into a revised time structure. It has also been recast to relate to Hightower's books and Byron's admiration for the knowledge derived from them. The second reference to the same episode occurs in chapter 17, also written on two paste-on slips, each of a different weight (MS 149, 150; T 372-73). The episode is now related to the birth of Lena's baby, and again Byron's respect for the book is evident, for he has complete confidence that Hightower can use it for the practical and life-giving ends Byron so desperately desires.

In the two stages of revision of chapter 3, Faulkner not only changed the center of consciousness for the purpose of enhancing Byron Bunch's role but also readjusted levels of time to balance the long tale of Hightower's misfortunes in Jefferson with the flashback glimpses of Joe Christmas and Joe Brown in the preceding chapter. Both chapters are brought to the point in time at which the present action occurs. But the third chapter carries the narrative one step further, to the next evening of the Sunday following the murder. The ending of chapter 3 prepares for chapter 4, in which the events of the additional thirty hours between the close of chapter 2 and the opening of chapter 4 are the subject. In addition, Faulkner's revisions result in showing Hightower and Bunch together in the brief flashback of chapter 3, in which each of the men comments on the quality of his own life and tries to understand something about the other's life, thus establishing a pattern for the subsequent dialogues between them.

The revisions of chapter 4 (MS 31-40) show the same pattern as those of chapter 2. Faulkner has recopied the first three and the last manuscript sheets and also the present manuscript page 35, which shows a canceled number 34. On the remaining sheets, the present page 34 and pages 36-39, he has salvaged large sections of a previous parchment draft by cutting it up and affixing the usable passages to new tissue pages. The three shades of blue ink are also present in this chapter.

Evidently, in chapter 4, as well as in chapter 2, Faulkner culled episodes from disparate parts of the earlier draft and combined them into one chapter in order to link more closely the LBH and the Christmas stories. I have described (chap. 2) the episodes in which Byron takes Lena to Mrs. Beard's boarding house on Saturday night. Such an episode may at one time have been much longer and formed an independent chapter. It appears to have been compressed in order to be reported after the fact by Byron to Hightower the following night.

Faulkner also added new passages on the base page and on the sheets of the tissue-type paper that he cut up and pasted to the new tissue-type sheets. The new passages display a pattern that suggests that they were added after he became absorbed with the Christmas story.

The first direct statement that Joe Christmas is a Negro occurs on the base page of 35 (T 83), a page without paste-on slips. Significantly, Bunch informs Hightower of the "fact" before telling him of the murder. Brown's first testimony that Christmas is a Negro also appears on the base page of manuscript page 38, and on the base page of manuscript page 39 the marshal implies that it is far worse to call any white man a Negro than to call him a murderer. Brown's insistence that Christmas is a Negro is continued in a tissue-type paste-on slip, along with Hightower's question "Is it certain, proved, that he has Negro blood?" (MS 39; T 91-93). Even Byron seems to assume here that it is true. These passages probably were added after the flashback was written. They underscore the Negro complications of the Christmas murder case and serve to show the responses of the actors of the LBH story to the character who became far more central to the novel.

These revisions illustrate the changed direction of the work after Faulkner had added the Christmas flashback. Others show the purposeful disruption of time sequences that may once have been developed chronologically but in which linear time was later shaped into a circle. By means of the ubiquitous world of the memory, which knows nothing of linear time, Faulkner compressed material that probably originally covered more of the surface of the manuscript. He used flashbacks and flashforwards to place these episodes into the denser context of memory.

Some Changes of Diction

It has been necessary to ignore many of the significant revisions of diction that occur in the manuscript and from the manuscript to the published text. But so much has been written about the Christian symbolism in *Light in August* that I have selected one interesting revision in the last chapter of the novel concerning the furniture repairer and dealer. Originally he was a cattle dealer returning with a newly purchased pair of Jersey calves (MS 183; T 468). It is hard to determine whether this change of occupation was made in the text for the practical reason that it would have been difficult for Lena to share her sleeping quarters in the truck with the calves or whether Faulkner wished to eliminate imagery that too obviously evoked the holy family. But the latter explanation seems consistent with Faulkner's association of Lena with Keats's pre-Christian Grecian urn and with a later comment that she had "something of that pagan quality."[20]

Perhaps to separate his pagans and martyrs, Faulkner also eliminated from the text the description of Hines's rapt and alert expression as that "of an ancient martyr among pagans" (MS 141). This deletion implies that Hines cannot be linked with Hightower as a martyr, nor can Hightower, the auditor of Hines's story and the implied pagan of the manuscript, share

---

[20]*Faulkner in the University*, p. 199.

with Lena her pagan quality. For Hightower's only fit place on the pagan urn would be in the deserted village, which does not appear on the urn at all, but for which Keats has evoked such haunting sadness.

Certain revisions of diction in the Christmas flashback should be noted, for they illustrate Faulkner's attempt to show, rather than tell, how Christmas responded to the passage from innocence to experience. By filtering the shock of Joe's final meeting with Bobbie through his sensory perceptions, later to be stored away in his memory, Faulkner found that he could eliminate many of the passages in which the narrator had explained and often overexplained. Thus, such lines and phrases as "but that was long ago. He had been a kid then, a child then" (MS 84) and "with the debris of all life talking about him" (MS 86) have not found their way into the novel.[21]

Instead, Faulkner showed that Joe was still a "child," a "kid," by introducing from the margin two references to Beale Street and noting that Joe had never heard of that infamous street of sin and pleasure (MS 84; T 199). The implied contrast between Beale Street and the "sinful" high school dance is left to the reader's perception.

The whole process of achieving manhood and the way in which Joe Christmas's psyche dealt with the painful lessons he learned has been adjusted toward delineating a more precise and consistent picture of the relationship between memory, the senses, and the knowledge derived from them. The following five examples should suffice to illustrate Faulkner's verbal sharpening:

1. Manuscript page 76 explicitly describes Christmas's hallucination about the urns: "He seems to see in the darkness all the nameless women in the world like an endless ⟨row of⟩ declining row of suavely shaped urns." The text eliminates the simile in favor of a metaphor: "he seemed to see a diminishing row of suavely shaped urns in the moonlight, blanched" (T 177).

2. Manuscript page 83 reads, "Where he would wait, and meet her in the days before his youth had died." The text de-

---

[21]The first quotation would have appeared in the last paragraph of T 198; the second would have been in the second paragraph of T 204.

scribes him as "less urgent perhaps but not less eager, and more young" (T 196).

3. "Knowing remembers a thousand grieving streets" (MS 87) becomes "knowing not grieving remembers a thousand savage and lonely streets" (T 207).

4. The process of memory, flying backwards, in the field-pea episode has been shifted from the third person of the manuscript to the first person of the text: "Then memory clicked. He could almost hear the sound as, his head bent, he listened to a monotonous, dogmatic voice" (MS 90) becomes "memory clicking knowing *I see I see, I more than see hear I hear I see my head bent I hear the monotonous dogmatic voice*" (T 217).

5. The last paragraph on page 217 of the text now begins, "More of him than thinking may have been absent"; manuscript page 90 explains: "More of him than the tasting sense of memory had come back."

In each of these revisions Faulkner has tried to communicate the complexity, multiplicity, contradictions and ambiguity of human experience. He has avoided the explicit statement that selects a single emotion or sensory response in favor of a more inclusive set of possibilities.

V

Ambiguities, Contradictions, and Inconsistencies

FROM THE PRECEDING description of the growth and development of *Light in August*, one fact is indisputable: Faulkner made many revisions in the manuscript itself and even more from manuscript to published text. But for one reason or another he failed to clarify certain narrative facts, thereby providing a fertile field for the critical argument that has persisted since the publication of the novel. If a comparative study such as this one, which entails a microscopic reading of both manuscript and published text, cannot settle these many factual disputes, it can at least identify the particular questions that can never be answered and also illustrate why the obscurity must remain.

But a distinction should be made at the outset between intentional narrative ambiguities and those inconsistencies and contradictions of vital statistics that remain in the text because of the peculiar nature of the process of its composition. Two different orders of means are involved in these categories. Nonetheless, the final function of both must be taken into consideration in interpreting and evaluating the novel, for any ambiguity, whether intentional or accidental, ultimately contributes to the total meaning of a work.[1]

---

[1] Gerald Langford takes Floyd C. Watkins to task for claiming that Faulkner's errors and inconsistencies in that novel are deliberate. Langford implies that the study of original manuscripts can correct such critical misinterpretations (*Faulkner's Revisions of "Absalom, Absalom!"* p. 3). Both critics seem to have fallen into the intentional fallacy; for, whether deliberate or not, all contradictions and inconsistencies of fact ultimately affect critical interpretations of the work. Statements such as Langford's are like saying that Cezanne meant to shadow his apples with green paint but had only blue at hand. Still, the fact of the blue paint remains in the painting and it is the blue with which a critic must contend.

In this chapter I shall discuss a series of ambiguities in the published text of *Light in August* which cannot be resolved but which have often been the basis for misreadings and resultant misunderstandings of the novel. Many critics, embroiled in the problems of trying to resolve some of the contradictions, have ended by providing simple solutions to questions that, because of the novel's theme, must remain complex and often para-doxical.

Ambiguities

Heading the list of unresolved ambiguities is the oft-debated question of whether Joe Christmas had Negro blood. The evidence cited in the preceding chapters shows that Faulkner removed most of the narrator's explicit statements on the subject and revised the manuscript to stress the fact that Joe himself did not know but was haunted all his life by the fear that he was a Negro. In the final version, neither Joe, the narrator, nor the reader can ever know if in fact Christmas had Negro blood. Still, "memory believes before knowing remembers" (T 111). The emphasis here is not on solving the riddle; in fact, Faulkner has purposely increased the ambiguity so that it can never be solved. The main issue concerns what the mind can believe without ever really knowing. When asked about Joe Christmas, Faulkner said: "I don't think he was bad, I think he was tragic. And his tragedy was that he didn't know what he was and would never know, and that to me is the most tragic condition that an individual can have—to not know who he was."[2]

A second significant point related to the Negro theme is that although Joe Christmas had not been identified as a Negro after he left the orphanage, no one in Jefferson ever doubted once he had committed murder that he was a Negro. Even Byron Bunch and Gail Hightower after hearing Brown's testimony agree that "even a liar can be scared into telling the truth" (T 93).

---

[2] *Faulkner in the University*, p. 118.

Other questions cluster around Christmas, too, such as whether he killed Simon McEachern.[3] Again, the point at issue is not the solution to this enigma but the fact that Joe Christmas does not know, but he thinks he killed his foster father. When McEachern last appears on the scene in chapter 9, manuscript page 81 describes him as walking "unhurried and absolved into the descending chair and peaceful nothingness." The published text adds "perhaps the nothingness astonished him a little, but not much, and not for long" (T 192).

Later Max asks Joe if he has "croaked" McEachern. In the manuscript Joe replies, " 'Croaked him?' " and the narrator explains that "he spoke in a fretted tone, as though he were being held and questioned by a child" (MS 85). As I noted previously (chap. 3), after copying out chapter 9, Faulkner may have added manuscript page 85 for the sole purpose of stressing Christmas's bewilderment at having to be concerned over a matter he considers so trivial. The text enlarges on the scene; Joe replies that he doesn't know anything beyond that he hit McEachern and "he fell down." He adds, "I told him I was going to do it someday," but he never knows whether he succeeded in carrying out his threat (T 202).

In this manner Faulkner has actually increased the factual ambiguity in order to convey to the reader the spectrum of Christmas's emotions: his detestation of McEachern, his inability to distinguish between his intensely subjective feelings and their objective results, and his naive devotion to Bobbie, which has blinded him to any realistic analysis of his own plight. Never at any point in the novel, although memories occasionally flood back, is Joe troubled about what happens to McEachern. Thus, the ambiguity about McEachern's death functions to alert the reader to focus not on the pragmatic fact but rather on Christmas's attitudes: his obsession about Bobbie that feeds his

[3]Floyd C. Watkins has observed that three scholars have discovered that Christmas killed McEachern, but Watkins notes that Faulkner leaves McEachern either dead or unconscious without specifying which ("Faulkner and the Critics," *TSLL*, 10 [1968], 327). The critics cited by Watkins are (1) Edward McCamy, "Byron Bunch," *Shenandoah*, 3 (Spring 1952), 11; (2) Frederick J. Hoffman, *William Faulkner* (New York: Twayne, 1961), p. 70; (3) Phyllis Hirshleifer, "As Whirlwinds in the South," *Perspective*, 2 (1949), 230.

already well-established misogyny and the disproportionate, almost humorous, scale of values that leads him to think, "Why, I committed murder for her. I even stole for her" (T 204).

Next, there is the enigma concerning Joe Christmas's motives for actually killing Joanna Burden, as opposed to his motives for wanting to kill her, just as he had wanted to kill McEachern. Despite his intuitions and premeditations, Christmas may actually have killed her in self-defense. The reader does not know, for the precise moment of the murder is not recorded.[4] When Christmas reaches Joanna's bedroom, he lays the unopened razor on the table. He stands beside Joanna's bed and watches with fascination "the shadowed pistol on the wall; he was watching when the cocked shadow of the hammer flicked away" (T 267). Immediately the reader is transported to the exterior view of Christmas, unaware that he is holding the pistol, standing in the middle of the road. He does not "remember having picked it up at all, nor why" (T 270). The author has made it structurally impossible to assign a simple motive to the murder. He has denied the reader a direct view of the actual act. Certainly it is not for narrative suspense that Faulkner has withheld the description of Joe Christmas's slashing Joanna Burden's neck, for the reader already knows that Joanna has been murdered. Furthermore, Faulkner has foreshadowed the murder in chapter 5 by showing that Joe thought, *"Something is going to happen to me. I am going to do something.... This is not the right one"* (T 97). But at the end of the chapter, Joe does not "think even then" that something is going to happen to him (T 110). Still, as he rises to enter the house he thinks, "Already in the past tense; *I had to do it. She said so herself"* (T 264).

Why does Faulkner portray such confusion in Christmas's mind? Why does Joe think of himself as both acting and being acted upon? Why does he watch not Joanna but the shadow?

---

[4]The only critic to my knowledge who questions whether Christmas murdered Joanna is Stephen E. Meats, who claims that the evidence against Christmas is entirely circumstantial and that the murderer could as well have been Brown. His argument is overly ingenious, but the conclusion is sound that Faulkner may have been trying to point out that "man knows so little about his fellows" (T 43) ("Who Killed Joanna Burden?" *MissQ*, 24 [1971], 271-77).

What is his purpose? And if murder was his intention, why does he stand by and permit Joanna to fire the first shot?

There is no single simple explanation for Christmas's compulsion to be present for the death tryst. He is driven by all the forces and furies that have controlled his whole life: outrage at compulsory prayer, fear of being a Negro, and the violence that has always been identified for him with the sex act. In addition, he is still seeking the clearly defined punishment that was denied him at the age of five. Even beyond these motives that memory "believes longer than recollects, longer than knowing even wonders" lies the large social issue of guilt and responsibility, of who is the victim and who the victimizer (T 111). In this novel the roles of predator and prey cannot be clearly assigned, for Faulkner has chosen to achieve his ends by drawing back from the murder and by closing the door to leave the reader as much in the dark as Joe Christmas. Both Joe and Joanna were drawn toward that fatal moment; yet she struck first. Perhaps, then, the de facto explanation may be that Joe retaliated by committing murder in his own defense.

But fact is only a part of the whole truth, the truth that includes everything from first to last causes. In end results and final outcomes, fact is often ignored or considered irrelevant, as Faulkner implies by showing the town's reaction to an alleged Negro who not only had a sexual relationship with a white woman but also killed her. There is no mistaking the irony at the end of chapter 12 where Joe tosses away the gun that had had two loaded chambers and says, "'For her and for me'" (T 270). Joanna's motives are perfectly clear, but Joe's are far more complex and therefore more ambiguous. He himself has only partial knowledge of why he acts, for he is absorbed by watching the shadow rather than the substance of reality. The reader knows more—knows that Joanna embodies all the forces that have shaped Joe's life and that her attempt to force him into the mold she has prepared will end in disaster. But the truth is many-faceted and even the reader can never know all of it. Consequently, Faulkner described in considerable detail the myriad paths that led to the dark house on that fatal Friday night in August, but he did not record what Christmas was thinking when he actually committed the murder.

Once Christmas has willingly surrendered at Mottstown, there is no further internal view of him. Hence, his motives for the second escape, in which he sought refuge at Hightower's house, are never fully understood. Only Gavin Stevens's explanation is proffered, and it rests on the assumption, shared with the white townspeople, that Christmas had Negro blood. It was the conflict of his mixed blood, according to Stevens, that prompted his escape and brought about his death. The black blood "snatched up the pistol," but the white blood "would not let him fire it" (T 424).

Stevens's theory is no doubt based on sincere sentiments, but they too emerge from what memory believes, not what Stevens knows. And memory believes that Joe's black blood is responsible for his violent instincts. Little does Stevens know that it is the violence of white society, composed of people like McEachern, Hines, the dietitian, Bobbie Allen, and Joanna Burden, that has forced Christmas to choose the road to murder. Hence, although Stevens's version may have provided one view of the truth in the earlier draft from which it was carried forward, it presents in the published novel a far different relationship to reality. Combined as it is in the same chapter with the portrait of the war-lover, Percy Grimm, it conveys the author's ironic implications that Stevens can never know the truth because there are too many preconceived barriers to its attainment. What Stevens unintentionally reveals are his own convictions, which he confuses with the truth; they are convictions shared by all of white society, the same convictions that convict Joe Christmas.

The motives of other characters are often even more opaque, such as Hines's motive in abducting Christmas after the scene with the dietitian. Since Hines is firmly convinced that Christmas's father was a Negro, why has he such a horror of his grandson's being placed in a Negro orphanage? In this instance, ambiguity apparently implies ambivalence.

Nor is there a satisfactory resolution to the puzzling question of how Hightower's wife actually met her end. Here the reader is given every reason to assume that her motive was suicide, but the precise fact is denied. Long after the event the townsman-narrator of chapter 3 says that Hightower's wife had "jumped

or fallen from a hotel window" (T 61). The fact that she had
written her real name on a piece of paper would indicate that
it was a premeditated act were it not for the additional information that she tore up the paper. As in many instances, the
conflicting impulses that motivate the characters result in
possible, or even probable, explanations of events, but the final
proof cannot be established. Something indefinite, uncertain,
always remains to tease or trouble. Hightower, however, believed
that it was suicide, for the burial "was not a funeral. He did not
take the body to the church at all" (T 63). Again, the author
stresses not the fact but what is engraved on the character's
mind.

There are also several conflicting predictions as to whether
Lena Grove will ultimately marry Byron Bunch. Hightower,
after delivering Lena's baby, thinks, *"That will be her life, her
destiny. . . . But by Byron engendered next"* (T 384). On the
same day he thanks God because Lena has refused Byron's
proposal of marriage and will continue to refuse, at least until
after she has seen Brown (T 390-91). Lena's motives for continuing the pretense of pursuing Brown are perhaps truthfully
explained by the furniture dealer, who says that she is just
enjoying herself for a little while before settling down for the
rest of her life (T 480). But whether she settles down as Mrs.
Bunch, the reader never knows.

Finally, the language at the end of chapter 20 lends itself to
two diametrically opposed conclusions as to whether Hightower
lives on or dies. This particular ambiguity has resulted in considerable critical dispute.[5] The author stated unequivocally, but

---

[5]Floyd C. Watkins quotes Faulkner, who said that Hightower did not die in the
novel. Watkins says that "at one point he thinks he is dying, but Faulkner does not
say or otherwise imply that he dies" ("Faulkner and the Critics," p. 327). Jeff H.
Campbell agrees that "there is nothing in the novel itself which makes such an
assumption necessary" ("Polarity and Paradox: Faulkner's *Light in August*," *CEA*,
34 [Jan. 1972], 31). Watkins cites the following six critics who assume that Hightower dies: (1) Robert D. Jacobs, "Faulkner and the Tragedy of Isolation," in
Southern Renascence, p. 182; (2) Norman Holmes Pearson, "Lena Grove," p. 5;
(3) Hyatt H. Waggoner, *William Faulkner: From Jefferson to the World* (Lexington:
Univ. of Kentucky Press, 1959), p. 115; (4) Robert M. Slabey, "Myth and Ritual in
Light in August," *TSLL*, 2 (1960), 335; (5) C. Hugh Holman, "The Unity of Faulkner's *Light in August*," *PMLA*, 73 (1958), 162; (6) Alfred Kazin, "The Stillness of

long after the book was written, that Hightower did not die.[6] The manuscript, however, as opposed to the novel seems more specific in backing up the author's declaration; in the manuscript, Hightower thinks, " 'Maybe I am dying,' " but in the text there is no uncertainty on his part, for the "maybe" is missing (MS 183; T 466).

The major action of chapter 20 is played out on the stage of Hightower's mind and memory, so that the significant factor may not be whether he dies but that he thinks he is dying. Still, the narrator explains that Hightower felt "himself losing contact with earth, lighter and lighter, emptying, floating," not that he felt *as if* he were losing contact with earth (T 466).

Perhaps the confusion concerning Hightower's death does not really affect the meaning of his life. Cleanth Brooks claims that aesthetically it does not matter whether Hightower dies in the end because he has broken out of the circle that confined him at the beginning of the novel.[7] But why, then, does he hear again "the wild bugles and the clashing sabres and the dying thunder of hooves" that still represent to him what is "left of honor and pride and life" (T 466-67)?

What do the wild bugles and the clashing sabers and the dying thunder of hooves finally mean to Hightower and to the significance of his life? They are the last words written about him and the images most frequently associated with him throughout the novel. Thus it would seem that nothing has changed and that he is still in the circle that has always confined him. Either he dies "into" his old dream or he continues living in it. Like Joe Christmas, he gains some self-knowledge, but he does not break out of the circle. Although the "wheel of thinking turns on" until "it seems to him that some ultimate dammed flood within him breaks and rushes away," his last thoughts return to the same mirage of honor and pride in life (T 464, 466).

Light in August," in *Twelve Original Essays on Great American Novels*, ed. Charles Shapiro (Detroit: Wayne State Univ. Press, 1956), p. 275.

I can add to the list: (1) Henry Campbell and Ruel Foster, *William Faulkner*, p. 35; (2) William H. F. Lamont, "The Chronology of *Light in August*," p. 360; and (3) Howard Nemerov, *Poetry and Fiction*, p. 254.

[6]*Faulkner in the University*, p. 75.

[7]*Yoknapatawpha Country*, p. 71.

Contradictions and Inconsistencies

Apart from the ambiguities relating to motivation or to final resolutions, there are contradictions and inconsistencies of narrative fact, which also inspire critical misinterpretation.[8] The most conspicuous of these inconsistencies, and the one that has provoked the most frequent misreadings, is the age of Joe Christmas at his death. Hastening to exploit analogies between Christmas and Christ, many critics have assumed that Joe was thirty-three when he died. Although it is patently impossible to specify Christmas's precise age, the published text provides ample evidence to refute the claim that Christmas died at thirty-three.

Other assumptions are predicated on insufficient evidence about such matters as the year in which the action of the narrative present occurs or the location of the McEachern farm. In fact, the items on this list are inextricably interwoven and cannot be untangled; nor can a single set of facts be established because of Faulkner's method of integrating his separately written segments into the novel as a whole. Hence, contradictions result from the extension of the Christmas flashback, the compression of the LBH story, the insertion of the Burden genealogy, and the revisions of point of view and levels of time. Although Floyd C. Watkins, in his quite correct claim that Faulkner has been much abused by critical error, states that "the critic is the source of the error, not the writer,"[9] the discussion to follow will illustrate that Faulkner was completely accurate only when he said that he often contradicted himself.[10]

In the earlier chapters of this study, narrative inconsistencies were cited to illustrate hypotheses about the stages of the novel's development. Approaching some of the same material from a different perspective helps to corroborate some of the earlier

---

[8] Richard L. Canary has noted many inconsistencies in *LIA* which he uses in his warning against the misinformation that often appears in so-called student aids, various guides, and notes on the novel, as well as in those on other works of literature ("Caveat Lector," pp. 370-79).

[9] "Faulkner and the Critics," p. 329.

[10] *Lion in the Garden*, p. 276.

speculations about the manuscript, although it does not necessarily clarify the confusion of factual matter in the novel, such as the problem of Joe Christmas's age.

Beekman W. Cottrell, focusing on the Christmas symbolism of the novel, repeats Richard Rovere's erroneous assumption that Joe Christmas was thirty-three when he was killed.[11] C. Hugh Holman, basing his theory of the unity of the novel upon the Christian symbolism, says that "Joe Christmas, at thirty-three as Gail Hightower had earlier prophesied that he would, becomes 'the doomed man . . . in whose crucifixion [the churches] will raise a cross.' "[12] William H. F. Lamont has attempted to correct this error and to reply to the critics who, as a result of incorrect readings, stress the Christ parallels in the novel.[13] Part of his argument is based on the information in the Hightower story that sets the novel in 1932. Working backward from that date, which he substantiates from the figures of the Burden genealogy, Lamont reconstructs the date of Christmas's birth and states as a fact that he died at the age of thirty-six. Unfortunately, Lamont ignores such matters as Joanna Burden's being both forty and forty-one at the same moment in time on the same page of the novel (T 227). He is also willing to take as fact Mrs. Hines's statement that Joe was conceived in December, but summarily disposes of the more confusing matter of her frequent repetitions when she pleads with Hightower that she had not seen her grandson since his infancy thirty years before, implying that Joe was thirty when he committed the murder. Although Lamont fails to establish the positive facts he asserts, his list of negatives does rectify many misconceptions about the novel. He proves that in the text Christmas was not thirty-three when he died, not born in December, and not crucified on Friday.[14]

---

[11]Cottrell, "Christian Symbols in *Light in August*," MFS 2 (1956), 207; Rovere, Introduction to *Light in August* (New York: Modern Library, 1950), p. xiii.

[12]"The Unity of Faulkner's *Light in August*," p. 158.

[13]"The Chronology of *Light in August*," pp. 360-61.

[14]Numerous other critics state that Christmas was thirty-three when he died. Among those who perpetuate the error *after* Lamont's correction are Carlos Baker, "William Faulkner: The Doomed and the Damned," in *The Young Rebel in American*

As we have seen, the Christmas chronology is a tangled affair and provides little help in reading the timetable to establish either Joe's age at his death or the date of the present action of the novel. According to Mrs. Hines, Joe Christmas was conceived in December (T 353); he was, therefore, born in September. He was taken to the orphanage by Hines on Christmas eve of the same year. The toothpaste episode occurred in October when Joe was five years old (T 113). Two weeks before Christmas of the same year and two months after the toothpaste episode he was adopted by McEachern (T 132, 134).

Many of the succeeding inconsistencies in time and chronology have already been listed (chap. 3) in the discussion of Joe's life with the McEacherns. These confusions are ultimately resolved by the narrator's strong statement that Joe was thirty-three years old when he ended his fifteen years on the paved street and arrived in Jefferson (T 213). According to this set of figures, if he was then killed in August either two and one-half or three and one-half years after the spring in which he reached Jefferson, he was either almost thirty-six or almost thirty-seven years old when he died.

Up to this point, the inconsistencies can be explained on the basis of the rearrangement of the earlier episodes of the McEachern period, compressed to accommodate the later addition of the Bobbie Allen romance. But more confusion is added with the details of the Joanna Burden affair.

Literature (New York: Frederick A. Praeger, 1960), p. 153, and Samuel A. Yorks, "Faulkner's Women, p. 122. Martin Green in his attack on Faulkner in general and on *LIA* in particular states that his grasp of facts is so loose that "we find a version of them in one part of a book which is hard to reconcile with the version given later on" (*Re-Appraisals: Some Commonsense Readings in American Literature* [1963; rpt. New York: Norton, 1965], p. 184). Unfortunately Green has chosen a bad example to prove his point: the position of Hightower's grandfather when he was shot. The town told Byron that he was shot from a galloping horse (T 57) and Hightower remembers that he was shot from the saddle of a galloping horse in a Jefferson street (T 452). The version of Cinthy, the Negro ex-slave, is that he was killed in a henhouse (T 459). Hightower *deliberately* chooses to believe Cinthy, even if she invented it (T 458), although he thinks that "perhaps some of them had already dismounted" (T 459). Green misses the twenty-to-thirty-year discrepancy, as well as the subtle point Faulkner makes about Hightower's character.

One reason that Joe Christmas's age at the time of his death cannot be precisely established is that the total duration of his relationship with Joanna Burden changes from one chapter to another. In addition, even if the reader takes the narrator's statement as fact that Joe was thirty-three years old when he reached Jefferson at the end of the street that ran for fifteen years, he must come to terms with a second street which ran for thirty years and formed a circle.

As for the duration of the affair between Joe and Joanna, it appears that Joe went to work at the mill in the spring of the year, three days after he arrived in Jefferson (T 225-26). In September the second phase of the affair began (T 226-27). Within six months, Joanna was completely corrupted (T 245). The last figure brings the affair to March, approximately one year after Joe had arrived in Jefferson. The second phase of the affair merged into the third gradually, toward the end of the summer (T 247). But it is not clear at this point which summer the narrator means, for as the second phase of the affair is drawing to a close Joanna, desperately desiring more time, thinks of how "her naked breast of three short years ago ached as though in agony, virgin and crucified" (T 250). It is questionable, therefore, whether this scene occurs at the end of Christmas's second or third summer in Jefferson. Moreover, the vague phrase "this was over a period of two years" could apply to either phase two of the affair or to the entire time that Joe had lived in Jefferson, since phase one began on the night he arrived there (T 247).

In September Joanna discussed the possibility of having a child with Joe. Immediately after Christmas she tells him she is pregnant; by January she is certain. One evening in February, the third phase begins (T 250-53). Two months pass during which Joe sees Joanna only once, to tell her that Brown is coming to live with him (T 254-55). It is now April and Joe has been in Jefferson either two or three years. One evening he returns to the cabin to find a note from Joanna. We know that the weather is still cold because Brown teases him with "this here's a cold night to be laying around on the wet ground without nothing under you but a thin gal" (T 258). On this night Brown follows Joe to the big, dark house and is soundly thrashed when Joe discovers him. On the same night Joe realizes that Joanna is not pregnant, but is in fact an old woman, too old to have a child. When he confronts her with this accusation, she strikes him and he retaliates in kind.

Joanna now begins her attempt to rehabilitate Joe. Each time she summons him to the dark house she attempts to convert him. Finally, in August, three months later, on the night of the murder, Joe finds himself sitting in the ruined garden, thinking of what Joanna had said two nights previously—that since he refused to save his soul there is just one other thing to do (T 264-65). Before rising to go into the house he remembers the wild period two years ago. That memory suggests that the third phase of the affair was conducted over a longer time span (T 266).

In this catalog of events it is impossible to discern whether the second phase of the affair lasted from approximately September to December of the following year, a period of about fourteen months, or whether an additional year was included in the so-called wild period, and another added to phase three instead of the six or eight months that chapter 12 seems to indicate. But if, as the narrator asserts, Joe had come to Jefferson in the spring, and phase two has begun six months later, in September, Joe must have arrived in Jefferson sometime in March. The third phase of the love affair obviously terminated with Joanna's murder in August; so Joe apparently spent either two and one-half, three and one-half, or four and one-half years in Jefferson. Yet repeatedly the narrator states that Joe had lived in Jefferson for three years (T 27, 268, 279). And Joe himself remembers in chapter 14 the food he had hurled at the wall of Joanna's kitchen three years before the murder, at the beginning of their affair (T 316).

There is another indication too that the third phase of the affair lasted two years instead of from February to August of the same year, as chapter 12 implies. In chapter 5, on the night before the murder, Joe thinks of his past sexual encounters with Joanna and repeats silently, "That was two years ago, two years behind them, now" (T 99). An additional confusing statistic occurs at the beginning of chapter 13, in which the people gather to watch the fire, "believing that the flames, the blood, the body that had died three years ago . . . cried out for vengeance" (T 273). The narrator in this instance must be referring to menopause as a symbolic death, but his use of "three years" adds still a third year to phase three.

Finally, questions arise as to why, on arriving in Mottstown, Joe thinks that "he is entering it again, the street which ran for thirty years" (T 321). If he is reckoning from the day he left the orphanage, he would be thirty-five at this moment. But if he is also subtracting his years with Joanna, he would be considerably older. It seems unlikely that Joe is including the Joanna period because on several occasions during his affair with her he had looked longingly at the street that symbolized to him the freedom to live his life as he preferred. Still, why does Joe think, on pages 250-51 of the text, " 'No, if I give in now, I will deny all the thirty years that I have lived to make me what I chose to be?' " Again, one does not know if Joe is thirty years old here, as Mrs. Hines's figures would indicate, or if he is computing those thirty years from the date he left the orphanage when he developed the pride and determination to be what he chose to be. In the latter instance he would of course be thirty-five at the time of his death.

The manuscript, as mentioned previously, does not use the phrase "all the thirty years that I have lived" but "a threat against that which he had spent 30 years in building." Hence, this latter confusion was contributed by the typescript and text.

Perhaps if the text were clearer about where the fifteen-year street with imperceptible corners began and how it varies from the thirty-year street of chapter 14, the question of Joe's age might be resolved. The circle formed by the street apparently ends in Mottstown (T 321). Did it begin there? The problem hangs on the lack of information about where the McEacherns lived and where the Hineses moved after leaving Arkansas and before going to Mottstown. The thousand streets that "ran as one street, with imperceptible corners and changes of scene," which Joe entered at the close of the Bobbie Allen episode, "was to run for fifteen years" (T 210). It ran into Oklahoma, Missouri, as far south as Mexico, north to Chicago and Detroit and then back south, and at last to Mississippi (T 211). When Joe reached Mississippi for the last time he was thirty-three years old. It is not, then, the same street that had run for thirty years and formed a circle. For the path Joe takes on the fifteen-year street cuts a zigzag pattern within the larger thirty-year circle, out of which Joe has never broken (T 321). The implication here is that this circle began and ended in or near Mottstown and that the fifteen-year street with its opposite sides of black and white was a flight made in the attempt to break out of the circle. Hence, it appears that Joe entered the circular cage when he reached what McEachern referred to as home.

In studying the series of inconsistencies relating to Joe's years in Jefferson, one might posit a stage of the novel in which Joe remained in Jefferson for three years *before* it was determined that he arrived in the spring. Certainly the images of the red dust, the cool "neversunned" earth, the crickets and insects, the frogs and fireflies that furnish the background for Joe's first days on Joanna's plantation do not agree with the cold night of a later description of April there (T 214-16, 258).

The spring-summer-fall pattern seems to have appealed to Faulkner because of its suggestive implications for the three-phased affair with Joanna Burden. As Peter Swiggart has noted of another section of the novel, "the symbolism is at odds with the chronology."[15] It is as if the words and images, the "rotten richness ready to flow into putrefaction," and "the shadow of autumn" at the close of stage two, shaped the poetic but chronologically confusing truth that prompted Faulkner to insert Christmas's spring arrival (T 247-48). At any rate, at this point in the novel the old, fecund, mellow earth takes priority over the Christian calendar.

The description of Joe Christmas's spring appearance in Jefferson has been written on the base page of manuscript page 93, which leads into the Burden flashback. Probably the page was recopied when Faulkner inserted into the three-phased love affair the tale of Joanna's ancestors. Since the Christmas flashback was first revised independently from the LBH story, the spring arrival may have been supplied at the time of copying out the earlier draft of the flashback; the author may well have overlooked the fact that he had said elsewhere that Joe arrived in

[15] *Art of Faulkner's Novels*, p. 146.

Jefferson about three years before the August of the narrative present. In any event, this later date provides a source of confusion as does the implication, also on a recopied base page, that by the time of the murder it had been two years since Joe had slept with Joanna (MS 43; T 99). These inaccuracies help to provide evidence, however, for the fact that these pages were rewritten after the flashback was extended, at the time Faulkner was trying to work it into the other plot of the novel.

The mystery of the precise location of the McEacherns' farm and of the railroad division point where Joe conducted his romance with Bobbie Allen is also difficult to solve. Faulkner seems to have taken particular trouble to keep the name of this town obscure. If it formed the first point on Christmas's circle, it must be Mottstown, although some critics assume that it is Jefferson. Perhaps, though, since the two towns are located so near each other, Faulkner referred to them almost as one when he wrote that Joe completed his thirty-year circle in Mottstown.

The farm to which McEachern took the five-year-old Joe is evidently a day's drive from Memphis, in the jolting buggy, drawn by the stout, well-kept team (T 135). Joe, shapeless and immobile, wrapped in a horse blanket, sitting beside his new father, is given lunch at noon from a "cardboard box containing country food cooked three days" before (T 134). If one assumes that the food was cooked the day before Simon McEachern's early morning departure and that he reaches Memphis in one day, adopts Joe Christmas and returns with him to the farm the next day, McEachern must live about a day's wagon-journey from Memphis.

The McEachern farm is in the country, five miles outside the unnamed town where Bobbie Allen lives. The town is a railroad division point, and the restaurant where Bobbie works is on a back street. It has a long wooden counter lined with backless stools, completely filled with male occupants. They are obviously not farmers, for they wear no overalls; they do, however, wear hats. They look "like people who had just got off a train and who would be gone tomorrow" (T 163).

Although the name of this town is never mentioned, it is obviously south of Memphis because Max, in his disgust at Bobbie's relationship with Joe, says, " 'Coming all the way down here from Memphis. Bringing it all the way down here to give it away'" (T 181). Strangely, although Jefferson is near Mottstown the name *Mottstown* does not appear in the seven chapters of the long Christmas flashback. Instead, when Christmas is put off the southbound freight train at Jefferson, he asks the Negro boy how far it is to the next town "'over this way,'" and the boy replies, "'Bout thirty miles, they say'" (T 213-14). And when he asks again, after he has murdered Joanna Burden, "'How far does this road go?'" he is given the name of the same town the Negro boy had named "three years ago, when he had first seen Jefferson" (T 268). The manuscript does not include the words "when he had first seen Jefferson" (MS 108).

But in the last one and one-half pages of chapter 14, Mottstown is mentioned seven times. It is rapidly identified as close to Jefferson at the point where Joe, riding in the wagon to Motts-town, thinks, "Jefferson is only twenty miles away" (T 321). From here on, Mottstown figures conspicuously in the story, but from the description given in chapter 15 it is difficult to ascertain whether it is the site of Joe's misspent youth. There is a railroad depot in Mottstown with a small cafe nearby, and a southbound train runs through Mottstown at nine o'clock. The train for Jefferson departs at 2:00 A.M., arriving there at 3:00 A.M. (T 341, 421).

Apparently the author preferred not to identify the town in which Joe and Bobbie played out their mournful romance. There are few details provided except the description of its itinerant male population that foreshadows Joe's future life. Besides the municipal clock in the courthouse tower, the country school-house where the dance is held, the dingy back-street restaurant, and the gravel road with its terrible little houses belonging to "people who came yesterday from nowhere and tomorrow will be gone wherenot," the town is given few physical characteristics (T 198).

Several critics, however, have assumed that it is either Mottstown or Jefferson. G. T. Buckley, in his attempt to prove that Holly Springs, Mississippi, rather than Oxford, was the model for Jefferson in *Light in August*, says that Holly Springs is nearer Memphis and that there is a direct rail connection to

Memphis.[16] A part of his evidence for concluding that Jefferson is based on Holly Springs is the fact that Max and Mame have dropped down to Jefferson and return to Memphis. This argument, of course, implies that the McEacherns lived five miles outside of Jefferson. Perhaps Buckley has based this assumption on the scene in which Joe upon his arrival in Jefferson at the age of thirty-three was eating the food stolen in Joanna Burden's kitchen when his "thinking fled for twenty five years back down the street" to the "monotonous dogmatic voice" and the "indomitable bullet head" of Simon McEachern (T 217).[17]

Ford and Kincaid also assume that Bobbie, Max, and Mame lived in Jefferson and identify Bobbie Allen as a waitress in a Jefferson restaurant of low repute.[18] It must be remembered, though, that this nameless abode of the McEacherns (and the others) was a railroad division point, but the fact that fast trains did not always stop at Jefferson is specifically mentioned by the narrator (T 280). This casts doubt on Jefferson's candidacy for the position. C. Hugh Holman, on the other hand, assumes that the restaurant owned by Max and Mame was in Mottstown and describes it as a carnal temple with Bobbie and the owners as priests of the world.[19]

The critical issue at stake in attempting to determine whether Christmas had ever lived in either Mottstown or Jefferson involves a major theme of the novel: the relationship between memory and responses to experience. Often in the novel Christmas remembers in some deep cavern of his mind without realizing or even knowing that he remembers. But when he eats the field peas cooked with molasses in Joanna's kitchen in

---

[16]"Is Oxford the Original of Jefferson in William Faulkner's Novels?" *PMLA*, 76 (1961), 452.

[17]Floyd C. Watkins disputes Lawrence Thompson's claim that Christmas "returned compulsively to Jefferson" (*William Faulkner: An Introduction and Interpretation* [New York: Holt, Rinehart and Winston, 1967], pp. 67, 75). Watkins says that Joe had never been to the town before ("Faulkner and the Critics," p. 321).

[18]Patricia Margaret Ford and Suzanne Kincaid, *Who's Who in Faulkner* (Baton Rouge: Louisiana State Univ. Press, 1963), p. 18.

[19]"The Unity of Faulkner's *Light in August*," p. 157.

Jefferson, he knows what he is remembering; he feels "memory clicking knowing" (T 217). His thinking flies back twenty-five years and he remembers the sound of McEachern's voice and the corner where he used to wait "for someone whose name he had forgot" (T 217).

It is quite possible that when Faulkner wrote those words he thought of Joe as having returned to the scene of his youth and specifically to Jefferson. Perhaps in one of the earlier versions, Jefferson was actually named as the town where he had lived with the McEacherns, for in the manuscript the first description of that town is found in the newest section inserted into the Christmas flashback, the first of the sheets lacking canceled number-sets and written in bright blue ink (MS 70; T 162-65). This section replaces six previous manuscript leaves.

But when he added to the text the information that Joe first saw Jefferson three years ago, Faulkner took pains to remove the suggestion that Joe was returning to his former home (T 268). Joe's arrival in Jefferson is described on manuscript page 89 as follows: "He did not know the name of the town, he didn't care. But he avoided it. He went through the woods and came to the road and looked about him." The text is even clearer: "He did not know the name of the town; he didn't care what word it used for name. He didn't even see it, anyway" (T 213). Such an explanation precludes any necessity to come to terms with visual memories. Nor is there any mention of Christmas's recognition of the town in the two chapters devoted to his life there. The tasting scene of memory, therefore, evoked by the field peas, in its present context must be read to refer to memories of having lived, not specifically in Jefferson, but somewhere in the South.

One wonders, though, why Faulkner avoided mentioning Mottstown by name anywhere in the Christmas flashback. Could he have been hinting that Joe had once lived there? When asked if he was "fixing to walk" to the nearest town, Christmas tersely replies, "No" (T 214). After the murder Joe is quite willing to be taken to the nearest town, although it is still not named (T 268). After his week in the woods, he finally arrives in Mottstown. As noted above, Mottstown is now named seven times in the last pages of chapter 14. After the youth says "Mottstown,

Dar tis," Joe can see "beyond the imperceptible corner" and enters again "the street which ran for thirty years. . . . It had made a circle and he is still inside of it" (T 321). The circle image, linked as it is with the first identification of Mottstown, seems to indicate that Joe is returning at last to the point at which the thirty-year street began.

The question of where the McEacherns lived has implications for the interpretation of the meaning of the street and the circle. And the problem of Joe's age is irretrievably bound up in these images. In the earlier chapters of this study I noted that the inconsistencies concerning Christmas's age shed light on the stages of compiling the manuscript. They also cast doubt on Faulkner's intention to closely identify Joe Christmas with Jesus Christ. Perhaps by noting that Christmas did not die on Friday at the age of thirty-three, a reader will be more likely to take Faulkner at his word: "Everyone that has had the story of Christ and the Passion as part of his Christian background will in time draw from that. There was no deliberate intent to repeat it. That the people to me come first [sic]. The symbolism comes second."[20]

The puzzling question of the exact year in which the action of the immediate present of the novel occurs is also entangled in the knotty problem of the exact age of another of its characters—this time Joanna Burden's age at her death. The most accurate information from which to infer the desired date is provided in the Hightower story, but unfortunately it conflicts with the already conflicting statistics of Joanna Burden's story.

To establish the age of Joanna Burden, one must examine the history of her family. Calvin Burden, Joanna's half brother, was born in 1854, for he was twelve years old in 1866 when his father, Nathaniel, returned to his own father, also named Calvin (T 231, 237). The second Calvin was killed at the age of twenty (T 235); the manuscript adds the date 1874 (MS 96). Joanna Burden was born fourteen years later, in 1888 (T 236).

About six months after Joanna first encounters Joe Christmas, she comes to his cabin and tells him her life story. "She told him that she was fortyone years old" (T 227). Had she been

---

[20] *Faulkner in the University*, p. 117.

born in 1888, this meeting must have occurred in 1929. However, as I mentioned earlier (chap. 3), the narrator informs the reader in a paste-on slip forming part of the same paragraph that even after "forty years" she spoke with a New England accent as plainly as her New England kin whom she had seen only three times "in her forty years" (T 227). In deference to this new vital statistic, the meeting must be placed in 1928. Turning back to page 219 of the text, the reader finds that it was not until many nights after their first meeting that Joanna told Joe she was forty years old. Since the intimacy between the two occurred on only the first three nights of the first phase of their affair, Joe's memory on page 219 must refer to the same confession of age that begins the second phase. But in the second allusion to the same night Joanna is forty-one (T 227).

Moreover, the published text adds the information that "within six months she was completely corrupted" (T 45), but that after "the black waters would drain away . . . the world would rush back: the room, the walls, the peaceful myriad sound of insects from beyond the summer windows where insects had whirred for forty years" (T 246-47). The latter reference to Joanna's age is even more confusing, because it occurs six months after the beginning of phase two during the second summer that Christmas has been living on her plantation.

If Joanna Burden was forty in September of 1928 when she began the second phase of the affair and if she was killed two years later in August, the date of her murder would be 1930. If she was killed three years after the beginning of phase two, the date would be 1931. However, if she had been forty-one when phase two began, the date of the talk in the cabin would have been 1929. Had she died two years later the date would be 1931, but if phase two had been protracted for one additional year the date of her death would have been 1932.

Unfortunately, there is no way to solve the problem of Joanna's exact age on that night in September or the length of the affair, for although Faulkner has been careful to name the months as they pass, he has avoided any specific mention of the precise calendar year. Turning back to page 42 of the text merely complicates the problem, for there, in the first reference to Joanna Burden, the narrator states "that it is now sixty years

since her grandfather and her brother were killed in the square."
If the duel had been fought in 1874, that event would place the
action of the narrative present in the year 1934. In the manuscript the duel was fifty years before, placing the current action
in 1924 (MS 19).

According to the section affixed to the manuscript page
numbered 93, Joanna was forty on the evening of the cabin
meeting. The date of her half brother's murder, 1874, also appeared in the manuscript in a new section (MS 96), but the fact
that Joanna was not born until fourteen years later is proferred
in one of the older paste-on slips (MS 97; T 236). In the manuscript, therefore, Joanna was definitely born in 1888. In the
previous version she was forty at the beginning of the second
phase, placing the date in the year 1928. But the new material
provided the confusion by making Joanna forty-one and the
year of the cabin meeting 1929. By removing from the text the
date of Calvin's murder, Faulkner left the precise date of his
birth in doubt; there remains only the statement that he was
twelve in 1866 when his parents were married. In addition,
Faulkner changed from manuscript to text the year of Joanna's
birth from "one" to "two" years after her parents' marriage,
although since no date is given for that marriage Joanna could
still have been born fourteen years after her half brother's death
(MS 97; T 238).

In short, to establish firmly the exact year of the fateful
August in which the two murders occurred is no simple task.
To paraphrase Hightower's paraphrase, there are more things in
heaven and earth too than fact (T 453). Still, although there is
some conflicting evidence, most of the statistics given about
Hightower point to the assumption that the action of the narrative present occurs in August 1932.

Both the narrator and Hightower himself inform the reader
that he is fifty years old (T 44, 345, 465). Moreover, there are
indirect statements from which the date of his birth can be
derived. The first occurs when Hightower remembers that he
was eight years old when he first saw, carefully folded and stored
in a trunk in the attic, the somber frock coat his father had
worn during the Civil War. His father had not worn it after the
day he returned from the war in 1865, and it had remained un-

touched in the attic for twenty-five years. When Hightower at the age of eight found the uniform, it must have been sometime during the year 1890, indicating that he was born in 1882. If he is fifty when he remembers the discovery that changed the course of his life, the year of the narrative present must be 1932 (T 443). A later reference substantiates this date at the point at which Hightower begins to understand the significance of his ancestor worship and the ways in which it has doomed his life; he thinks that symbolically he died twenty years before he was born (T 452). Identifying so closely with his grandfather, Hightower realizes that, figuratively speaking, like his grandfather he too was shot in the henhouse during Van Dorn's raid on Grant's stores, which occurred in Holly Springs, Mississippi, in December of 1862.[21] If Hightower was actually born twenty years later he would indeed have been born in 1882.

Conflicting data are garnered in chapter 2 of the novel from the townsman who tells Byron when he first comes to Jefferson all about Hightower. In this chapter Hightower is reputed to have been "born about thirty years after the only day he seemed to have ever lived—that day when his grandfather was shot from the galloping horse" (T 57). However, since this information comes from a less reliable witness, and since to take it seriously would place the novel in the year 1942, ten years after it was published, it is wise to ignore it when searching for reliable data. In examining the inaccuracies or inconsistencies in the novel, it is always necessary to consider the source of the information and to distinguish among those narrators who may be reliable and those who are not. As the misinformation stands in chapter 2, it reinforces the sort of violation of fact and truth that characterizes what the town believes.

Suggestions that Hightower is fifty years old occur in leaves of the Virginia manuscript that have been recopied from a previous draft. But there are certain discrepancies, sometimes appearing in the passages taken from earlier drafts, which make that figure doubtful because the events and dates of Hightower's residence in Jefferson are somewhat cloudy. In a single page, the friend who shows Hightower's house to the stranger says

[21]T[homas] M. S[paulding], "Earl Van Dorn," *DAB* (1936).

that he had come to Jefferson about twenty-five years before and that no one had been inside his house in twenty-five years (T 54). But in the series of episodes in which the congregation watches Hightower's wife with dismayed amazement and finally sends her to a sanitarium just a few months before her death, it is implied that Hightower was the minister of one of the principal churches for at least two years (T 57-64). During this period the house has been entered by the ladies who call on Hightower and even take him food while his wife is in the sanitarium (T 57, 60).

After Hightower resigns his pulpit but refuses to leave Jefferson, his harassment begins. It is not clear how long it persists, but on page 67 Byron suggests that people forget a lot in twenty years. At this point one can assume that Hightower's period in the ministry and his persecution by the townspeople lasted approximately five years and that he has lived in Jefferson for twenty-five years in all. On the other hand, in chapter 16 Hightower has not needed a watch or clock in twenty-five years, since he has been living "dissociated from mechanical time" (T 346). In addition, Miss Carruthers, who was once the organist in his church, has been dead for twenty years, although he does not know it (T 346). And in chapter 17, after delivering Lena's baby, Hightower returns home and builds a fire in his stove "as clumsily after twentyfive years as on the first day he had ever attempted it" (T 382). He has been a man "who for twentyfive years has been doing nothing at all between the time to wake and the time to sleep again" (T 383).[22] These figures indicate that Hightower had lost his wife and his church twenty-five years previously, rather than that he had arrived in Jefferson twenty-five years before the novel begins. Although they do not actually conflict with the date thus far assigned to the action of the novel, they are somewhat disturbing in their inconsistency and suggest the recourse of examining the manuscript.

Originally, on manuscript page 19, Hightower had come to Jefferson thirty years previously, but the figure has been adjusted in both the manuscript and the text to read "twenty-five"

---

[22]The inconsistencies in the form of my references to the number twenty-five follow the published text.

(T 43). And on the purple ink sections of manuscript page 24, Hightower's wife went bad on him twenty years ago. The text has been changed to "twenty-five" and adds "that was right after he came here" (T 54). No one had been inside the house in twenty years (MS 25). In the pasting inscribed in light blue ink, the color that first introduces Byron Bunch in chapter 3, Faulkner originally wrote that Byron thought "people forget a lot in 25 years." The text reads "twenty years" (MS 29; T 67).

Apparently Hightower was originally an older man who had lived in Jefferson for thirty years and had been retired from the ministry for twenty or twenty-five of them. But when the new Christmas material was added to chapter 2, Faulkner compressed the time span to balance the chronology of the two stories, reducing the thirty years of Hightower's life in Jefferson to twenty-five.

In addition, when he included the actual pages of the purple ink draft in chapter 3 of the manuscript, Faulkner blurred the facts, changing the manuscript's "twenty years" since Hightower's wife had gone "bad on him" to the twenty-five of the published text and adding to the text the phrase that it was "right after he came here" (T 54). He also corrected the originally accurate phrase employed in the manuscript, to the effect that it had been twenty years since anyone had entered Hightower's house, to the twenty-five of the text (T 54). The correction from twenty-five to the twenty of Byron's comment about people's memories has also been made for the text and is perfectly accurate as it now stands, indicating that Hightower has been retired from the world and that people have been ignoring him for twenty years.

This figure tends to provide further evidence for the statements in my earlier chapter that Faulkner's purple ink draft was the first to have been written and that Faulkner compressed it after extending the Christmas story. He changed his time span, as well as his narrator, when he introduced the new material and sifted the older passages through Byron Bunch's consciousness. But when the author copied out chapters 16 and 17, he must have neglected to make the corrections, for in that section Hightower has been retired from the pulpit for twenty-five years, or from the very moment he presumedly reached Jefferson. This anachronism substantiates the assumption that the episodes in these chapters were a part of the shorter version of the novel—the version lacking the Christmas flashback.

Since the events of chapter 20 show no such inconsistency, that chapter must have been more carefully revised than chapters 16 and 17. Thus one can conclude, based on the dates of Hightower's birth derived from chapter 20, that Hightower was fifty years old on that fateful Monday in August and that the action of the narrative present occurred in the year 1932.

Readers of the novel, nevertheless, must have noticed that Hightower is described in terms that make him appear far older than the fifty years attributed to him. It is hard to imagine that a man of fifty would have seemed so old to an author who was almost thirty-five when he created the character.[23] Presumably, Hightower's sedentary life caused him to age prematurely and to appear "flabbyjowled and darkcaverneyed" with a "flabby and obese stomach like some monstrous pregnancy" (T 290, 291). Ordinarily, though, even an inactive man of fifty would not fit the following description, with its metaphysical simile so strained as to verge on the ludicrous:

His mouth is open, the loose and flabby flesh sagging away from the round orifice in which the stained lower teeth show, and from the still fine nose which alone age, the defeat of sheer years, has not changed. Looking down at the unconscious face, it seems to Byron as though the whole man were fleeing away from the nose which holds invincibly to something yet of pride and courage above the sluttishness of vanquishment like a forgotten flag above a ruined fortress. (T 343).

Nor would Byron Bunch, who will never see thirty again (T 42) and who is almost twice as old as Lena's twenty years (T 389), be likely to think of a man of fifty as the extremely old man Hightower appears to be in Byron's eyes (T 369, 372).[24]

---

[23]Faulkner may have written the earlier drafts of the Hightower chapters when he was younger than thirty-five.

[24]Lena is twelve when she goes to live with her brother and twenty when she first climbs out of the window. This would make her either twenty or twenty-one in the narrative present. Her brother is forty, twenty years her senior (T 2-4).

Even though Faulkner may have merely carried over his earlier version of the minister, so powerfully felt and expressed, the picture in the final version of the now prematurely old, grotesquely obese, myopic man serves to heighten the inner truth of the character. Ironically, despite his living for so many years "out of time," he has aged. Hightower, a man frightened and shattered by life, disgustingly dirty, and repellently obese, lives completely for the pride and glory he takes in the cavalier grandfather who, in contrast to his grandson's stagnant existence, had ridden in the cavalry during the Civil War when he was even older than the Hightower of fifty.

Internal evidence has helped to confirm assumptions about the external conditions under which the novel was written. The process might now be reversed to hazard a conjecture as to the date of the present action of the novel. Faulkner started to write, synthesize, and revise the Virginia manuscript on August 17, 1931. That day was a Monday, often a favored day to begin a project. Ordinarily, such a fact would be insignificant. But as the revisions demonstrate, Faulkner, in unifying the strands of the novel, carefully rearranged the events so that Joe Christmas dies on Monday, Lena's baby is born on Monday, and Hightower's hour of truth apparently occurs on Monday.

Thus, given all the conflicting data, including the fact that the Hightower story places the book definitely in 1932, it seems unlikely that Faulkner intended to set the action of the novel in the future. It is more probable that when he began the Virginia manuscript he had in mind, if not on paper, Monday, August 1931, for the climax of the novel.[25] Since he composed

---

[25] One very bad guess at the date is made by Beach Langston, who says that "for those who like to press coincidence, there is an enticing fact that in the year 1927— a good date for the setting of *Light in August*—the feast day of the Assumption of the Virgin (August 15) fell on a Monday, the very day when Lena prepared to leave the world of Jefferson . . ." ("The Meaning of Lena Grove and Gail Hightower in *Light in August*," *Boston Univ. Studies in English*, 5 [1961], 50). Langston has obviously picked this date to suit his thesis that Lena incorporates the Virgin Mary and her avatar, Diana of the Grove. But Langston must have chosen his date with the text closed, because Lena left Jefferson three weeks after the baby was born (T 470). Since the baby was born ten days after the murder was committed (just after midnight on a Friday in August), it would have been impossible for Lena to have left Jefferson on August 15.

the final draft in a period covering both years, it appears that the year in which it is set shifted with the process of composition. The most that can be said, therefore, is that the narrative present of the novel coincides with the period of its composition, in the early thirties of the twentieth century.[26]

From the investigation of this level of fact, it is obvious that Faulkner was not as deeply concerned with accuracy as with poetic truth. Being the "sole owner and proprietor" of the world he created, he could juggle dates and places according to his own inclination.[27] He was not a systematic writer, but, as he often said, was carried forward by inspiration, rarely knowing in advance where his characters would lead him. It might seem, therefore, that my theory of the development of the novel relies too heavily upon narrative inaccuracies and insignificant details, were it not for the patterns these inaccuracies form.

Thus, the contradictions of narrative fact in the published text serve to reinforce certain of the conclusions previously drawn from a close examination of the manuscript. They illustrate the compression of an earlier, shorter draft of *Light in August* made to accommodate the addition of the Christmas flashback and the author's attempt to balance the yearly and daily events of Christmas's life with those of the world around him. Even though this attempt was not always successful, one can conclude that the implications of the parallel stories are of primary importance to the total meaning of the work.

Although many inconsistencies and contradictions of fact remain in the novel, Faulkner was wrong when he said: "I'm telling a story—to be repeated and retold. I don't claim to be

---

[26]Although I have not examined the manuscripts and published texts of Faulkner's other novels as closely as *LIA*, I have noted that the narrative present of many of them concurs with the period of composition and particularly of revision. For example, three sections of *TSATF*, published in 1929, are dated 1928. *Sanctuary*, published in 1931, is set in 1930. The action of *Intruder in the Dust*, published in 1948, occurs at a period near that date, for it seems to be a response to the agitation during that period for new Civil Rights legislation. Edmond L. Volpe has pointed out that even in *The Reivers* present time is the time of composition, for the novel is subtitled "A Reminiscence" (Volpe to Walker Cowen, July 6, 1973).

[27]Faulkner drew a map of Yoknapatawpha County for *Absalom*, under which he wrote those words.

truthful. Fiction is fiction—not truth; . . . Thus I stack and lie at times, all for the purposes of the story—to entertain."[28] Faulkner was wrong because fiction is not opposed to truth but to fact, and great fiction contains and expresses truth. Although William Faulkner on occasion may have stacked his facts, he never lied about his truths or ceased to strive in his fiction to communicate those truths.

[28]*Lion in the Garden*, p. 277.

VI

Summary and Conclusions

ALTHOUGH WILLIAM FAULKNER disliked being called a literary man and occasionally referred to himself as a farmer, the revisions of the manuscript of *Light in August* testify to his having been a skillful craftsman who revised the novel with scrupulous attention to the most minute detail. In spite of having overlooked several minor discrepancies on the novel's factual level, he had infinite patience in working and reworking his material until he had molded it into the particular form he considered most satisfying and significant.

In the attempt to trace Faulkner's complicated maneuvers, I have described and interpreted the evidence of the manuscripts in order to formulate a series of hypotheses about the genesis and development of the novel. These hypotheses have been derived from observing the mechanical means by which Faulkner assembled the Virginia manuscript, as well as from the patterns of narrative inconsistencies, some of which remain in the published text. I have also drawn upon four early worksheets that do not form part of the Virginia manuscript, changes of pagination in the typescript, and verbal differences from manuscript to text.

In this final chapter, I shall sum up my hypotheses and the points about the novel that the study of the manuscript has revealed. These hypotheses fall into three general categories: (1) the content and structure of previous drafts of the two major sections of the novel, the narrative present and the Christmas flashback; (2) the time order and the types of revisions; (3) the effects of the revisions on the published novel. Although I shall refer to various drafts, I am by no means implying that these drafts were complete versions of the novel. To the contrary, in many instances they consisted only of single episodes, or fragments of episodes, or merely new material to provide transitions between segments of previous drafts or rearranged episodes. There appears, moreover, to be little first-draft material of significance in the Virginia manuscript. Comparing its pages with the pages in Texas leads to the conclusion that most of its leaves have been copied out from previous, preliminary versions.

The manuscript includes every manner of revision: copied-out leaves, paste-on slips carried forward from previous drafts and subdrafts, repagination, new insertions (most frequently appearing on the base page but occasionally added in new paste-on slips), margin insets, and minute changes of a single word. For that reason, the precise time order of the revisions and repagination, although fairly obvious at some stages, is impossible to determine.

The Content and Structure of Previous Drafts

The basic assumption on which this study has been developed is that Faulkner had written a nearly completed version of the novel's narrative present before he composed the Christmas flashback. The author compressed and reordered the episodes of the narrative present when he combined them with his separately written-and-revised story of Christmas's childhood, adolescence, and manhood. Before the flashback was written, *Light in August* began with the opening passages of the present chapter 3, concerning Gail Hightower in his study. Most of the episodes in which Hightower figures were part of that version, which has been carried forward to the repaginated leaves of the Virginia manuscript by means of paste-on slips or copied-out passages. Worksheets now in the collection of The Academic Center Library at the University of Texas show that Faulkner had written a preliminary treatment of Hightower's history, parts of which, in revised form, appear in chapters 3 and 20, of both the Virginia manuscript and the published text.

The first meeting between Byron Bunch and Lena Grove, now to be found in chapter 2, was also a part of the earlier version. This meeting may have been followed by the episode at Mrs. Beard's boarding house, which was originally presented as a dramatic scene, not recounted by Byron to Hightower in his study. A version of Christmas and Brown at the planing mill existed, but it was not related through Byron's mind and memory. Nor did it occur in the same chapter as Byron's meeting with Lena and the narrator's brief summaries of the lives of Byron, Hightower, and Joanna Burden.

Diction changes from manuscript to text in the first scene between Byron and Lena suggest that this hypothetical draft of the narrative present did not include chapter 1, portraying Lena on the road to Jefferson. But there is every indication that there was a version of Christmas's activities during the twenty-four hours before the murder. These episodes were probably followed by the scenes (now at the end of chapter 12 of both manuscript and text) of Christmas's wild ride in the car driven by the young white boy and his companion and of Christmas's subsequent disposal of the pistol, which, until that moment, he did not realize he held.

In addition, the earlier version included all the episodes of the search for Christmas, now occurring in chapters 13 and 14, as well as some version of Christmas's week in the woods. These episodes, however, were not in their present order. Also present were the Mottstown episodes, the Hineses' visit to Hightower, the birth of Lena's baby with Hightower's assistance, Byron Bunch's ministrations, his departure, his fight with Brown, and his return to Jefferson.

Joe Christmas in the previous version sought refuge in Hightower's house and was killed there. Gavin Stevens also proffered his explanation of the motive for Christmas's escape on the way to the courtroom. There is no evidence, however, that Lena's departure from Jefferson with Byron and the baby was part of the novel before the Christmas flashback was added.

This version of the events of the narrative present was organized around a different time structure from the ten-day period of the final version. Christmas may have committed the murder at midnight on a Saturday; he definitely appeared in Mottstown on a Saturday and was killed on a Wednesday. Nor did his death occur on the same day as the birth of Lena's child.

More of the story was narrated by a character-narrator (perhaps Byron Bunch), who employed colloquial and substandard diction. Less of the story was retold, after the event, to Gail Hightower in his study. There were transitional passages between the sections devoted to Bunch, Hightower, and the sheriff, and those scenes that directly presented Joe Christmas. As in the published version, nothing of the matter of Christmas was known to the people of Jefferson except that he was a mill hand, rumored to be a bootlegger involved in violent acts. But in contrast to the completed novel, the reader was offered only brief glimpses into his mind during the twenty-four hours before the murder and in the week following it.

In that version Joe Christmas was described not only by Gavin Stevens but also by the omniscient narrator as definitely possessing Negro blood. And at the time of his death, Christmas thought of himself as being thirty years old. So did his grandmother, although there was some ambiguity as to whether he was actually the Hineses' grandson. Hightower, on the other hand, having lived in Jefferson for a longer period of time, was probably nearer to sixty than to the fifty of the published text.

It appears that Faulkner took this version of *Light in August* and added to it the Christmas flashback, which he composed and revised independently. The flashback was written in three major stages, but not in the order in which the episodes finally occur.

Stage one included the scenes at the orphanage, the abduction, the adoption, the arrival at McEachern's farm, the catechism lesson, and the first initiation into sex. These sections were probably composed in a linear time structure and ended with Christmas's determination at the age of fourteen or fifteen to escape from the McEacherns. At that period of composition, Mrs. McEachern may have played a smaller role.

In the next stage Faulkner supplied the details of Christmas's affair with Joanna Burden. He probably composed their story as a separate, discrete unit, combining it later with the history of the Burden family, also written independently. The manuscript shows how Faulkner inserted the Burden flashback into the Christmas flashback to make it appear as if it were being narrated to Christmas by Joanna. Still later the author separated the Christmas-Burden story into two chapters and added the tale of the visit to the graves, which haunted Joanna all her life.

The Bobbie Allen episodes now found in chapters 8, 9, and 10 form the final expansion of the Christmas flashback, which also includes the heifer–new suit affair at the end of the present chapter 7. Christmas's first possible homicide forms part of that expansion. It is hard to discover to which period of composition the scenes of Christmas on the fifteen-year-long street belong, for they have been revised and copied out to link the McEachern-Allen period with the Burden-Jefferson years. But the leaves on which the scenes are inscribed were probably not originally part of the same chapter in which Christmas is deserted by Bobbie and her friends, for the final scene of their disappearance was once a part of the preceding chapter.

The Time-Order and Types of Revisions

Except for the substitution of six new manuscript leaves in chapter 8 and some additional changes in chapter 6, Faulkner engineered all the structural revisions of the Christmas flashback before he combined it with the rest of the manuscript. He made extensive changes in the order of episodes in the orphanage scenes and the scenes of the early McEachern years. Certain episodes were compressed and reordered to occur as significant memories or as predictions offered by the omniscient narrator in the form of flashbacks or flashforwards. For example, Joe's memories of Alice were probably inserted into the abduction scene to illustrate an illusionary hope. His future hostility to the McEacherns as well as his search for identity are foreshadowed by the rearrangement of the end of chapter 6 to show that Christmas did not yet bother to think that his name was not McEachern. His forlorn hope was dramatized by inserting the later episode of the arrival at the farm into the earlier adoption scene.

Passages were transferred from previous positions to form the present chapters 6, 7, and 8. One passage concerning Christmas's life with the McEacherns even found its way into the manuscript version but not the text of chapter 5, which is not a part of the flashback. The heifer–new suit motif was added to chapter 7 to link it to chapter 8, and the whole of chapter 8 was reset into a flashback, related on the last night Joe spent with the McEacherns.

After composing the last extension of the flashback, Faulkner added new material to increase the ambiguity about McEachern's death. He separated the scenes of the last encounter with Max, Mame, and Bobbie into two chapters, altering the point of view to filter their voices through Joe's consciousness. The author also adjusted Christmas's age when he arrived in Jefferson from thirty to thirty-three and revised the last two leaves of chapter 10 to include veiled references to Bobbie Allen. But he neglected to adjust subsequent references to Christmas's age, thereby creating the confusion that has misled so many readers.

The Burden genealogy may also have been lengthened to include Joanna's traumatic memory of her visit to her brother's and grandfather's graves. Added phrases and changes of diction show that Faulkner heightened the Negro theme throughout the flashback, particularly emphasizing the Burden attitude that resulted in Joanna's obsession. In other respects Faulkner increased the ambiguity about Christmas's Negro blood and muted his memories of having been called a Negro at the orphanage. At no point does the narrator of the flashback assert that Christmas was a Negro. Instead, the development of his ambivalence and his fear concerning that possibility are carefully traced.

After reworking the structure of individual chapters of the flashback and reordering the sequence of events, Faulkner tried to adjust the chronology of chapter 12 to make it consistent with the more objective view of those same years provided in chapter 2. He did not, however, provide an accurate timetable, as the preceding chapter of this study illustrates. Nor did he clarify the mystery of Christmas's car, which is never mentioned in chapter 12, nor develop in that chapter the violent episode on the road to Memphis, so frequently mentioned in chapter 2.

A final revision was effected in chapter 8 after Faulkner had joined and paginated for the last time the two massive sections of his novel: the Christmas flashback and the narrative present. In this revision he added six new pages to chapter 8 in order to juxtapose Joe's sacrifice of the sheep to his first tryst with Bobbie Allen.

In general, in revising the flashback, Faulkner shifted chronology and point of view, juxtaposing particular memories to the events colored by those memories. He added passages to emphasize the racial and religious themes of the novel and to increase parallels between Mrs. McEachern and Joanna Burden. He heightened the ambiguity about Christmas's Negro blood by stressing that Christmas himself could never know the truth but would be forever obsessed by the fear that he was part Negro. Several revisions, described in earlier chapters of this study, also show that the author wished to portray Christmas as a more sympathetic character. In fact, the whole thrust of the flashback seems to be toward that end.

In combining the seven new chapters devoted to Joe Christmas with the rest of the novel, Faulkner may have begun by writing new pages at the beginning of chapter 5 in which he made overt references to the McEacherns, Bobbie Allen, and Joanna's having prayed over Joe. During this stage of composition, the author may also have experimented with the position of the chapter, placing it temporarily in chronological order where the new references would have been recognized by a reader. At this point, two of the seven manuscript leaves carried forward intact from the preflashback draft and now found in chapter 12 may still have been part of chapter 5 (MS 108, 109; T 267.21-270.31). The transitional passage, found in the manuscript only, that links the beginning of chapter 5 with the end of chapter 4 may have been supplied to help orient the reader, for at that writing many more pages may have intervened between the two chapters.

When he added the Christmas flashback, Faulkner seems to have compressed his earlier draft of the narrative present to accommodate the newer material. He also had to decide at what point to turn from Christmas's pursuers and focus instead on the fugitive. As a result, he made the numerous revisions indicated by the six numbered sets on the leaves of the manuscript from chapters 7 through 12 and by the arrangement of the slips pasted to the two types of papers of the chapters that precede and follow chapter 5 through 12. In addition, he made further structural changes in chapters 5 and 6, possibly supplying new material at the beginning of each, which meant retyping parts of the transcript. (For the typescript he drastically changed the paragraphing and diction, too.) Although most of the manuscript revisions involve the compression and the changed order of episodes, certain passages cited previously seem to have been added to emphasize theme and to define character more sharply.

The canceled number-sets point to the assumption that the manuscript was once arranged so that more of the details of the search for Christmas preceded the flashback. These episodes were reassembled to form the present chapters 13 and 14 in order to stress the action-reaction relationship between the LBH and the search-for-Christmas stories. New pages protracting the dialogue between Bunch and Hightower were added to the present chapter 13. The search episodes of chapter 14 were combined with at least two previous versions of Christmas's week in the woods; the flight episodes were then revised again. One version may have been written before Faulkner composed the flashback and another after its first expansion, for Christmas's memories of the meal set out for him on Joanna's kitchen table and the dishes he hurled against the wall have been inscribed on a parchment-type paste-on slip in that chapter (T 316). The passages conveying his changed attitude toward Negroes and toward his own possible Negro blood seem to have been added after the flashback was written. Finally, the tenses and the chronology of events were rearranged to give the impression of blurring into each other as Christmas tried to recall his peregrinations in the woods.

In reworking the events of the week of the search for Christmas, Faulkner also reshaped the chapters preceding the flashback. Chapter 2 was rewritten to occur as a three-year flashback, remembered by Byron Bunch on the day he first encountered Lena Grove. The references to Hightower were introduced, and the pattern of his and Bunch's dialogues established. Since the novel no longer began with Hightower in his study, salient facts about Hightower were provided in chapter 2, as well as concise information about Bunch and Joanna Burden.

Byron Bunch became the center of consciousness in most of chapter 3, a shift that enhanced his role in the novel. Also evident in chapter 3 are not wholly successful attempts to alter the time span of the Hightower biography so that it would parallel the Christmas flashback. Chapter 4 was assembled from separate narrative units to link Hightower to both the Lena-Bunch romance and the Christmas-Brown murder story. The point of view and time structure were again altered to relate Bunch's and Hightower's reactions to each other as well as to the lurid events under discussion.

There is also evidence to show that Faulkner tried various arrangements of the chapters following the flashback. When more of the flight-and-pursuit material now in chapters 13 and 14 preceded the flashback, the present chapter 15, in which Christmas appears in Mottstown, may have followed directly after the conclusion of the flashback. And before the episode of Christmas's death was finally placed to occur in the same chapter with Gavin Stevens's explanation of it, the death scene may have more closely followed the Hineses' story of their grandson's birth.

The manuscript leaves of chapters 17 and 18, which relate the birth of Lena's baby from both Hightower's and Bunch's points of view, show drastic revision. At one point the two chapters seem not to have been separated. The time structure, moreover, of chapter 17 has been altered to record mental time and to alternate between Hightower's and Bunch's reactions to the birth of the baby.

Hightower's musings and memories of chapter 20 have been interrupted by reminders to the reader that the former minister is sitting alone in his study, long after some of the events he recalls. These late revisions seem to have been carried out after Faulkner had decided on the narrative order of the other episodes, for he has inserted one passage into the manuscript and a second in the text to establish the fact that Hightower's head is now bandaged. These references subtly allude to Hightower's earlier encounter with Christmas and his pursuers.

The author's last revisions of the Virginia manuscript were the new pages juxtaposing the scenes of the killing of the sheep to the first assignation between Bobbie Allen and Joe Christmas and the insertion into chapter 1 of the comparison of Lena Grove to "something moving forever and without progress across an urn" (T 5).

In short, the following general stages of revision are apparent in the manuscripts of *Light in August*.

1. The composition of most of the episodes of the narrative present

2. The copying-out of those episodes

3. The composition of the Christmas flashback in three separate stages

4. The revisions of individual chapters within the flashback

5. Two or three additional revisions of chapters 5 and 6, the final one carried out after the typescript was begun

6. Six separate stages of revision in the draft of the narrative present to combine it with the Christmas flashback

7. The rearrangement of the chapter order of the present chapters 15 through 19

8. Revisions of narrative order and of point of view within chapters 17, 18, and 19

9. The removal of six manuscript sheets from chapter 8 and the addition of six newly composed ones

10. The addition of the urn passage to chapter 1

11. The changes of diction and paragraphing from the Virginia manuscript to the typescript

The six separate stages of revision Faulkner engineered to combine his two parts of the novel probably included the addition of chapter 1, the new, copied-out leaves at the beginnings of some of the chapters (such as the new opening leaf of chapter 15, which contributes to the confusion about the day Christmas appears in Mottstown), the compression of episodes of the narrative present, and the introduction of new material to relate it thematically to the Christmas flashback.

Within individual chapters, at various stages of revision, Faulkner expanded certain episodes, such as the second dialogue between Bunch and Hightower in chapter 13, the additional leaf to increase ambiguity about McEachern's death, and the episodes between Christmas and Mrs. McEachern that emphasize her psychological kinship with Joanna Burden. He also added the slip in chapter 16 in which Mrs. Hines expressed doubt about her grandson's racial heritage. At some point the author provided the new material found only in the manuscript in chapter 5, including one large paste-on slip dealing with Joe's memories of his life with the McEacherns. Furthermore, he may have shifted the position of that chapter several times.

From manuscript to text, Faulkner removed the transitional passages at the beginnings of chapters 5 and 13 and Joe's explicit memories in chapters 5 and 7. By not carrying forward the omniscient narrator's specific references in chapter 5 to Christmas's Negro blood, the author increased the ambiguity about Christmas's racial composition. And by his changing Christmas's age at his death and the day of the week on which he died, the Christian symbolism was muted. The change from manuscript to text of the profession of the narrator of the final chapter, who originally had been a cattle dealer carrying cattle in his truck, also eliminates a former identification of Lena, Bunch, and the baby with the holy family.

The Effects of the Revisions

Process criticism, or a study of revisions, can provide a useful critical tool by comparing several versions of a work and by identifying the choices and changes made by its creator. Because of Faulkner's by now well-documented habit of working in small independent units, the final order of those units is of major significance to the meaning of the work. As Faulkner said: "Unless a book follows a simple direct story line, such as a story of adventure, it becomes a series of pieces. . . . It takes a certain amount of judgment and taste to arrange the different pieces in the most effective place in juxtaposition to one another."[1] He was, in fact, an artist in montage.

Certainly Faulkner was not a systematic writer, as he was the first to agree. He did not "lay out a plot or synopsis first"; he claimed that he had no order, knew nothing about plots, sometimes wrote his stories backwards and then disciplined himself to give them "something of unity."[2] He said that the story of *Light in August* began with "Lena Grove, the idea of the young girl with nothing, pregnant, determined to find her sweetheart."[3]

[1]*Faulkner in the University*, p. 45.

[2]Ibid., pp. 193-94, and *Faulkner at West Point*, pp. 80-81. *A Fable* is the only novel for which Faulkner is known to have made an outline.

[3]*Faulkner in the University*, p. 74.

Yet in two versions the author actually began the novel with the character of Gail Hightower.[4] And when he finished it, he had magnified enormously the role of Joe Christmas.

The study of the manuscript reveals that Faulkner did indeed arrange his "different pieces" into a novel with judgment and taste, putting them in the most effective place in juxtaposition to one another. Although all critics do not agree, many share my view that he achieved a satisfying and significant form for the expression of his content. After many struggles and various experiments with the order of the narrative, the following time scheme emerged:

Chapter 1:   The same Friday as the murder, a few minutes past midnight, to the following Saturday noon

Chapter 2:   A three-year flashback preceding a meeting on the same Saturday afternoon

Chapter 3:   A flashback of about twenty-five years preceding a meeting on Sunday of the same week

Chapter 4:   A meeting on the same Sunday, in which the dialogue provides narrative detail of the episodes of that day and the preceding one

Chapter 5:   The twenty-four hours before the murder

Chapters 6-12: A flashback of about thirty years ending on the night of the murder, including a flashback reaching over three generations.

Chapter 13: The Saturday morning after the murder through the Wednesday following it

Chapter 14: The Wednesday after the murder to Friday morning

Chapter 15: Friday morning to 2 A.M. Saturday morning

Chapter 16: A flashback to a period about thirty-five years before the Sunday evening on which it is narrated

Chapters 17-19: Monday, ten days after the murder

Chapter 20: The same Monday, containing a flashback reaching over three generations

---

[4]The Texas manuscript may have been the beginning of a short story rather than of a novel.

Chapter 21: Three weeks after the death of Christmas and the birth of Lena's baby

It is this final order of Faulkner's series of pieces that conveys much of the meaning of the novel. The manuscript provides the pattern for the careful balancing of the flashbacks with the episodes of the narrative present, often achieved by the use of dialogue or within the context of memory so that one episode is framed by another. In this way Faulkner clearly conveys his omnipresent theme of the presence of the past in the present. His juxtapositions illustrate how the personal histories of many of the characters affect their present plights, as well as linking the dilemmas of these characters to the historic past of the nation. The arrangement of the final chapters, in which Christmas's death, the birth of Lena's baby, and the resolution of the Hightower story all occur on the same Monday, makes it possible for Hightower's mind and memory to penetrate to the deepest time level of the novel until he perceives the significance of the events, in the distant as well as the immediate past, in which he has been either a participant or a witness.

The revised time scheme also serves to call attention to Faulkner's counterpointing of the LBH story to the Christmas story and illustrates how the pieces of both plots were assembled to imply significant parallels among the characters. For example, while Lena is sleeping at the Armstids on the Friday night of the murder, Christmas, for the final time, is entering Joanna Burden's house. When Lena moves to the cabin, Christmas is fleeing from his pursuers. The awkward situation of the former and the dangerous one of the latter meanwhile are discussed by Bunch and Hightower, both of whom ultimately become involved directly or indirectly with Lena and Christmas.

By analogy Christmas is compared and contrasted to Lena in parallel actions involving windows, food, shoes, and, at the end of chapters 1 and 14, wagons. The later revisions in which the urn imagery was inserted into chapter 1 provide a contrasting tableau to the picture of the cracked urns of chapter 8, exploiting the dramatic differences between Christmas, the bough that was felled, and Lena, the eternal grove. Although the setting and time structure preclude a meeting between Mrs. McEachern and

Joanna Burden, the two women share a proclivity for conspira-
torial secrets and unpredictable behavior. The experiences of
Hightower's and Joanna's forebears mirror each other in providing
a historic context that includes both the South and the North.

Within individual chapters the juxtaposition of the pieces of
both plots and the strategic shifts of point of view show how
the author succeeded in exploiting the ironic implications of his
pattern. For instance, in the final version of chapter 14, the
posse pursues a criminal presumed to be exceedingly dangerous,
but when the criminal is viewed more intimately, he is revealed
to be trying to give himself up. Similarly, the combination in
chapter 2 of the flashback (portraying Brown as his fellow
workers see him) and the first Lena-Bunch meeting presents two
vastly different views of Brown and adds the new component of
dramatic irony to the already present element of suspense.

The removal from manuscript to text of transitions between
the objective view of Christmas, as seen by the actors of the narrative present totally from outside, and the subjective view,
which focuses on Christmas's personal experiences, memories,
deceptive hopes and longings, suggests a deliberate dissociation
between the Christmas of his own story and Christmas as catalyst of the LBH story. The complete lack of evidence, moreover,
in the Virginia manuscript of any draft in which a meeting
between Christmas and Lena was even considered indicates that
the pattern of the novel precludes such a meeting. The manuscript, therefore, illustrates the means by which the separation
of characters as well as plots was maintained.

The study of the manuscript demonstrates, too, how carefully
in the process of revision Faulkner increased the ambiguity
about Christmas's Negro blood and transmuted a story about a
black man who could pass for white into a story of a man who
did not and could never know who or what he was. The final
order of chapters and the passages added when the pieces were
assembled sharpen the ironic edge of this ambiguity, for once
Christmas has committed a murder, it is immediately assumed
by the formerly unsuspecting members of the white community
that he is a Negro. Thus Gavin Stevens's explanation of Christmas's black violence appears not only naive but egregious when

it serves to introduce, in the same chapter, the horror of Grimm's self-righteous white violence.

In composing the Christmas flashback and inserting it into the earlier draft, Faulkner not only magnified Christmas's role but used his personal story to illuminate by implication all the other characters in the novel. The Christmas drama becomes the focus of eight and one-half chapters and Christmas himself is the topic of conversation or the target of pursuit of eight more. Of the remaining chapters, chapter 18 culminates in the report of his death, and chapter 20 ends with a vision of Christmas. Chapters 1 and 21 refer to him indirectly, in the image of the smoke in the former and in the latter in the question that Lena so deftly avoids about the murder. Only chapter 3, which contains the earliest material in the manuscript, lacks any reference to Christmas. But a passage describing Hightower's delivery of a stillborn Negro baby carries pertinent implications for thematic and narrative foreshadowing.

The flashback, as previously noted, increases the reader's sympathy for Christmas and puts his death into a broader context. It also serves to enhance the meaning of Hightower's memories at the end of the novel of his own childhood, young manhood at the seminary, and subsequent years in Jefferson. Comparing the text with the early Texas version of parts of the Hightower story clearly illustrates the subtlety and depth of meaning gained by the final placement of that episode.[5] Revisions previously described show how Hightower's character was altered in earlier chapters to include a new humanitarianism that prepares for his epiphany at the end.

Thus the manuscript records the means by which its author juxtaposed scenes from the LBH story to those of the Christmas story, increased the ambiguity and the irony, added parallel

---

[5]Carl Benson contends that Hightower is the central figure in the narrative sense and the moral protagonist in the thematic sense; that it is Hightower who is contrasted to Joe Christmas, not Lena to Christmas, as many other critics assume. ("Thematic Design in *Light in August*," *SAQ*, 53 [1954], 540-55). Faulkner himself later substantiated this interpretation. In answer to a question as to why he put the chapter about Hightower's early life at the end of the novel, he said, "It seems to me that was the most effective place to put that, to underline the tragedy of Christmas's story by the tragedy of his antithesis" (*Faulkner in the University*, p. 45).

actions, blended memories of the past with present impressions, altered point of view, introduced new characters as well as enlarging the roles of characters carried forward from earlier drafts, and employed motifs to unify the disparate actions of the extended time span of the Christmas flashback.

As a result, the novel became not only the story of the effect of a murder upon a community and in particular upon three innocent bystanders but also the anatomy of the society of which those bystanders were a part, the same society that had created the murderer. An examination of the final placement of Faulkner's series of pieces and his large, separately composed segments shows that he was absorbed with the problems of adjusting levels of time and of finding the best moment to turn from the pursuers of the narrative present to the fugitive of the long flashback. The dissociation of the two suggests that the novel is constructed by means of two complementary plots set into the frame of the first and last chapters, depicting Lena arriving in, and departing from, Jefferson. Taken together, the revisions show how Faulkner achieved this double-plot structure and how the incorporation of the flight into the two parallel and interlocking pursuits changed not only the pattern but the themes of the book.

The novel opens with Lena's pursuit of Brown, intensified by the relentless exigencies of nature, her pregnancy and the imminent birth of the child. Bunch successfully impedes her from immediately achieving her goal, the discovery of Brown, but is impotent in preventing the birth of the child. Hightower fails to dissuade Bunch from becoming involved with Lena but succeeds in aiding the natural event of the birth of the baby.

The second strand of this story is the search for Christmas, in which Brown is a principal actor and in which Bunch and Hightower are nonparticipants but function as a profoundly affected chorus, commenting on the manipulations of the demons and demigods whose struggles will ultimately affect their fates. Lena remains oblivious to her role in this drama, protected and shielded from the truth by Bunch. It is Brown who serves as the link between the two strands of the LBH story, as well as the link between these characters and Joe Christmas.

The higher series of canceled numbers in chapters 7 through 12 indicates that many of the passages now presented in the two chapters following the flashback once preceded it. Had this arrangement not been altered and had all the forays in search of Christmas preceded the flashback, as well as Lena's move to the cabin by means of which she edges slightly closer to Brown (or at least to some knowledge of his former life), the emphasis would have been placed more firmly on the elements of suspense. The reader would have been propelled along by such questions as these: Will Lena find and confront Brown? Will Bunch defy Hightower and keep Lena shielded from the knowledge of Brown's involvement with Christmas and the murder? Will the posse find Christmas and release Brown? The movement of the novel, then, would have been one of headlong pursuit, interrupted only by a brief change in focus from the pursuers to the pursued until the latter had voluntarily surrendered.

Such a version, of course, would have achieved intense dramatic irony from the juxtaposition of the two strands of the pursuit plot. Lena's slow but certain progress toward Brown would be contrasted to his frantic endeavors to find Christmas and claim his reward. In fact, the wordplay on the various kinds of rewards in store for Brown serves to bear out one of the underlying motifs of this story of pursuit and capture.

But with no loss of irony Faulkner has ultimately chosen to arrest the force of the events of the narrative present by employing a counterforce. Opposing the theme of pursuit is the theme of flight. For from the beginning of the Christmas flashback until his ultimate death, the story of Joe Christmas is one long persistent flight. It is probably no coincidence that Joe Brown, the only character who is both fleeing and pursuing, serves as the link between the two stories. Although Byron Bunch manages to draw the Hineses into Lena's affairs and to involve Hightower in both her and Joe Christmas's fates, it is actually Brown who is a major actor in both the pursuit story and the flight.

When one considers, then, that Faulkner interrupted the pursuit story shortly after it began with the long history of the pursued, it is clear that he was building a double-plot structure based on two sides of the same coin—or, in Keatsean terms, the same urn. And just as in Keats's poem the poet unifies the two tableaux on the urn in his own imagination, Hightower's revelatory vision at the end of the novel gathers up most of the characters on his painful wheel of thought.

Finally, the close comparison of manuscript to text as a whole has led to a series of assumptions about the ambiguities, contradictions, and inconsistencies remaining in the text. The preceding chapter traces these narrative problems and concludes that many of them cannot be solved. For example, although it is certain that Joe Christmas is not thirty-three at the time of his death and therefore does not parallel Christ in that respect, Christmas's exact age cannot be determined. Nor can the reader know whether Christmas kills McEachern or whether in fact or in fancy Hightower dies. And the reader must always share with Christmas his own doubt and confusion about his racial identity.

Furthermore, the author's methods of composition illustrate how the more trivial factual contradictions occurred. For instance, the inconsistencies pertaining to Hightower's and Joanna Burden's ages result from the synthesis of older and newer passages in the manuscript. Conversely, the turning away from climactic scenes, such as the murder and the distancing of Christmas's last escape, are deliberate, so that specific motivations for key actions must always remain obscure.

In sum, a study such as this one, which attempts to discover the entelechy of the work by examining the author's many revisions, should lead to a fuller understanding of what is acknowledged to be a major work by a major author. It can more closely describe and identify the form of the whole by observing how the separate, discrete parts of the work were ultimately fused into a single novel. Perhaps, too, it can illustrate how the meticulous work habits of a highly gifted teller of tales transformed those tales into a profoundly probing study of human experience. Most of all, it can attest to the sanity of true genius.

Appendix

1. Faulkner's pagination of the Virginia manuscript

All the canceled numbers on the Virginia manuscript have been transcribed as accurately as possible in table 1. Faulkner's vertical columns are reproduced as follows: his top number appears in the first left column of the canceled number section of the table. Reading from left to right, one should visualize a vertical column in order from top to bottom inscribed on a single page.

Ditto marks have been used for those pages that have both canceled roman and arabic numerals. In addition, because some pages have many more canceled numbers than other pages, blank spaces have been left in some of the columns so that a reader can more easily observe the consecutive number-sets on the many successive pages of the manuscript.

Table 1. Faulkner's pagination of the Virginia manuscript

Final pagination		All canceled numbers						
Ch. no.	Page no.							
I	2							
	3							
	3							
	4-12							
II	13-23							
III	24[a]							
	25[b]	3						
	26-30							
IV	31-34							
	35	34						

[a]On page 24 the number 2 is written in purple ink and the number 4 in dark blue-black. At the top of this page, in black ink, is written "Gail Hightower in his study, alone."

[b]The number 3 is written in purple ink and canceled in dark blue-black. Number 25 is written in dark blue-black.

Table 1 (cont.)

Ch. no.	Page no.		All canceled numbers				
	36-40						
V	41-49						
VI	50-58						
VII	59[c]	VIII	IX	IX	XI	X	
	"	62	39[d]	47	61	72	69
	60	63		48	62	73	70
	61	64		49	63	74	71
	62	65		50	64	75	72
	63	66		51	65	76	73
	64	67		52	66	77	74
	65	68		53	67	78	75
	66	69		54	68	79	76
	67	70		55	69	80	77
	68	71		56	70	81	78
VIII	69	XII	IX[e]	XI			
	"	72		57	71	82	79
	70						
	71						
	72	41[f]					
	73						
	74	71[g]	73[g]				
	75						

[c] The roman numerals on MS page 59 appear in the following arrangement:

~~VIII~~	VII
~~IX~~	~~XI~~
~~IX~~	~~X~~

The number XI was probably the first written and canceled, for it appears in the customary place of the chapter numerals when there is only one such number, the final one.

[d] This number is dubious because it is obscured by an ink blot and not canceled in the customary way.

[e] Number IX was probably the first to be written and canceled, for it appears in the center of the ruled partition, which always indicates the beginning of a new chapter.

[f] This number pertains to the passage written underneath the first paste-on slip. It is a discarded beginning to chap. 5, which, in its final form in the MS, begins with MS page 41.

[g] The number 71 has been changed to 73 as follows: 7̷3. The number 3 is written over the number 1. The top margin is bisected for a new chapter, but there are no canceled roman numerals.

Table 1 (cont.)

Ch. no.	Page no.	All canceled numbers						
	76[h]	79	79	64	78	89	86	78
	77	79	80	65	79	90	87	
	78	80	81	66	80	91	88	
	79	81	82[i]	67	81	92	89	
	80[j]	82	83	68	82	93	90	
IX	81	XIII	XI[k]	XII				
	"		84	69	83	94	91	
	82	74	85	70	84	95	92	
	83	88[l]	86	71	85	96	93	
	84		87	72	86	97	94	
	85		88	73	87	98	95	
	86		89	74	88	99	96	
X	87	XII[m]	XII	XIV	XIII			
	"		90	75	89	100	97	
	88		91	76	90	101	98	
	89		92	77	91	102	99	
	90		93	78	92	103	100	
XI	91	XIII[n]	XIII	XV	XIV			
	"		94	79	93	104	101	

[h]The canceled numbers on this sheet appear as follows:

79   78
79
64
78
89
86

[i]The number 82 of this column is slightly to the right of the rest of the column.

[j]The column of canceled numbers on this page is irregular.

[k]The roman numeral XI was probably the first to be written and canceled.

[l]Number 88 is slightly to the left of the rest of the column.

[m]The column of canceled roman numerals is arranged as follows:

XII   XIII
XII
XIV

The number XIII is between the two XII's but is adjacent to the column. Number XIII was probably the first to be written and canceled.

[n]The column of canceled numbers is arranged as follows:

XIII   XIV
XIII
XV

The second number XIII may have been the first written and canceled.

Table 1 (cont.)

Final pagination		All canceled numbers						
Ch. no.	Page no.							
	92		95	80	94	105	102	
	93	100	96	81	95	106	103	
	94	96	97	82	96	107	104	
	95		98	83	97	108	105	
	96		99	84	98	109	106	
	97		100	85	99	110	107	
	98		101	86	100	111	108	
XII	99	XIV[o]	XIV	XIII	XV	XIV	XVI	
	"		102	87	101	112	109	
	100		103	88	102	113	110	
	101		104	89	103	114	111	
	102		105	90	104	115	112	
	103	107	106	91	105	116	113	
	104		107	92	106	117	114	
	105		108	93	107	118	115	
	106		109	94	108	119	116	
	107		110	95	109	120	117	
	108	VII[p]						
		111[q]	96	110	35	43	121	118
	109	112	97	111	36	44	122	119
XIII	110	VII[r]	XV	VI				
	"	112	45	43	34			
	111	113	46	44	35			
	112-16							
	117	116						
	118							
	119	122						

[o] These canceled roman numerals form two parallel columns of three numbers each. The second number XIV is placed so that it appears to have been written first.

[p] The top margin is not bifurcated so that this leaf was probably not intended for the beginning of a chapter. Faulkner wrote in black ink above the horizontal line: "Escape of Christmas into the country, first night."

[q] MS pages 108 and 109 provide numbers to complete the number sets, but because the two pairs of lower numbers are placed in the center of the column, the table does not reflect the pattern of the continued series as clearly as elsewhere. The two pairs of low canceled numbers are slightly to the right of the remainder of the column and probably were the first to be written.

[r] The canceled roman numerals are written:

VII
XVI   VI

From their position in the margin it is hard to tell which was written first. Above page 110 is written: "The week of the hunt for Christmas, from the fire to his disappearance [?] at the cotton house."

Appendix

Table 1 *(cont.)*

Final pagination		All canceled numbers					
Ch. no.	Page. no.	40	59	57	48	123	123^s
	120	40	59	57	48	123	123^s
	121	41	60	58	49	124^t	
	122	46[?]	61	59	50	125^u	
		42					
XIV	123-30						
XV	131	XVI^v					
	"	123					
	132	124					
	133	121	125				
	134	126					
	135	127					
	136	128					
	137	129					
	138	130					
XVI	139	126					
	140-46						
	147	XVII					
	"	146					
	148						
XVII	149-56						
XVIII	157-67						
XIX	168	XVII					
	169-74						
XX	175-83						
XXI	184	182					
	185-87						

^{s}This column is divided into two as follows:

4̶0̶	1̶2̶3̶
5̶9̶	1̶2̶3̶
5̶7̶	120
4̶8̶	

The uncanceled number 120 is the final number of the leaf as it now appears in the MS.

^{t}These numbers appear as follows:

4̶1̶	1̶2̶4̶
6̶0̶	
5̶8̶	
4̶9̶	

^{u}These numbers are placed in the same position as those in the preceding note. Number 125 is adjacent to number 42.

^{v}There is an ink blot over the roman numeral I of this number, but it appears to cover a number I, so that the canceled number would have been XVI.

Table 2. The canceled numbers of chapters 7-13 and chapter 15 rearranged into consecutive sets

Final pagination		The five continuous number-sets					Additional sets				
Ch. no.	Page no.										
VII	59	62	47	61	72	69					
	60	63	48	62	73	70					
	61	64	49	63	74	71					
	62	65	50	64	75	72					
	63	66	51	65	76	73					
	64	67	52	66	77	74					
	65	68	53	67	78	75					
	66	69	54	68	79	76					
	67	70	55	69	80	77					
	68	71	56	70	81	78					
VIII	69	72	57	71	82	79					
	70										
	71										
	72										
	73										
	74										
	75										
	76	79	64	78	89	86					
	77	80	65	79	90	87					
	78	81	66	80	91	88					
	79	82	67	81	92	89					
	80	83	68	82	93	90					
IX	81	84	69	83	94	91					
	82	85	70	84	95	92					
	83	86	71	85	96	93					
	84	87	72	86	97	94					
	85	88	73	87	98	95					
	86	89	74	88	99	96					
X	87	90	75	89	100	97					
	88	91	76	90	101	98					
	89	92	77	91	102	99					
	90	93	78	92	103	100					
XI	91	94	79	93	104	101					
	92	95	80	94	105	102					

Table 2 (cont.)

Final pagination Ch. no.	Page no.	The five continuous number-sets					Additional sets				
	93	96	81	95	106	103					
	94	97	82	96	107	104					
	95	98	83	97	108	105					
	96	99	84	98	109	106					
	97	100	85	99	110	107					
	98	101	86	100	111	108					
XII	99	102	87	101	112	109					
	100	103	88	102	113	110					
	101	104	89	103	114	111					
	102	105	90	104	115	112					
	103	106	91	105	116	113					
	104	107	92	106	117	114					
	105	108	93	107	118	115					
	106	109	94	108	119	116					
	107	110	95	109	120	117					
	108	111	96	110	121	118	35	43			
	109	112	97	111	122	119	36	44			
XIII	110			112			34	45	43		
	111			113			35	46	44		
	112-118										
	119									122	
	120						40	59	57	123	48
	121						41	60	58	124	49
	122						42	61	59	125	50
XV	131				123						
	132				124						
	133				125						
	134				126						
	135				127						
	136				128						
	137				129						
	138				130						

Table 3.   Concentration of the canceled roman numerals of the Virginia manuscript

Canceled numerals	Chapters											
	VII	VIII	IX	X	XI	XII	XIII	XIV	XV	XVII	XVIII	XIX
VI							VI^L					
VII						VII^L	VII^L					
VIII	VIII^H											
IX	IX^H IX	IX^H										
X	X^H											
XI	XI^H	XI^H	XI^H									
XII		XII^H	XII^H	XII^H XII								
XIII			XIII^H	XIII^H	XIII^H XIII	XIII^H						
XIV				XIV^H	XIV^H	XIV^H XIV XIV						
XV					XV^H	XV^H	XV^H					
XVI						XVI^H			XVI^H[a]			
XVII										XVII^H[b] MS 147		XVII^L

NOTE: *H* designates a higher, *L* a lower, canceled number than the final pagination.

[a] A blot follows XV, probably covering the I that would make the numeral XVI.

[b] This number does not appear on the first page of the chapter.

Table 4. The canceled numbers of the Virginia typescript

Chap. no.	Final pagination	−1	−2	+1	+2
II–IV	31-104		29-102		
V	105-16				
	117			118	119
	118			119	120
	119			120	121
	120			121	122
	121			122	123
	122/123			123	124
VI	124-32			125-33	
	133			134	
	134-40				
	141			142	
	142-50			143-51	
	151			152	
VII	152-67			153-68	
	168			169	
	169	168		170	
	170	169		171	
	171	170		172	
	172			173	
	173			174	
	174	173		175	
	175	174		176	
VIII	176			177	
	177			178	

NOTE: The final numbers were written by hand in blue-black ink, except where there are no canceled numbers, in which case the page number was typed.

The canceled number-set one digit lower than the final number (−1 col.) was written in blue-black ink and canceled by hand. The −2 col. and +1 col. numbers were typed and canceled by hand in blue-black ink. The +2 col. numbers were typed and canceled by hand.

Table 5. Types of paper in the Virginia manuscript

Chapter no.	Base page pagination and thickness 0.003 mm.	Base page pagination and thickness 0.004 mm.	Paste-on slips: number per page and thickness 0.003 mm.	Paste-on slips: number per page and thickness 0.004 mm.
I		2		1
		3		2
		3		
		4		
		5		
		6		
		7		
		8		
		9		
		10		
		11		
		12		
II		13		
		14		
		15		
		16		
		17		1
		18		
		19		
	20			1
	21			2
	22			2
	23			
III		24		
		25		
	26			2
	27			2
	28			2
	29		2 A & C	2 B & D
	30		1 A	1 B
IV		31		
		32		
		33		
	34		2 A & C	2 B & D
		35		
	36			4
	37			2
	38			1
	39		2 A & C	1B
		40		
V		41		

Table 5 (cont.)

Chapter no.	Base page pagination and thickness		Paste-on slips: number per page and thickness	
	0.003 mm.	0.004 mm.	0.003 mm.	0.004 mm.
		42		1
		43		1
		44		3
		45		3
		46		2
		47		2
		48		2
		49		1
VI		50		
		51		
		52		
		53		2
		54		3
		55		2
		56		1
		57		3
		58		2
VII		59		
		60		
		61		
		62		3
		63		
		64		2
		65		1
		66		1
		67		3
		68		
VIII		69		2
		70		
		71		2
		72		2
		73		2
		74		1
		75		1
		76		
		77		
		78		
		79		
		80		
IX		81		
		82		1
		83		
		84		

Table 5 (cont.)

Chapter no.	Base page: pagination and thickness		Paste-on slips: number per page and thickness	
	0.003 mm.	0.004 mm.	0.003 mm.	0.004 mm.
		85		
		86		
X		87		1
		88		
		89		
		90		
XI		91		1
		92		1
		93		1
		94		2
		95		3
		96		1
		97		3
		98		
XII		99		
		100		2
		101		
		102		2
		103		2
		104		
		105		
		106		
		107		
		108		
		109		
XIII		110		
		111		
	112			1
	113			1
		114		
		115		
	116			2
	117			2
	118		2 A & C	1 B
	119			1
		120		
		121		
		122		
		123	1 B	1 A
		124	3	
		125	2 A & C	2 B & D
	126		3 B, C & D	1 A
	127		2	
	128		1 C	2 A & B

Table 5 (cont.)

Chapter no.	Base page: pagination and thickness		Paste-on slips: number per page and thickness	
	0.003 mm.	0.004 mm.	0.003 mm.	0.004 mm.
	129			2
	130			2
XV		131		
	132			3
		133		1
		134		
		135		
		136		
		137		
		138		
XVI		139		
		140		
		141		
		142		
		143		
		144		1
		145		
		146		
		147		
		148		
XVII		149		1
	150		2 A & B	2 C & D
	151		1 B	2 A & C
		152	1 B	1 A
		153		
		154		
		155		
		156		
XVIII	157			1
		158		1
		159		
		160		
		161		
		162		
		163		
		164		
		165		
		166		
		167		
XIX		168		
		169		
		170		
		171		
		172		

Table 5 (cont.)

Chapter no.	Base page: pagination and thickness		Paste-on slips: number per page and thickness	
	0.003 mm.	0.004 mm.	0.003 mm.	0.004 mm.
XX		173		
		174		
		175		
		176		
		177		3
		178		
		179		
		180		
		181		1
		182		
		183		
XXI		184		
		185		
		186		
		187		

NOTE: The letters following the numbers indicate the position of the pasting on the manuscript leaf. For example, if there were four sections affixed to the base sheet, and they were arranged so that the first and third measured 0.003 mm., the table would read 2A & C; if the second and fourth measured 0.004 mm., the table would read 2B & D.

Index

Index

Q2